## PRAISE FOR *FLOATING IN DARKNESS*

"Ron Garan's awe-inspiring *Floating in Darkness* is literally the story that could inspire us all to follow the path of miracles he has so elegantly described. Garan's call to action could help us on our journey of personal and social transition, enabling us to move toward a more peaceful, just, sustainable, healthy, and joyful world. This book kept me up at night." – Deepak Chopra, MD, Author

"Ron Garan has led an exceptional life, a life full of extraordinary challenges, determination, bravery, and achievement. Sitting in the cockpit of an F-16, he was a potential instrument of war, yet today much of his work is as an instrument of peace. In *Floating in Darkness*, he takes us with him on his remarkable inner and outer journey. From fighter pilot to astronaut, to peace and climate envoy, and now to space entrepreneur, we get to know this unique man, to understand who Ron is, and to familiarize ourselves with his story, both from inside and out. This is one hell of a ride!" – Peter Gabriel, Grammy Award-winning Musician, Humanitarian, and Activist

"In *Floating in Darkness*, Ron Garan shares his experience from space. We cannot share the ride with him, but we can share his thoughts. This book is about sharing his thoughts. Ron has felt the potentials of planet Earth, a bright future that is ours if we want it. A future filled with peace and harmony with the Earth and each other. A future where every person is regarded as a precious member of our one human family." – Muhammad Yunus, Nobel Peace Prize Laureate

"Little more than 500 human beings have the grit, the persistence, and the talent ever to have flown in space. A far smaller number have the poetry to tell the tale of that journey.

You can either go to space or you can write with true artfulness about it, but you can't do both. That, at least, is the common rule, but Ron Garan is the rare exception to it. In *Floating in Darkness*, he gives us the astronaut's perspective in the lyricist's voice – challenging all of us to think about our Earth, our species, our strengths, our failings, our hopes for our world and our future off of it in a new way. The vast majority of us will never float in the darkness Garan and only a few others have, but we can all experience it by proxy, thanks to Garan's words." – Jeff Kluger, *Time* Magazine Editor at Large, *New York Times* Bestselling Co-author of *Apollo 13*

"Read this perfectly inspiring poet's floating journey into space. Astronaut and master storyteller Ron Garan will make you feel alive and thankful you are on Spaceship Earth. Ron unlocks the secrets to understanding our complex yet enchanting and delightful universe. A must-read for anyone who wants to improve their future and our world." – Mark Victor Hansen, Co-creator of the *Chicken Soup for the Soul, One Minute Millionaire, You Have a Book in You*, and *Ask!* Series

"I first met Ron Garan and his lovely wife, Carmel, in the summer of 1990 when we were young captains in the Air Force. Ron was our weapons and tactics officer responsible for preparing an F-16 squadron for combat. Our success as a squadron during Operation Desert Storm is directly attributable to his passion for excellence and keen ability to get the best out of everyone he meets. No surprise that he went on to become one of our most thoughtful and successful astronauts. Just as he led all of us in the crucible of combat, he led his international teammates in the unforgiving crucible of space exploration. Ron Garan is an American hero I am proud to call a friend and his book captures the essence of what a life of selfless service can mean to our world. Fascinating read!" – General David L. Goldfein, 21st Chief of Staff of the US Air Force

"*Floating in Darkness* does what all great literature should do . . . it makes us examine ourselves, our lives, and our role in a larger society. It forces us to the realization that our actions have an impact on others and the world we inhabit. Powerful lessons for all." – Jon Landau, Academy Award–winning Producer of *Titanic* and *Avatar*

"*Floating in Darkness* is a riveting must-read for navigating our time of fear and upheaval – vividly describing dogfights, seafloor living, space flights, and spacewalks. Ron Garan generously shares his deeply personal journey of overcoming seemingly impossible obstacles and temptations to live out many people's wildest dreams. In doing so, he gained a profound perspective on the unity the world truly needs. It is a story of a life well-lived, his amazing career, his love for his family, his friendships, and love for the planet, which is a true inspiration to lift our spirits during these dark times." – Emilie Sydney-Smith, CEO, ExO Works

"Ron is one of the very few human beings who have been able to see our home planet from the vantage point of space, but he is the only one who is able to take you on this journey with him enabling you to rediscover yourself as he did. *Floating in Darkness* is not just about space, it's about traveling within and seeing the world for the first time. It is about finding the light inside you and letting it illuminate the world. Ron found that light on the ISS and now he is shining that light through his hopeful and beautifully written book. *Floating in Darkness* illuminates a bright future for all of us if we can see past what divides us and celebrate what connects us – our home, our Earth. I hope it becomes required reading for all students." – Anousheh Ansari, CEO of XPRIZE, Serial Entrepreneur, and First Female Civilian Space Explorer

"Ron Garan – family man, decorated fighter pilot and astronaut, American hero – raises us, through his own awakening journey, to a greater perspective of a world caught in doom, division, war, and political polarization. The realization that we are 'One' and are all interconnected should transform the way we look at reality and interact with each other; this is what Ron Garan defines as the Orbital Perspective. This inspiring new book, written in his unique poetic style, is an exciting and necessary *Leap of Awareness* to heal the world from a divisive, flat (two-dimensional), and limited point of view." – Paul Drouin, MD, President of Quantum University

"Even among astronauts, Ron's view of the world stands out. Ron writes with passion, empathy, and deep affection for humanity. Ron's books are must-reads." – Dylan Taylor, Founder of Space for Humanity, Chairman and CEO of Space Voyager Holdings, Former Global President of Colliers International

"Ron Garan is a storyteller of our times. He not only writes about the journey of evolution but is also a firsthand partici-pant in that compelling adventure. As an astronaut and fighter pilot, he uses his skills as an author to communicate what he is learning and shares that knowledge with his readers. We live in a period of history when a rise in nationalism and inward-thinking challenges our ability to progress the human condi-tion. This is why *Floating in Darkness* offers us an opportunity to widen our understanding of the entire planetary system and our membership within it." – James Chau, Host of *The China Current*, WHO Goodwill Ambassador

"Astronauts have a unique perspective. By this, I don't mean they've read more books or been exposed to more ideas. I mean LITERALLY: they have stood outside the Earth and looked back at it. From this, they must know something we don't, akin to what the Greeks call katalepsis – a truth from which nothing can dislodge us: that we are all connected. Ron Garan is such a person. An astronaut, philosopher, and writer, in *Floating in Darkness,* he offers us a phenomenological account of his inner world as he marvels at the outer world, from perhaps the most glorious of perspectives." – Jason Silva, Filmmaker and Futurist

"*Floating in Darkness* relays the experience of an astronaut who boldly journeys beyond the experience of the Overview Effect and into territory usually reserved for contemplatives and adepts of wisdom traditions. Poetic, profound and powerful. This book is an essential read." – Guy Reid, Filmmaker and Director of *Overview* and *Planetary*

"At a time where it often feels we are growing further apart—through social distancing, the internet, or partisan politics—*Floating in Darkness* provides a much needed unifying message. Through the lens of Ron Garan's vast life experience, this book reminds us of what is truly important and emphasizes the critical necessity of collective action in a way that is profoundly inspiring. Ron has a tremendous ability to inspire through storytelling. Although so few of us will ever experience travel in space, Ron's work helps us learn life lessons that only come from seeing our beautiful planet from so far away. We are all lucky to call planet Earth 'home,' and this book provides a vision of how we can make it a fairer, more compassionate, and more sustainable place to live." – Kate Robertson and David Jones, Cofounders, One Young World

"I am grateful and blessed to call Ron, his wife, Carmel, and their sons family. We first met in August 2000 when Ron and I were selected as NASA astronauts. Over the past twenty years, Ron and I trained together and spent eighteen days on an undersea mission. While we never flew in space together, we supported each other every step of the way as astronauts. More importantly, though, is our bond as family. In Ron's latest book, *Floating in Darkness,* he shares not only the awe and wonder of spaceflight but also the stark contrast of the beauty of Earth from space to the challenges of life on Earth—and he does so through a memoir that can help us all better understand our relationship with and responsibility to each other as a planetary family." – Former NASA Astronaut Nicole Stott

# FLOATING IN DARKNESS

## A Journey of Evolution

## RON GARAN

# Floating in Darkness: A Journey of Evolution, 2nd Edition

ISBN 13: 9781571022783
Library of Congress Control Number: 2020947326

Printed in China


First Printing: 2021


22 21 20 19 18     5 4 3 2 1


Cover design by Lightfarm Studios, Milton Menezes, Dragan Bilic,
and Tarver Lowe

Interior design by Michael Grossman

*Floating in Darkness* edited by Cheryl Ross

"One" Music by U2 Words by Bono (c)Universal Polygram Int.
Publishing, Inc. on behalf of Universal Music Publishing Int. B.V.
Used by Permission - All Rights Reserved

info@newepochpublishing.com
orders@newepochpublishing.com

To all those seeking the light of truth and who have the courage to peel back the layers of reality.

# CONTENTS

*Silent singularity*
*Timeless existence*
*Dormant blueprints lying in peaceful readiness*
*Yet to be fulfilled plans waiting for an other*

# The Red Shift of an Expanding Universe

✦ In a single flash, the dark and still universe explodes in an exponential fury of light and energy. Specific points of matter align under the careful supervision of an invisible design. Creative intuition seamlessly merges with disciplined focus, forming specific points of universal matter. Each point of matter is imbued with an important predestined and necessary purpose that serves a greater plan—a note in a grand and ancient symphony. As more matter organizes into groups and functions, an altruistic hierarchy develops. At the top of the hierarchy, groups transmit and receive the most precious natural resource in the universe: information.

Information ripples in waves and bursts from all points and in all directions. Individual points of matter communicate with each other over vast distances—a cosmic dance. As the complexity of the material universe reaches critical mass, a primordial certainty echoes throughout creation in a loud, simultaneous proclamation:

*We are one!*

A silent sleep then gently descends upon the creation.

***I am awake.***

For the first time, I realize that the communication I experience constantly is coming from me. *I am awake* is my first acknowledged thought.

*I am alone.*

If my awareness comes from me and there is nothing else, am I alone? Is my awareness all that exists?

I hope not. I long for others. I long to belong.

*I feel.*

I feel something pushing against me that makes me wonder if I have boundaries. It seems that there may exist an *other* that is not me. It seems that this other just put pressure on me, which I suppose means I must have boundaries. Through touch, I can also determine this other's boundaries—the boundaries of my universe.

### March 14, 1961

In the News: *A B-52 bomber carrying nuclear weapons crashed near Yuba City, California today, the second such crash in two months. The previous crash of a nuclear weapon–carrying B-52 occurred in late January near Goldsboro, North Carolina.**

*I hear.*

Not long ago, I started hearing things other than my thoughts. None of what I hear makes any sense. Could there be more to reality than what I sense? Another world? Others like me somewhere? Am I hearing the thoughts of others?

### April 12, 1961

Breaking News: *Russia has put the first man in orbit around Earth and returned him safely. A Soviet Air Force major, Yuri Gagarin, 27, father of two, circled Earth in 89.1 minutes before returning, the official Russian news agency Tass reported. Gagarin had launched from a top-secret Soviet military installation within the Kazakh Soviet Socialist Republic and later landed at 2:55 EST. Upon his return, Gagarin commented, "I saw for the first time how beautiful our planet is. Mankind, let us preserve and increase this beauty, and not destroy it!"**

The sounds I hear have changed. Until recently, they seemed strange, distant, and random, but now I occasionally hear muffled thoughts. I can't make sense of the sounds, but they definitely resemble the pattern of my thoughts.

### I see.
For the first time, I realize that I have been floating in darkness. I didn't know what darkness was until I saw light. Now, my world cycles between periods of complete darkness and a perceptible dim red glow. Within the red glow, I can make out shapes. I can determine the direction of sound. I am beginning to see my world.

### May 5, 1961
*The United States' first space man, Alan B. Shepard Jr., rocketed briefly across the threshold of space today and landed safely after a 5,100-mile-an-hour journey that carried him 115 miles high and 302 miles downrange. The pickup occurred at 10:53 a.m., 19 minutes after the Redstone booster blasted off from Cape Canaveral at 10:34 a.m. The 37-year-old navy commander's good condition was evident throughout the flight when Shepard reported such things as, "What a beautiful sight!" in describing Earth below.*\*

### I love.
Ever since I first saw light, I have felt something I can't fully explain. I feel that I am wrapped in warmth and well-being, that I am protected and cared for. I am starting to believe that I'm not alone. A strong desire to be with others is awakening within.

### May 14, 1961
*Today, as a Greyhound bus arrived in Anniston, Alabama, carrying so-called Freedom Riders, an angry mob of about 200 white people surrounded the bus. The driver continued past the local bus station, followed by the mob in automobiles. When the bus's tires blew out,*

*a firebomb was thrown into the bus. The Freedom Riders, who had been seeking to test the segregation of interstate transportation facilities, escaped the bus as it burst into flames only to be brutally beaten by members of the surrounding mob. Other Freedom Riders traveling on a second bus arrived in Birmingham, Alabama. An angry white mob, many of whom brandished metal pipes, beat those riders too. Birmingham Public Safety Commissioner Bull Connor said he knew that violence awaited the Freedom Riders but that he posted no police protection at the station because it was Mother's Day.\**

It is becoming clear to me that I am indeed hearing the thoughts of others. I don't know what they are saying, but I can tell when they are happy and when they are sad.

Why are these others such a mystery to me? Why can't I see them or speak to them? Are they like me? I don't know who I am or what I am, but I love where I am. Whenever I feel the slightest need or discomfort, I am immediately soothed. I feel constant sustaining and protecting energy flowing to me. I suspect there's a larger world than what I'm presently experiencing.

**August 13, 1961**
*In the early hours of the morning, the quietness of East Berlin's deserted streets was shattered by screaming sirens as police cars sped through the city. This occurred shortly after the Communist Warsaw Pact States declared that effective controls must be put into force on the borders of West Berlin because of a "perfidious agitation campaign" by the West. As of now, the border between East and West Berlin is effectively closed. East German troops are standing guard at the Brandenburg Gate, the main crossing point between the Eastern and Western sectors. This will affect thousands of East Berliners who daily commute to work in the Western sector. The closing of the border came after East Berliners had waited nervously yesterday for the Iron Curtain to ring down on refugee escape routes to the West.\**

I realize now that I live in two worlds. One is a world of alternating darkness and dim red light, where everything is familiar, comfortable, and right. But every now and then, I feel this familiar world slipping away. All that is familiar starts to vanish only to be replaced with a new world that has no boundaries. This other world is the opposite of familiar, and everything is novel and exciting. In it I see a blur of red, purple, blue, orange, green, and turquoise, each in turn becoming dominant. Here, I have freedom to do whatever I like. Here, I see many others with unique forms.

Somehow, I communicate with these others effortlessly. I hear their thoughts. They hear mine. It's as if their thoughts are mine and mine are theirs. Though they are separate from me, an unbreakable force binds us. In this boundaryless world, we can simultaneously understand how everything is intimately tied together and dependent on each other while not losing the realization of our own distinct existence.

Normally, just when I really start to get used to this boundaryless world, the world of alternating darkness and dim red light creeps back in and I return to the familiar, comfortable, and right. But just now, while deep into the world without boundaries, I feel vibrations.

These vibrations are barely perceptible and don't distract me from enjoying the freedom of the boundaryless world. Slowly and steadily, however, they increase in strength to a crescendo and then decrease beyond my perception, over and over. I imagine a giant being many times bigger than my entire world slowly approaching me, coming so close that I feel I can reach out and touch it. I haven't yet worked up the courage to reach out before the vibrations retreat. I am not sure which one of my worlds I'm in.

I feel stronger and faster vibrations. They jolt me back into the certainty of the world of alternating darkness and dim red light. Suddenly, things no longer feel familiar, comfortable, or right!

The vibrations become almost unbearable and push me in from all sides. They squeeze me so tightly that I feel part of me spilling outside of my boundaries. Just when I think I'm about to turn inside out, the world around me expands back to its usual size. Then it shrinks again, this time around the top of my head. *What's happening?!*

Suddenly, my head feels cold. The rest of me, however, feels squeezed and hot. *Am I dying?* My world is crashing in on me. If this continues, I will surely cease to exist. I want this to stop. I want to return to the familiar, comfortable, and right.

Then harsh, colorless radiant light engulfs me, and I am no longer squeezed at all. I am bathed in cold white light coming from every direction streaming over and around me. I can now clearly hear thoughts that are not my own. I still don't know what they're saying, but for the first time, I am sure they are not from me.

Although I am no longer being squeezed, my insides are pulling in from my core. A great pressure is building up outside of me that could destroy me. I need to fight to stay alive. To survive, I must let go. But how? The link between me and from where I came must be severed, and that terrifies me.

Then the link is cut, and like that, a part of me opens up and the great pressure enters me. I feel relief. For the first time, I hear something that I know is coming from me. I find myself taking in some substance from outside of myself and giving it back, all accompanied by a strange, loud sound. What is this substance? Where does it come from? It seems to be keeping me alive.

I am being held. I now fully understand that I am not alone. There are others out there. You are one of them, and I am sharing this story with you and all the *others*. An *other* is looking at me. I see joy, love. I stare back at this other and notice that the bright white light is softly dimming. I feel myself slowly being pulled back to the world without boundaries.

**October 30, 1961**

*Russia has exploded the world's largest ever nuclear device, provoking widespread condemnation from around the world. Called the Tsar Bomba, it is believed to be 50 megatons, equivalent to 50 million tons of TNT. This caused the biggest ever man-made explosion in history. The test, the 26th in the current series, was carried out over the Arctic island of Novaya Zemlya despite repeated objections from the West. Shockwaves from the explosion were first picked up at the seismological institute at Uppsala in Sweden at 0830 hours GMT.\**

# Starting Conditions

✦ The origin story of my evolution began in the embryonic ocean of my mother's womb. Nine months later, I left the familiarity of this maternal ocean for solid ground. Nineteen years later, I extended my life into the ocean of air blanketing our planet. Twenty-seven years later, I climbed above the ocean of air and my life was elevated into space.

Humanity's origin story begins in the prehistoric ocean of Mother Earth. Four billion years later, life was compelled to claw itself out of the familiarity of the ocean for solid ground. Life left the relative ease of the ocean for the promise of something better, fighting the crushing gravitational pull of the planet the whole way. The journey out of the ocean led to new adaptations, including the arrival of humans. Four hundred million years after life transcended the oceans, humanity extended itself into the ocean of air blanketing our planet. Fifty-eight years later, humanity elevated itself above the ocean of air and into space. Detaching ourselves from the planet enabled us to look back and see what we have always been: one single human family with a common origin and shared future.

On May 31, 2008, my story intersected with humanity's origin story when I became the 478th person to leave the planet. This intersection coincided with humanity and all

life on Earth facing a crisis that threatens the very survival of
life here. A crisis that humans must overcome. A crisis that
requires a giant leap in humanity's evolutionary process.
A life-or-death crisis that humanity can solve only by transcending individual and collective ego and embracing the
true nature of its interdependence with every living thing on
the planet and the planet itself. The crisis? We must evolve,
see, understand, and act on the fact that we are all part of one
human family, or we will perish.

On the news today, you will not see many, if any, stories that
illustrate humanity's evolution toward a more unified existence. Instead, the news bombards us with examples pointing
to humanity's devolution to more primitive forms. It shows
a rampant divisiveness fracturing our species along national,
parochial, partisan, racial, and religious lines.

The news doesn't reflect the complete reality of the story.

An awakening consciousness, a blossoming unity, could help
us overcome the divisive darkness—a darkness that surrounds
us because we, like the prisoners in the allegory of Greek philosopher Plato's Cave, are blind.

The prisoners in Plato's Cave lived their entire lives chained
inside of it, facing a wall. They could see only the shadows
cast upon the wall, nothing more. Sounds that emanated from
behind them echoed off the walls, leading them to believe that
the shadows were making these sounds. They believed in the
shadows because they had never seen anything else. They knew
no better life, so they did not desire to leave the cave.

One day, one of the prisoners broke free of his chains and
found another world where his eyes slowly adjusted, and he
discovered that reality was not as he thought. He then realized
that the shadows he had seen his whole life were mere projec-
tions of this outside world, which was superior in every way to
his old home. With this new knowledge, he sympathized with
those still trapped in the cave and desired to bring them out of it

and into the light . . . the light of sixteen sunrises illuminating an awe-, wonder-, and miracle-filled world . . .

This book is that true story.

# PART 1

# EPOCH A: SHADOWS ON THE CAVE

*"The art of war is of vital importance to the State. It is a matter of life and death, a road either to safety or to ruin. Hence it is a subject of inquiry which can on no account be neglected."*
— **Sun Tzu,** ***The Art of War,*** circa fifth century BC

# CHAPTER 1

# Mutually Assured Destruction

✦ My Casio G-Force digital watch silently rolls to thirteen hundred as I drive northeast on Taxiway Alpha under a dreary grey sky. The sun must be shining brightly high above my olive-green pickup truck, but unfortunately, a blanket of clouds, thousands of feet thick, separates me from the warmth of that inexorable sunshine. I imagine climbing in a fighter jet steeply through the towering white columns of billowing cumulus clouds and blasting through into the radiant sunlight. Instead, on this day, March 19, 1986, on Hahn Air Base in West Germany, I must stay firmly planted on the ground.

Today is not the day to fly. If I end up in the air today, it will be bad news for all of us—very bad news. I resolve myself to my dreary grey ground-level fate as a great mystery gnaws at me like an unscratchable itch, which I try to ignore. I pass through double gates in a perimeter fence adorned with swirls of concertina wire and video cameras perched atop it at intervals. I notice a camera is panning left, following me through the gate. I look directly into it, offer a lazy wave that I hope conveys "I'm on your side," and as I continue to drive, questions about the great mystery break through my defenses: *Why are any of us here? Is there a purpose to our existence?* As fast as my musings surface, I beat them back to the dark recesses of my mind. I don't have time for these thoughts. Why do they even matter? More important and practical things are at hand.

The windsock is lined up perfectly with Runway Zero-Four as I step out of my truck with a siren on the roof and the words "Alert Force" stenciled on a door. Cold, fresh air stings my face, and I instinctively inhale, filling my lungs with the lingering, cold, and damp Hunsrück winter. Winter is all I've known of life in West Germany. Will it ever start to warm up in this little slice of German countryside? With resolute duty and a little pride, I approach a TAB-VEE that contains an F-16 Fighting Falcon multirole fighter jet, known to those who fly it as the Viper.

A TAB-VEE is a hardened shelter designed to protect my aircraft from a Soviet attack. At one point during my brief time here at Hahn Air Base, I was told that TAB-VEE stands for *tactical air base hardened structure*. The "TAB" part makes sense—*tactical air base*. The "VEE" part is open for debate. Some say it's the Roman numeral "V," indicating that the design is in the fifth generation of aircraft structures. Others say that in the design specifications manual for US bases in Europe, the hardened aircraft shelters are located under tab "V." Regardless of the origin of the name, the TAB-VEE in front of me is a rounded structure of thick, reinforced concrete with iron blast-proof doors nestled among indigenous trees and vegetation in an attempt to blend into the beautiful surrounding landscape.

Towering about fifty feet above the TAB-VEE stands a guard shack elevated on a steel structure. It reminds me of the fire lookouts I've come across in my travels. But, in this case, the lookouts are not searching for forest fires. Near the top of the shack, a lone armed sentry stands on a catwalk that protrudes from the structure on all four sides. My eyes follow down past 137 steps of a metal staircase that wraps around the exterior of the shack's steel legs to ground level. There I see another sentry standing in front of the TAB-VEE.

I approach it, avoiding the occasional patches of snow, and the ground-level sentry snaps to attention. It is the sentry's responsibility to ensure that no unauthorized personnel gain access to what's inside the TAB-VEE—using lethal force if necessary. He flashes a signal that I return with an appropriate response. This allows me to get close enough to display my alert area badge. "Good morning, Airman Smith," I say as I give him my name and explain that I'm starting my alert force tour. His name is not actually Airman Smith, but for the sake of this story, and so as not to reveal classified information, let's just call him that. "Good morning, sir."

Strapped to the belly of the F-16 inside the TAB-VEE is a thermonuclear weapon that, according to unclassified sources, carries explosive power at least an order of magnitude higher than the yield of the bombs dropped on Hiroshima and Nagasaki combined. Of course, I can neither confirm nor deny any of this. If our national leadership determines that a nuclear attack is warranted, all the pilots who "sit" nuclear strike alert are prepared to drop these weapons on predetermined targets at a moment's notice. Most of the pilots here understand that for the vast majority of those flying the missions, it will be a one-way trip. But I don't think that would be the case for me. I'd probably survive.

I'm a typical young fighter pilot, a little cocky, and I tend to think of myself as seemingly indestructible. Despite the fact that I fly the most badass fighter in the world, somewhere very deep inside me exists a subtle certainty that barely rises above the noise level of my fighter pilot ego. The reality that I am, in fact, mortal is a basic truth that I easily suppress.

All fighter pilots are given a call sign or nickname. Mine is "Agent." On the right sleeve of my flight suit, I wear the patch of the 496th Tactical Fighter Squadron, "The World's Finest." My left sleeve boasts the patch of the 50th Tactical Fighter Wing, which depicts a griffin facing forward and breathing fire, its wings spread, while a nuclear mushroom cloud blooms behind it. The griffin's right talon holds an olive branch, denoting peace, while a lightning bolt springs from its left talon, symbolizing the strength and power of our unit's aircraft. Our wing patch is also prominently displayed on the front gate of the base, leaving little doubt about the nature of our mission.

It's no secret that we have nukes on base. Nukes at Hahn go all the way back to the 1950s, when famed test pilot Chuck Yeager sat nuclear alert here and served as a squadron commander.

"Airman Smith, let me ask you a question. Now that you see my face and have seen my alert area badge, and you know that I am authorized to approach this area and the aircraft, what will you do during this alert tour if you think I fail to reply with the proper signal as I approach?"

The airman, wearing an impeccable uniform and looking like he can't be more than nineteen, thinks about it. He looks at his locked and loaded M-16 rifle and then replies excitedly, "I'll shoot you."

"No, that's the wrong answer. Let's try that again. You recognize my face. You know via my alert area badge that has a photo *of my face* that I am authorized to be here. If I fail to reply with the proper signal, what will you do?"

Now, a little less sure of himself, he replies, "Uh, I'll shoot you?"

After a few more iterations, I get a somewhat unconvincing assurance that Airman Smith will not shoot me at a distance, and thus begins my first tour as the nuclear alert force commander. In this case, I am the commander of all the pilots who, at this moment, are on nuclear alert at Hahn, which, counting myself, adds up to a grand total of two—two very inexperienced, brand-new first lieutenants in way over our heads.

As a twenty-four-year-old first lieutenant, I'm charged with ensuring that *all*—aka both—of our alert force aircraft and pilots are ready to take off and head to our targets within minutes of hearing the scramble sirens go off, or, as we like to say, "if the balloon goes up." This is a reference to the large balloons that were raised on steel cables above British cities during the Second World

War to indicate an imminent attack. If a strike is ordered, a chain of events will be set in motion that will unleash unimaginable destruction thousands upon thousands of times more powerful than the most powerful man-made explosion to date.

I'm reminded that the very day I was born, October 30, 1961, the Soviets exploded a fifty-megaton weapon called the Tsar Bomba that, to this day, remains the most powerful man-made explosion in history. Strapped to my aircraft, right now, is a weapon not unlike that history-making bomb. If I were ordered to drop my bomb, it wouldn't break the old record for the most powerful man-made explosion. But when you consider that each of our aircraft carry similar weapons, and that countless nucle-ar-armed aircraft and missiles would launch from air, land, sea, and from under the sea, the cumulative effect of what we would unleash would obliterate the record. No doubt we have enough destructive power to annihilate every living thing on the planet. Of course, all these weapons are matched with weapons on the Soviet side. If the balloon goes up, we and the Soviets together would likely unleash enough destructive power to destroy every living thing on Earth many times over.

But all this destruction is not for me to think about. In fact, it is our job here on the nuclear strike alert force to make sure that doesn't happen. We are the point of the sword of the mutually assured destruction deterrence. Our job is to make sure the Cold War doesn't turn into a hot war.

I love my country. I understand that the threat the Soviet Union poses cannot be taken lightly or underestimated. We must stand firm against its aggression. If the balloon goes up, I will be faced with a choice: follow orders and wreak unthinkable death, destruction, and suffering on countless people, or not follow orders and potentially allow unthinkable death, destruction, and suffering to rain down on the United States and our allies. As I enter the alert facility, I think, *This is the world we live in. I have no control over it. I just work here.*

Nuclear alert is, for the most part, endless boredom interspersed with periodic terror. Every once in a while, we get scrambled and we never know until we get to our aircraft if we're in the midst of a drill or the balloon just went up. I walk down a narrow corridor with dark wood paneling stretching on either side from the floor to about halfway up the wall. Above the paneling peeks exposed concrete painted a color I can describe only as puke-yellow.

I enter my assigned quarters, and some aircraft maintenance guys down the hall in the breakroom shout that they're about to watch *Jaws* and ask if I want to join them. The alluring smell of microwaved corn dogs and popcorn trails their words down the hall and into my awareness. Suspecting, and hoping, that we are beginning one of those periods of intense monotony, I agree.

One of the guys pops the movie into our breakroom VHS player. My attention focuses on the opening beach party scene. But soon, after the late-night giant-fish-chomp-fest scene and as the last bit of winter chill is extracted from my bones by the heat of clanking steam radiators, my mind drifts away from the movie to thoughts about the path that brought me here.

I was born into a nation in turmoil. Several years after my birth, the US officially entered the Vietnam War. Throughout most of my childhood, I wondered if I was going to have to ship off to Vietnam when I was old enough to join the fight. I would classify my years up to the end of elementary school, for the most part, as normal. The boundaries of my known universe expanded from just me, to, at birth, me and my mom, and rapidly grew to include my father and extended family.

I was a happy and inquisitive toddler, always looking for a path around or over obstacles, always seeking to understand how things work. I was constantly trying to expand the radius of my world, ignorant of the perilousness of that pursuit. I was also a quiet child who often seemed to be deep in thought. Occasionally, I was content to take a break from the rigors of expanding my kingdom in order to just sit back and observe what was going on around me.

During my first five years of life, my mom, dad, and I lived in an apartment complex on Caryl Avenue in Yonkers, New York. The halls of the red brick complex seemed to always smell of cooked cabbage. Caryl Avenue forms the southern boundary of Yonkers with the northern boundary of the New York City borough of the Bronx, one of the few areas in the world where you have to put a "the" in front of the name.

Just behind our apartment complex was the Bronx's Van Cortlandt Park. I loved its wide-open spaces, but what I remember most was its smell, a pungent odor that was a cross between sulfur and dead fish. Occasionally, the aroma of onions and hot dogs from a Sabrett hot dog cart would pierce the fishy, chemical veil.

Van Cortlandt Park in the 1960s was a crime-ridden, polluted relic of a former urban oasis. Large portions of Tibbetts Brook and Van Cortlandt Lake were so contaminated that people who came in contact with the water would almost certainly get sick. Crime was also a big issue, which led golfers who played there to abandon traditional foursomes for more squadron-sized units. Some players added a nightstick to their collection of clubs or hid Mace in their golf bags.

For the most part, I was oblivious to the crime and violence. However, when I was about three, the hazardous nature of my little universe became very clear. My mom was carrying me down a long, dark stairway to the basement storage room of our building. She slid her key into the lock, but the door pushed open before she turned the knob. Inside the dark, musty, cramped room cluttered with tenants' belongings, dust gleamed in the light rays entering the darkness from small ground-level windows. My mom put me down to begin her search to retrieve an item, and in that instant the sound of crashing glass sprang from a far corner.

Mom quickly scooped me back up into her arms. She was frightened, which made me frightened. She backed toward the door when a hooded figure leaped out from the darkness and headed right toward us. Mom froze in terror as the figure bolted past us, out the door, and up the stairs. Apparently, we had stumbled upon a burglary in progress. Fortunately, we were not hurt.

Though I was only three, I remember that incident because it was so life-changing. It opened my eyes to a more complicated world. Up until that run-in, I viewed people outside of my tribe as friendly helpers and caregivers. But the fear that I experienced and the fear that I saw on my mom's face exposed me to the reality of the danger of others. I learned to be somewhat suspicious of people outside my small circle of familiar faces. My universe demarcated between *known others* who I could trust and *unknown others* who I shouldn't trust. In spite of this, I remained outgoing and always tried to break through boundaries to make friends with everyone I met.

The burglar encounter revealed a silver lining, however: the addition of a new family to our circle of trustworthy *known others*. After my mom's heart rate and blood pressure returned to normal, she knocked on the door of the building's superintendent, Johnny London, to report the incident.

Mr. London's wife, Ruth, answered. She had a reputation for being a tough, no-nonsense woman, and others had warned Mom to keep her distance from her. The Ruth answering the door that day, however, was the exact opposite. After my mom told her the story of our basement encounter, Ruth comforted her in a way that led to a deep, longtime relationship between our two families. My mom was only about twenty-two at the time. Ruth's welcoming motherly compassion touched a chord in her heart.

Our family's friendship with the Londons lasted for years and included vacationing with them on Long Island, New York. Thinking back on our friendship with the Londons, who are African American, makes me recall that I didn't really see racism as a child. I grew up in a racially integrated area and had friends and neighbors who came from many different ethnic, religious, and national backgrounds. Only later in life did I grasp that some people treat others differently because of perceived differences such as skin color. For the most part, the racism of the 1960s was beyond my awareness. The cancerous racism of the '70s and the racism that continues to this day, however, were and are very much present in my mind.

Suddenly, my rumination about my years growing up pauses when I'm pulled back into *Jaws* by a summer beach scene that reminds me of a typical summer day I spent on Long Island. Ominous *Jaws* theme music plays while the underwater camera pans around the legs of unsuspecting humans, legs that I imagine would be irresistible to a shark looking for a snack. I know this scene is going to lead to some serious blood in the water, so I focus less on the story the film is telling and instead evaluate Steven Spielberg's cinematography.

At the moment, the film's hero, Chief Brody, is keeping a watchful eye over scores of vacationers frolicking in the surf as unknowing shark bait. Just as an unsuspecting victim gets gobbled up in gruesome fashion, Spielberg employs a powerful cinematographic technique known as a dolly zoom. When Chief Brody realizes that a shark attack is underway, the camera's lens zooms away from his face at the same time and rate that the camera moves toward him on a dolly.

The dolly zoom is employed to enhance the emotion of the scene as the foreground stays in the same position while the background appears to stretch, giving a sense of height. I marvel at how powerful it is to zoom out while keeping the details of the scene in clear sight. The continuous perspective shift unveils a new reality. With a dolly zoom, the subject's place in the universe is challenged by continuously changing his spatial relationship with everything around him.

Critiquing Spielberg's use of the dolly zoom technique provides only a momentary reprieve from the pull of reminiscing. I remember when I was thirteen, swimming in the Atlantic Ocean the summer that *Jaws* came out. The movie's menacing theme music played in my head as I imagined what my legs must look like from underwater to the shark that was almost certainly lurking somewhere nearby. That movie really changed how I saw the ocean.

Lazy shark-free summer days swimming in the Atlantic are wonderful childhood memories, but an event behind one of my most vivid remembrances occurred on July 20, 1969. Most of my extended family was gathered at a restaurant in Yonkers to celebrate the fiftieth wedding anniversary of my great-grandparents, John and Pelagia Garan. Just eight years earlier, my grandfather Joe Garan beamed with pride as the news of Yuri Gagarin's historic first spaceflight spread. As the story goes, his father, after immigrating to America from Russia, thought the name Ivan Gagarin sounded too Russian, so he changed it to John Garan. Naturally, once the news of Gagarin's flight was known, we all became instantly related to Yuri Gagarin.

My family's supposed name change and relationship to Gagarin are almost certainly not true, but that didn't stop some in our family from taking deep pride in the accomplishment of the Soviet cosmonaut. But on this night, we were celebrating another historic first—the first landing on the moon.

A little after 4 p.m. Eastern Time, most of the partygoers headed down to a damp, smoke-filled basement bar to watch the landing on a small, grainy black-and-white television.

*Eagle, Houston. You're GO for landing. Over.*
*Roger. Understand. GO for landing. 3,000 feet. PROGRAM ALARM.*

The methodic beeps of what I later found out were called Quindar tones, along with the serious, all businesslike discussions of alarms and low-fuel states, made we wonder whether the astronauts would make it to the lunar surface. Would they survive? I wondered what they might be thinking at that moment and noticed that my heart was beating faster and my breathing had increased.

*Roger. 1201 alarm. We're GO. Same type. We're GO.*

*Eagle, looking great. You're GO.*

*100 feet, three and a half down, nine forward. Five percent.*

*Okay. Seventy-five feet. There's looking good. Down a half, six forward.*

*Sixty seconds.*

*Down two and a half. Forward. Forward. Good.*

*Forty feet, down two and a half. Kicking up some dust.*

*Thirty feet, two and a half down. Faint shadow.*

*Four forward. Four forward. Drifting to the right a little. OK.*

*Down a half.*

*Thirty seconds.*

It was being reported that the spacecraft could run out of fuel at any second. My heart pounded, and my palms sweated. I looked around the room to see every member of the Garan clan transfixed on this small television beaming images from a desolate rock 250,000 miles away. It felt as if the entire world was holding its breath.

*CONTACT LIGHT.*

*OK. ENGINE STOP.*

*ACA – out of DETENT.*

*Out of DETENT.*

*ENGINE ARM – OFF.*

*We copy you down, Eagle.*

*Houston, Tranquility Base here. THE EAGLE HAS LANDED.*

*Roger, Tranquility. We copy you on the ground. You got a bunch of guys about to turn blue. We're breathing again. Thanks a lot.*

The room erupted in cheers. People hugged. Tears streamed down the faces of adults that I imagined had never shed a tear in their lives. I dove right into the celebration, shaking hands and giving hugs. After our cheering started to die down after what seemed like an eternity, we heard that the astronauts were ready to leave their spacecraft.

Packed into this small bar with most of my male relatives and a few of my female relatives, including my mother, we watched those first footsteps on the moon. The sight mesmerized me and filled me with excitement and determination. As the astronauts explored the lunar surface, a phone call between them and President Richard Nixon was broadcasted.

President Nixon congratulated the crew, saying, "As you talk to us from the Sea of Tranquility, it inspires us to redouble our efforts to bring peace and tranquility to Earth. For one priceless moment, in the whole history of man, all the people on this Earth are truly one."

Astronaut Neil Armstrong replied, "Thank you, Mr. President. It's a great honor and privilege for us to be here representing not only the United States, but men of peace of all nations and men with interest and curiosity and men with a vision for our future."

I was only seven years old at the time, but on some level, I felt as if humanity had just become a different species—a species no longer confined to our planet. This awareness surged through me like electricity. I retreated to a corner of the room, where I sat in awestruck silence trying to come to grips with the singularly momentous event I had just witnessed. I felt as if I was floating on a sea of possibility. I felt a conviction growing deep within me, a conviction that rapidly reached critical mass and exploded in an announcement to anyone within earshot that I was going to be an astronaut someday and that I too would travel to and explore space. I imagine similar scenes were playing out at that moment all around the world. For me though, looking back on that night, that moment seemed like a calling. An intense, indescribable desire to explore space was born within me.

I carried the dream of becoming an astronaut throughout my childhood, or at least until high school, when the dream temporarily receded into seemingly unobtainable obscurity. But before I put that dream on the back burner, I would always answer the inevitable question, "What do you want to be when you grow up?" with the truth, "An astronaut." This would normally lead to a pat on the head and a follow-up question: "What do you want to be if you can't do that? What do you really want to do?"

Deep within me I started to understand the draw of the sea that compelled the early explorers to set out from the comfortable and familiar to discover new worlds. I wanted to join that long line of explorers that set out from the shore and into the unknown.

Throughout my early childhood, occasionally teachers brought a black-and-white television into the classroom. I would always get excited when I heard the squeaking wheels of a giant TV stand being rolled into the room because often that meant we were going to watch a rocket launch or some exploration of the moon.

Periodically too, various teachers yelled out, "Duck and cover! Duck and cover!" This was our cue to climb under our desks and bury our heads in our hands. Once while under a desk, I wondered how hiding there would actually protect any of us from a nuclear attack. I thought, *Why would anyone want to kill us all?*

✦

It's been a few days since I watched *Jaws*, and my tour as the alert force commander this round ended at noon today. Except for some issues arising from allegedly purchasing the wrong kind of beer for the squadron bar, the time was uneventful. In addition to occasionally serving as the alert force commander, I am the "Snack O," the guy charged with the solemn responsibility of ensuring that the snack bar for the 496th Tactical Fighter Squadron is properly stocked with the latest selection of treats and beers.

Now, I'm off to the squadron to get in a quick practice dogfight with my buddy Captain John "Gilly" Gillen. Gilly, a Chicago-born and-raised former South Beach, Miami lifeguard, is one of the most unforgettable people I have ever met. A younger and better-looking version of the comedian Rodney Dangerfield, he is one of those rare people who fully lives moment to moment, always looking for ways to maximize the fun factor of each second before it passes. Gilly's fun maximization is not just for himself but for everyone within his "fun radius," normally defined as ten to twelve feet.

After taking off together in close formation, Gilly and I head to our designated training airspace. Once we're above a cloud deck, he porpoises his jet to signal that I move out from my position, about three feet from his wingtip, to a wider position. Every once in a while, the sun peeks though gaps in the clouds and illuminates the beautiful German countryside rushing below us at more than 400 miles per hour. We pass the Mosel River with its numerous bends and switchbacks dotted with quaint German villages, many beautiful churches, and the occasional ruins of medieval castles. The Mosel River Valley is steep terrain that seems to be covered in a tightly woven fabric. Upon closer inspection, it becomes clear that its precisely spaced and arranged weaves are actually countless rows of grapevines of the many fertile Mosel vineyards.

*Ron Garan sits in an F-16 parked in front of a TAB-VEE at*
*Hahn Air Base, West Germany, circa 1987.* Credit: US Air Force

The one-seater F-16 I'm piloting provides a wonderful vantage point to take in the sights. I love flying it. My seat is reclined thirty degrees to help me deal with the high g-forces experienced when maneuvering, and my entire upper body is extending into a glass bubble canopy, which gives me an unrestricted 360-degree view around the jet. I don't feel like I'm riding in this F-16. I feel as though I'm wearing it, as though it's part of me.

Sitting in my glass-enclosed recliner, I'm connected to the aircraft through the sidestick controller in my right hand and the throttle controlling 24,000 pounds of thrust in my left. At the moment, this jet has more thrust than it weighs, meaning if I wanted to, I could accelerate going straight up—at least for a little while. On both the control stick and the throttle are myriad switches and buttons for controlling the aircraft's various weapon systems. My legs extend through holes cut into the dashboard, with my feet resting on the aircraft's rudder pedals, which really just serve as footrests, since the onboard computer is controlling the rudder for me. The computer is affection-ately known as "HAL," after the computer in the classic Stanley Kubrick film *2001: A Space Odyssey.*

After arriving in the training area, Gilly and I turn our jets ninety degrees to the right and then back ninety degrees to the left while pulling six to seven g's to ready our bodies for the violent forces we are about to experience. A "g" represents the pull of gravity, the weight of an object. Standing on Earth, each of us experiences the force of one g, which we call our weight, which pulls us down and keeps us grounded to the planet. Flying straight and level in an aircraft, we also experience one g, which pushes us down into our seat. But when we turn the aircraft sharply, centripetal force multiplies our weight. If I weigh 180 pounds and pull two g's in a turn, my weight effectively doubles to 360 pounds. If I pull nine g's, my weight would shoot to a whopping 1,620 pounds!

"One's ready," Gilly reports.
"Two's ready," I reply.
"Turn away!" Gilly commands.

Gilly and I turn about forty-five degrees away from each other, and the space between us increases rapidly. When Gilly's jet appears to be a small dot, I hear his crackling transmission in my helmet: *"Turn in. Fight's on!"* I slam the throttle full forward and pull four g's to center the speck that is Gilly in the middle of my heads-up display—HUD for short—a device on top of the control panel that allows us to simultaneously monitor the outside world while monitoring aircraft and weapons parameters. As more jet fuel explodes in my aircraft's exhaust nozzle, the jet accelerates. The distance between Gilly and me closes rapidly. Just before we pass, I turn as hard as I can right at Gilly. The g-meter in my HUD snaps to "9" as Gilly starts his turn toward me. We pass, glass bubble canopy to glass bubble canopy, at a relative speed of almost a thousand miles per hour. We're close enough so that I can see Gilly's kneeboard card, a piece of paper with mission information, strapped to his right thigh.

I continue turning into him as hard as I can as my peripheral vision turns black, as if I'm looking through a tunnel. My sinus bones feel like they're being wedged down into my front teeth by my brain, which is now nine times heavier. I constrict my leg and abdomen muscles to force the blood back into my brain, and the tunnel opens back up. Meanwhile, Gilly is still turning as hard as he can toward me. I try to put an imaginary pole that extends vertically from the top of my aircraft slightly in front of and below Gilly's aircraft as clouds and the German countryside spin below us in a blur of alternating green and white. I imagine that four decades ago, scenes like this were playing out between Mustangs and Messerschmitts, but back then, real bullets were flying from their nose-mounted machine guns.

I'm starting to gain slightly on Gilly as we approach our second pass. We're not traveling in exactly the opposite direction now, and I see more of the top of Gilly's aircraft, which indicates to me that I am starting to gain the advantage. Gilly now changes his game plan and takes his jet straight up, as do I. A choice now faces me: give up some of my turn advantage and put myself between Gilly and a nuclear reaction a million miles across and ninety-three million miles away in the hope that Gilly will lose sight of me in the sun, or press the small advantage I have and continue the hard turn. I go for the sun.

If I'm successful, I will see Gilly continuing his turn inside of mine and this will all be over quickly. Unfortunately, this is not the case today. Gilly's aircraft gets really thin. I can only make out the nose and bubble canopy. My move didn't work. He's pointing right at me.

Time for plan B. I pull as hard as I can back toward him, and again we pass canopy to canopy, this time with me pointing straight toward the earth and Gilly pointing straight toward the sun. This particular engagement has resulted in a standstill. No one is the victor. After several more dogfights, the clouds below us start to turn orange as we chase the sun back to base. I honestly cannot imagine life being any better than this. I once wanted to be an astronaut, but why would I trade flying like this every day for maybe flying once every few years?

While we've been out having fun—um, I mean sharpening our combat skills—the weather has deteriorated significantly. Gilly and I each take our turn flying an instrument approach back to the runway. Here's where sitting in a recliner in a glass bubble may not be the best idea. I block out all the disorienting visual stimuli and focus on my gauges and instruments. I could swear that I'm in a steep left turn, but my gauges all indicate that my wings are level. Here's where seat-of-the-pants flying will turn you into a smoking hole in the ground.

I pop out of the bottom of the clouds at 160 miles per hour, about 200 feet above a typical dark, wet, and foggy Hahn Air Base runway. After landing and braking my aircraft to a controllable speed, I clear the runway and head to parking in my designated TAB-VEE. *All in a day's work*, I think.

Being a fighter pilot in a frontline squadron does mean we work hard, but it also means we play hard. This Friday night, as all Friday nights, starts out in the squadron bar. The camaraderie of a fighter squadron is a powerful force. Being included in the unique and exclusive fraternity of fighter pilots is to be included in a long line of strong-willed, self-confident, type-A personalities that goes back all the way to the First World War. The Friday night camaraderie consists of song and drink and tales of past conquests and other victories. Being a fighter pilot means having self-confidence that borders on egotism. But bragging is tolerated only after you have demonstrated skills to back up your ego and only when you devote them to the service of your squadron mates.

Belonging to this elite group is another in a long line of tribes that I've infiltrated since my youth, when my us-versus-them days began. As I socialize with my pilot buddies, my mind wanders back to that time . . .

At some point during my elementary school years, I transitioned from being an outgoing kid who tried to make friends with everyone to a kid who didn't know where he belonged. As kids in the neighborhood and my classmates started to form into groups and cliques, places began to emerge where I was welcome and where I was not. Not being included in various seemingly infinitely important groups made me question my own worth. Compounding this prepubescent drama? My family owned a junkyard, which meant that my father would occasionally bring home what we called "junkyard clothes."

Junkyard clothes were normally procured by my grandfather, who bought large blocks of excess items that couldn't be sold. Occasionally, that meant that I and my brothers, who were born after me, would wear uncool clothes to school. This certainly meant that we lost points in the never-ending quest to fit into the "right" groups.

The demarcation into the world of us versus them reached a head in middle school. A catalyst of the new hormones surging through my veins helped to characterize me during my middle school years as a little terror. To accelerate the transition from boyhood to manhood, I revolted against authority, all authority. I did more and more disruptive things to be accepted into the "most desirable" groups. The boundaries of my universe rapidly became the groups that I belonged to.

My entry into the bad boys of middle school club was solidified one day when I skipped one of my many after-school detentions to run home, grab my minibike, and ride back to school. Backing the bike up to the open window of the detention hall, I revved up the engine until the hall filled with exhaust and everyone had to be let out.

My bad behavior played out in the streets too. Coming of age in New York in the '70s meant that arguments were settled with fists, and I was no stranger to getting into a fight or two. So, to reduce the chance of being on the receiving end of a pride-destroying left hook, I started formal boxing. In 1975, at the age of fourteen, I boxed under the tutelage of famed boxing coach Charlie Caserta at the Cage Rec in White Plains, New York. The seventysomething Mr. Caserta's appearance and soft raspy voice evoked Mickey, Sylvester Stallone's trainer in the movie *Rocky*. Mr. Caserta coached a string of champions, a string that started in 1927 and included WBO World Middleweight Champion Doug DeWitt, a childhood friend of mine that I introduced to the Cage Rec and Mr. Caserta.

I'm sure the long public bus ride every day from Yonkers to White Plains and all the time I spent in the boxing ring kept me out of a great deal of trouble. But growing up in New York meant sometimes trouble still found me in the streets. I don't remember ever starting a fight, but I don't remember ever backing down from one either. Fighting was a way to prove you were tough, that you were more a man than a boy. Even though my boxing skills enabled me to stick up for myself, I didn't care for the unchecked violence of a street fight.

In one particular incident, I never got the chance to use my boxing skills. Walking home from a night out when I was sixteen, I heard someone from across the street call out, "Hey, Garan, come over here!" Under a streetlight stood five guys that I knew. I played on baseball and football teams with some of them. Some I considered friends.

The ringleader who had called me over was a good six inches taller than me and probably a hundred pounds heavier. "Garan, we hear you're a Jew. We fucking hate Jews," he said as I approached the group.

My mom is Jewish, and my dad is Catholic. I grew up with little religious training or tradition and didn't identify with any religion. Being a smartass kid, I responded, "Yeah, I'm a Jew. So what?" One of the guys shouted, "You fucking jewboy!" As I turned to see which one of the derelicts said that, a bright flash exploded on my left side. Pain radiated through my face and into my neck. Instantly, I remembered some random, long-forgotten dream as my vision rapidly dulled. My knees buckled as another bright flash and another random, forgotten dream rose into my consciousness. The earth rotated ninety degrees, and the Yonkers pavement rose up to meet my body and head.

Apparently, as I had looked away, the ringleader coldcocked me with a right cross and left hook. I lay in the street for a moment, fighting to stay conscious. My fight-or-flight reaction kicked 100 percent into fight mode. But just as I was struggling to get to my feet, strong kicks began to hit me from every direction. I struggled to protect my head as more and more kicks and blows rained down on me. Between the sound of boots slamming against my head and body, I heard laughter and a string of anti-Semitic heckling.

The onslaught continued until I might have lost consciousness. When I realized that the kicks and punches had stopped, I opened my eyes to see that everyone was gone. For a little while, I lay in the street bruised and bloodied, wondering what the hell just happened. *Why did these guys all of a sudden turn on me? Why didn't the guys I thought were my friends stick up for me? Why did I let my guard down? What would make them want to attack me? What did I ever do to them?*

I occasionally went to the same Catholic church as some of these guys, including the ringleader. But somehow, they had gotten it into their heads that I belonged to a group where the membership meant I deserved to get my ass and face kicked. I sat there stunned and hurt, physically and emotionally. They had violently attacked me, not for anything I had done or said but simply because they perceived me to be not only outside their group but a member of a group they deemed repugnant.

Looking back, I am thankful for this incident. This ass whooping increased my loathing of bullies of all forms. It allowed me to experience what it means to be persecuted, and it forever lit a flame in me to stand up for the disenfranchised. To this day, I cannot understand what would make someone act the way those guys did. Unfortunately, that type of bigotry and hatred is seen all around the world and in many forms. That ignorance is a cancer that not only ruins or ends the lives of those persecuted, it also severely limits our ability to progress as a society and as a species. So, as a fighter pilot, I'm grateful to be in a position to defend the defenseless if I'm ever called.

As opposed to street fighting, which at times might have been a necessary evil to maintain my place in the "lord of the flies" pecking order, as a teen I loved being in the ring. Everything felt so simple in that sixteen-foot by twenty-foot rectangle of combat. My opponent and I—my skill, speed, strength, and determination against his—were all that existed in there.

Early on, it became apparent that success in the ring was directly related to how much I trained and how hard I trained. It was a wonderful lesson in self-discipline and the value of hard work. I learned that I could feel the pain in training or feel a lot more pain later in the ring. When I was in it, it was all about scoring more points than my opponent. This usually meant hurting the other guy while trying to avoid getting hurt myself.

I fought on the amateur circuit for a few years and had fights throughout Westchester County and the boroughs of New York City. I would classify my short-lived boxing career as slightly better than mediocre. Although I won a lot more fights than I lost, including a preliminary bout knockout win in New York's Junior Olympics, I never really made it to the big stage before a more violent sport started to capture my fascination—football.

My reminiscing ends once all the male-bonding rituals at the squadron bar are complete and we move on to the larger Friday night celebration at the officers' club. The Hahn O Club is a fairly mundane one-story building on the outskirts of the base. It looks like it was built with the understanding that it would be there only temporarily. A few years before I arrived here at Hahn, members of a West German terrorist group calling itself the Revolutionary Cells attacked the club. Inside it, they planted five bombs concealed inside fire extinguishers with timing devices, but only two exploded. The explosions coincided with antinuclear protests at nearby Ramstein Air Base. Luckily, no one was hurt. This incident, even though it was a few years ago, gives the area the feel of a combat zone.

This evening, O Club routine starts out like any other until I survey the bar and, across from it, spot an unfamiliar face belonging to an attractive brunette wearing the rank of second lieutenant. Even though the Air Force is trying its best to mask her beauty with an unflattering uniform and requirements to keep her dark hair in a bun, her charm is clearly shining through. *Why have I never met her before? Who is she?* I can't stop staring at this woman.

This second lieutenant has a face of an angel and a smile that knocks the wind out of me. Our eyes lock. It sounds corny, but it's as if in this very moment, a spotlight shines down on her from heaven and I can hear a choir of angels singing in rapturous melodic harmony. OK, I just made up most of that last part, but I still have to go over and speak to her, and it's not just because she's one of only about four eligible female officers on a base of several thousand men.

"Hi, I'm Ron. Are you new here?"

"Yes. I just arrived two days ago. My name is Carmel," replies the angel in a sweet but strong and confident voice that hints at a Brooklyn accent and penetrates my senses. Her name tag shows that her last name is Courtney. She is even more beautiful close up, and her eyes are that much more mesmerizing. They hypnotize me, and I feel as though I'm pulling nine g's and experiencing tunnel vision. All I see are those eyes. The inner rims of her irises are brown, but toward the outer edges, green mixes with brown and each iris is framed by a dark ring. *She has kaleidoscope eyes! I'm meeting an angel with kaleidoscope eyes!*

Apparently earlier today, Lieutenant Carmel Courtney was walking toward the base hospital to report for duty when the fighter wing commander walked up to her and instructed her, only half-kidding, to go to the O Club tonight, "and that's an order!" Besides being a nurse, I don't know who this Carmel Courtney is, but it doesn't take long to realize that there is something special about her. As we talk, I find that I'm not only attracted to her physically but also to her character. I sense that Carmel is a rare mix of kindness, toughness, and moxie, and I believe that her chosen profession of nursing likely illustrates a caring nature. I have a strong feeling that this angel will be in my life, in one way or another, for a very long time.

Some months later, I'm boarding a train at the Frankfurt Train Station with Gilly, several of our squadron mates, and their wives. I've been dating Carmel since almost the time we met, but unfortunately, she's not with us. I and the others are on our way to participate in a program that allows service members and their spouses to see the Berlin Wall and pass through Checkpoint Charlie to experience East Berlin. It's sort of a way to show us what we're fighting for. Our train pulls out at sunset from the nineteenth-century transportation hub as we pass under massive, adjoining circular and vaulted glass ceilings. *This must have been an easy target in World War II.*

A couple of hours into the journey, we pull into a desolate East German train station under the cloak of darkness. A lone light shines down onto the concrete platform blanketed in a dense fog. Two soldiers, rifles strapped across their backs, smoking cigarettes, begin to carefully examine our train from the platform. The dark, foggy scene reminds me of a Humphrey Bogart movie. This is the perfect introduction to East Germany. After arriving in Berlin, we check into a hotel not far from Tempelhof Airfield, which will be our first stop tomorrow.

The next day, we arrive at Tempelhof just after 0900 as the first stop in a tour of several historic sites before we will head over to the eastern part of the city. The massive semicircular structure of the main terminal building silently declares the collapse of a diabolical plan for world domination. The airfield is named for the land it was built on in the 1920s, land that originally belonged to the Catholic crusaders, the Knights Templar in medieval Berlin.

Tempelhof also whispers witness to the positive qualities of humanity. It is the site of the 1948–1949 Berlin Airlift. In response to a Soviet blockade of West Berlin, Western allies organized the airlift to carry supplies to West Berlin's people. Over the course of one year, aircrews flew over 200,000 flights, providing nearly 9,000 tons of needed supplies each day to the West Berliners. Undoubtedly, this effort saved many lives.

The next stop in the western part of the city is the Berlin Air Safety Center. Housed in the Kammergericht building, the center is responsible for coordinating all air traffic in and out of Berlin. It is a beautiful nineteenth-century five-story structure made of sandstone and basalt. Stately colonnades frame the imposing entrance. Inside, all the halls and rooms are richly decorated with elaborate woodwork, sculptures, and paintings— that is, until we reach the main office.

The office is a mundane, bureaucratic-looking room barely big enough to fit its four desks, which are situated to form the shape of a cross. On each desk stands a flag from each of the nations responsible for controlling Berlin's air traffic—France, the United Kingdom, the United States, and Russia. After introductions, Gilly asks why there is no German representative. The British controller from the Royal Air Force shoots back, "Because we won the war!"

Seated at the USSR position is a former fighter pilot in the Soviet Air Force who seems like he'd rather be somewhere else. We explain to the Russian major that US Air Force pilots have a Friday afternoon tradition of going to the officers' club bar and engaging in some liquid camaraderie after the day of flying is done. He shares that the same thing occurs in the Soviet Air

Force. Since today is Friday, we suggest that he take us to nearby Wittstock Air Base, home of Soviet MiG-29 fighter jets, so that we can toast our former WWII allies. All he musters is a shake of his head and replies, "I don't think that's a good idea."

After visiting various war memorials around the city, our last stop before heading east is the eighteenth-century Brandenburg Gate. Separating us from its neoclassical columns is the massive Berlin Wall. Staring at the foreboding graffiti-filled barrier, it moves me to learn that it was established the year I was born. I have never known a world where Berliners were free to cross from one side of their city to the other.

Unlike Berliners, we, as members of the allied forces, are free to cross into and out of the eastern part of the city. Kitted out in our dress-blues service uniforms, minus our name tags, we make our way to Checkpoint Charlie and approach the small, unremarkable guard shack in the middle of Frederick Street. A foreboding symbol of the division of Cold War Berlin looms: a sign in English, Russian, French, and German that reads, "YOU ARE LEAVING THE AMERICAN SECTOR." The simple, impermanent guard shack in the American-occupied sector symbolizes the allies' view that the Berlin Wall is not a permanent or legitimate border.

We pass through the American side of Checkpoint Charlie and cross into "no-man's-land" on our way to the more permanent and elaborately fortified East German checkpoint. I can almost feel the weight of two and a half decades of tense stalemate. One of the most dangerous standoffs of the Cold War occurred at Checkpoint Charlie two days before I was born. In response to East German officials denying Americans the right to enter East Berlin, the US put on a show of force and deployed ten M48 tanks into positions around the checkpoint. The Soviets responded by deploying thirty-six T-55 tanks nearby and then further deployed ten tanks forward to confront the American tanks.

The two sides stared each other down for sixteen hours with the ignition of World War III hanging in the balance. President John F. Kennedy averted the crisis when he convinced Soviet leader Nikita Khrushchev to withdraw the Soviet tanks. Once they had withdrawn, the American armor also left the scene.

The ease with which we pass through the East German side of Checkpoint Charlie shocks me—East German guards nonchalantly wave us through the heavily fortified embankments. *Will it be as easy to pass back through in the opposite direction when we return?* I wonder. Passing into East Berlin is like passing from one world into another. The colorful and vibrant West Berlin that we left behind serves as a shocking contrast to dull and grey East Berlin.

After a few hours taking in the sights and shopping with an insanely favorable exchange rate, I wander into an East German record shop to see what kind of music folks listen to on this side of the Iron Curtain. The only Western music I find is the blues. I assume that's because the genre depicts the economic pitfalls of Western capitalism on minority populations and fits well with the party line.

Afterward, we stop into an East Berlin pub for a few beers and are amazed when the total bill turns out to be considerably less than an American dollar. We leave the equivalent of a few dollars as a tip, which, based on the exchange rate, is probably a week's salary for the waitress. From the window as we leave, we see her jubilantly wave her tip in the air.

As night approaches, we head back toward Checkpoint Charlie. We cross the street leading to the East German side of the checkpoint when I spot standing on the corner a twentysomething woman and a girl of about five dressed in rags. As long as I live, I will always remember the look this young mother and child are giving me. With simply a gaze, they are communicating a clear and strong longing to cross into the Western sector, a silent scream to take them with us. Obviously, I can't do that. I wonder what their lives must be like.

We cross through the East German checkpoint, and I feel a pang of guilt and deep appreciation for the freedom I was born into, freedom that I don't think I will ever take for granted again. Arriving back into the Western sector, I feel relief as the weight of East Berlin's oppressive gloom lifts from my soul. If the Air Force sent us on this trip to show us what we're fighting for, it has succeeded.

It's a typical Saturday afternoon near the town where I live, Traben-Trarbach, and I'm sharing it with Lieutenant Carmel Courtney. Now, more than a year has passed since we began dating. I'm in love with her. I love everything about her. She is the best friend I've ever had. When I'm with Carmel, the whole world seems perfect, and today is no exception.

Carmel and I spent the day at various wineries and are now sitting on a horseshoe bend of a sunny bank of the Mosel River eating spaghetti ice—ice cream made to look like spaghetti, with vanilla for the pasta, strawberry syrup for the sauce, and coconut shavings for the cheese. It's one of those days that makes me thankful to be alive . . . thankful to be alive and sitting next to Carmel.

On a ridgetop overlooking the river valley, the ruins of Grevenburg Castle tower above us. "I wonder what life was like for people who lived in that castle," Carmel says as she gazes at it. It looks like it has to be at least 500 years old. All that's left is a lone two-story stone wall, with arched doorways on the first floor and arched window frames on the second. Obviously, the wall was once a very small part of an enormous fortification.

I answer Carmel, "I don't know, but I bet it was pretty good for some and not so good for others."

"Do you think it was just neglected and decayed into ruins or that it was destroyed by invaders?" Carmel asks with a smile that says she already knows the answer.

"Destroyed is my bet," I say as I imagine what the castle might have looked like in its heyday and what violence led to its demise. I hold Carmel's hand as our gazes shift back to the river that carved out this beautifully rugged terrain, both of us pondering the suffering that must have taken place on that ridgetop.

"I can imagine you in that castle back in the day, slinging frosty pints of brew, wearing a sexy beer fräulein outfit," I say in a feeble attempt to change the mood.

"I suggest you keep your imagination to yourself if you want to live to see another day," replies my angel with kaleidoscope eyes.

All of my first impressions the night we met at the O Club have turned out to be true. Carmel's genuine kindness puts everyone at ease, but a deep-rooted strength informs it. I've discovered that we both share a distaste for bullies and that Carmel stands up for the disenfranchised with a vengeance. I wouldn't want to get on her bad side.

Many times, I've seen her stick up for the enlisted troops in her charge when she felt they were being treated unfairly by others in her unit, and I've seen her cut off at the knees others who have acted maliciously toward her or her colleagues. I'm sure that at least part of her strength to stand up to do the right thing comes from growing up in Brooklyn in the '60s and '70s, but I think the core of her character comes from an other-worldly source. Simply put, I think she was born tough and that her experiences have imbued her with the indomitable traits of loyalty, fairness, dedication, beauty, and love of life.

As for Carmel's saintly quality, an action she took a few months ago perfectly illustrates it. Carmel was driving by herself through the German countryside not far from our current location when she spotted an elderly woman lying in the road. People were milling about concerned but doing nothing. Carmel pulled over and administered first aid to the semiconscious woman, who she would later learn had been hit by a car. As she cared for the woman, she directed bystanders to call an ambulance. Carmel stabilized the woman's condition and stayed with her until the authorities arrived. No doubt her cool and precise reaction to this challenging situation made a big difference, so much so that the mayor of the town sent a proclamation of gratitude to our base commander, thanking Carmel for her action. This led to Carmel being awarded a flight in the back seat of one of our two-seater F-16s. She relished flying aerobatics and pulling nine g's.

I think on this and realize that I am drawn to Carmel's wisdom and quiet strength and that we have become more than two people dating. We are two people who have each other's back. We are two people who are starting to realize that we have complementary imperfections.

As I look out at the Mosel River pondering where Carmel's and my relationship will lead, I also contemplate the history of this little part of the world. I'm struck by the beauty of this river valley. *Why wasn't it enough for Hitler? Why did he try to take over the world when the Germans were already living in this paradise?* The sobering contradiction between the striking natural beauty of Germany versus its horrible past is particularly poignant as we sit on the peaceful banks of the Mosel with spaghetti ice in our bellies and the sun on our faces.

A couple of months later, I'm part of a tactical formation about 100 feet above the North Sea with Gilly leading and another pilot line abreast about 3,000 feet off Gilly's right wing. I'm about a mile back, between the two of them, with Captain John "Simo" Simonetti flying 3,000 feet off my left wing. About ten minutes ago, we took off from Aalborg Air Base near the Northern Coast of Denmark and headed north. Our target is a Norwegian F-16 base near Oslo. The low sun from the west is making a spectacular light show. Red-orange sunlight illuminates the rooster tails of water our four F-16s are kicking up as we travel at about 500 miles per hour.

*Left to right: Captain John "Simo" Simonetti, Captain John "Gilly" Gillen, and First Lieutenant Ron "Agent" Garan stand outside a Norwegian F-16 squadron building at Rygge Air Base, circa 1987.* Credit: US Air Force

About fifteen minutes later, we all successfully hit our target and by that, I mean we land at Rygge Air Base in time to go hang out with the Norwegian F-16 pilots in their squadron bar. Tomorrow, two Norwegian F-16s will lead our four F-16s on a low-level tour through the towering Norwegian fjords. This is all part of a tradition that Gilly, Simo, and I started about a year ago.

Simo, who is much older than his boyish face would indicate, is a perfect "partner in crime" as he is the second-most "live in the moment and squeeze everything you can out of life" kind of guy—second only to Gilly, of course. About once a month, Gilly, Simo, and I take out our F-16s for a weekend cross-country. A cross-county is a mission that originates at our home base and ends with us landing elsewhere. Occasionally, another pilot will tag along to make an even four-ship, what we call four aircraft flying in formation together.

Although many pilots supplement their flight hours by flying to other US bases around Europe, what sets our cross-countries apart is a self-imposed rule that we can stop for gas at any base we want, but any overnight stays have to be at a non-US base. We all believe that part of the opportunity of living and serving in Europe is to share in the European culture. On one cross-country trip, we ate breakfast at a Spanish base on the South Coast of Spain, lunch at a Belgian Air Force base near Belgium's border with France, and dinner at a Norwegian base near the Oslo Fjord.

On another trip, after getting some gas at an Italian Air Force base in Naples, Gilly—impressed with the service the Italian enlisted guys provided—decided to give an impromptu airshow for the locals. After a formation takeoff with me on Gilly's wing, we circled around and dropped down to not more than a hundred feet off the ground. Traveling at about 400 miles per hour approaching the base, Gilly transmitted over the radio, "Burners ready now." With that, Gilly slammed his throttle into full afterburner, rocketing his jet toward the base.

I slammed my throttle full forward too in order to stay in formation with him, tucked in tight on his right wing. The Air Force base passed in a blur. Troops on the ramp waved to us, or maybe they were bushes. Then we skimmed over the rooftops of the ancient city of Naples as clotheslines strung between buildings whipped by, way too close below us. In seconds, we were out to sea. It would have been impossible for us to have gone unnoticed to anyone living within a few miles of our flight path. We never heard anything about that one. Somehow, we avoided creating an international incident.

These trips are really opening up my eyes to how other people live, think, and enjoy life. I cannot imagine life being any better than this. I live in a beautiful place and have a girlfriend I adore and a job that I can't believe I'm getting paid to do. Whatever it is I've been working my whole life toward, I think I may have arrived.

✦

Today, November 12, 1987, marks a transition in my life. I received word that I'm being transferred from Hahn Air Base to the 17th Tactical Fighter Squadron, aka "The Hooters," as in an owl, at Shaw Air Force Base in Sumter, South Carolina. It'll be a few months before I ship out. Hopefully, that will give me enough time to make some major decisions.

The biggest thing on my mind is whether Carmel and I should take a go at a long-distance relationship or if I should ask her to marry me and come with me to South Carolina. Carmel and I are perfect for each other. I am in love with her, and somehow I know deep inside that I will always be in love with her. I have fallen in love with every aspect that makes Carmel *Carmel*—the kind and caring way she treats people no matter who they are or their situation, the way she puts others first, and the generosity of her heart. She's utterly unimpressed with status or celebrity, instead gravitating toward people who exhibit simple goodness and people who need help. She always shares an uplifting smile with others that can pull them from the darkest depths. I have fallen in love with that smile and her laugh. Her smile seems to shine from her heart, and her laugh is the most beautiful sound in the universe.

I have fallen in love with the way she looks at me. That someone so beautiful and pure of heart loves me makes me feel good about myself. I can't imagine my life without her. I picture myself growing old with her. But at the moment I'm only twenty-six, and marriage is a huge step that I didn't think I would take for a while. The squadron ships off tomorrow for a month-long training deployment to Spain, so this should give me some time to think.

After a few weeks in Spain, I conclude that I want to ask Carmel to marry me. She's my soul mate, the person I want to build a life with and grow old with. I want to fully meld my life with my love's. If she says yes, my life will be even more complete than I thought possible. Not long after I arrive at this conclusion, on what is now Christmas Eve, back in West Germany, I prepare to ask Carmel to marry me.

I am more than a little nervous. I know I'm making the right decision, but it's still a huge move. Whatever Carmel's answer will be, my life will forever change. I have had serious relationships before, but this one is different. Tonight could potentially mark the moment when my existence becomes deeply intertwined with another's. Tonight could potentially start me down a path where my entire life, career, happiness, and being become intimately, and I believe eternally, joined with another soul.

As the moment of truth arrives, I step to the edge of the high dive. I can almost feel a soft breeze caressing my cheeks as I survey the landscape of my life and savor these last moments of what I hope is about to become my former life. With my toes hanging over the edge, I take a deep breath and leap. I set in motion a carefully concocted plan that will forever remain a private moment between Carmel and me that concludes with me presenting her a diamond ring to match her character, exquisite yet understated. Time comes to a complete stop as we hold each other for a while. As we drift back down to reality, I ask, "So, what's your answer?"

# CHAPTER 2

# Risky Business

✦ Our four F-16s pull into the arming area of Runway Two-Two Right at Shaw Air Force Base. One by one, our arming crew removes safing pins from our practice bombs. Today, I'm checking out a pilot to be a four-ship flight lead. My job is to ensure that he can lead a four-ship to the bombing range safely and effectively.

Outside of my glass bubble canopy, the temperature soars in the high nineties on this sunny, humid South Carolina afternoon in mid-September 1988. Inside, it's cold enough to freeze meat, just the way I like it. A steady stream of chilled, condensed water vapor spews from the air-conditioning vents.

I prop my elbows up on the canopy rail so I can keep my hands in clear view of the arming crew. Nobody wants to be underneath an aircraft and have the pilot accidently drop a couple of bombs onto the ramp. As I wait for the crew to arm my bombs, I think about the monumental event that is picking up speed on its march toward me. In a mere seven weeks, Carmel and I will marry. It's going to be great seeing family and friends. Some of our friends from Hahn will be there too. I don't really know Carmel's family, so it will be wonderful to spend a little time with them. And I'm really looking forward to our honeymoon in the Bahamas. I'm thrilled about all that is soon to unfold.

Although nothing ever felt so right and I love Carmel with a passion stronger than I knew existed, I'm still a little apprehensive. I believe with all my heart in the *until death do you part* bit, but that's a little sobering. I haven't fully figured out what it means to give yourself to someone completely, but what I do know is that Carmel is that someone for me. What's in store for us? Where will our life take us? Wherever we're heading, I'm grateful that Carmel and I will be going there together.

We're all armed up. The flight lead, called "Lead" for short, radios the tower for takeoff clearance. Lead taxis his aircraft on the left edge of the runway, which in this case is the upwind edge. His wingman pulls up along the centerline, leaving just enough room for me in the number three aircraft to pull in between the wingman and Lead. My wingman is the farthest downwind aircraft. Lead extends his gloved right hand in a circular motion, signaling everyone to push up the throttle to 80 percent power while holding the brakes. The force of the thrust pitches all four jets down toward the asphalt. It takes a great deal of force on the brakes to keep the jets from lurching forward.

When everyone's engine is checked at 80 percent power, Lead salutes, releases his brakes, and slams the throttle into full afterburner to start his takeoff roll. We plan to join up into a tight formation once we're all safely airborne. I watch as Lead's exhaust nozzle expands as successive stages of raw fuel are ignited in it. Fifteen seconds later, Number Two follows Lead down the runway, and fifteen seconds after Number Two, it's my turn.

I feel a sense of relief in my thighs now that I no longer have to hold the brakes as I slam the throttle into full afterburner. *I'll have to remember to point out to Lead that he needs to position himself downwind next time so we're not all sitting in his jet wash*, I think. As the jet approaches takeoff speed, I check on the position of Lead and his wingman and plan my approach to rejoin. I pull back on the sidestick controller and twelve seconds after I released the brakes, the aircraft leaps off the runway at 180 miles per hour, still accelerating rapidly.

At about ten feet above the runway, I raise a handle to retract the landing gear into the aircraft's fuselage, then I feel a "pop." *What was that?* BOOM! My head slams back into the headrest, and my feet fly off the rudder pedals. *What the hell?* The engine is still running, so what else is going on? I need to get to "low key," a position where, if the engine fails, I will have enough altitude to deadstick the jet in for a landing.

Fighter jets have an emergency stores jettison button that, if pushed, will eject everything that the jet is carrying under its wings. Today, I have over three tons of stuff weighing me down. In front of me, rush hour traffic surges on Highway 441, Patriot Parkway. I elect to keep my stores with the aircraft.

I start a climbing left turn to get to low key when it becomes apparent that my jet has no usable thrust. Airspeed is decreasing rapidly. I'm pointing directly toward a trailer park as the aircraft starts to settle back toward the ground. I've got to minimize the aftermath of a jet that's about to crash!

Off to the left, I spot a more sparsely populated area, and I turn the jet toward it. Then, farther to the left, I see an isolated wooded area. I attempt to point the jet toward the woods, but it goes out of control and slices back to the right. The ground starts to rush up to meet me, and I realize that since the jet is no longer doing what I'm asking of it, there's no reason for me to be here anymore!

I loop each of my thumbs through the underside of a yellow ejection handle between my legs and grip it tightly. I pull as hard as I can and wonder if I waited too long.

Suddenly, time slows to a crawl. The canopy peels back from the instrument panel in slow motion. Air pressure pushes past my neck under my oxygen mask as the jet starts to retreat toward Earth from between my legs and feet. The jet becomes smaller and smaller as rockets under the ejection seat fire to decrease my own plunge toward Earth to a survivable rate.

I start to assess where the jet is heading as I weightlessly free fall. *Come a little left, a little more,* I silently command in an attempt to will the jet to a good spot. Relief takes over as I see the aircraft, *the aircraft I was just sitting in,* head toward an open field. Suddenly, I feel as if a hand has reached down and yanked on my harness. My weightless experience comes to an abrupt end as my parachute opens, slowing my harness with me in it to a gradual, peaceful descent.

With time still crawling at an inconceivably slow rate, I see the jet crash in the field I was hoping for. A fireball slowly blossoms to consume everything in its path, and undecipherable debris spins out in superslow motion from the blast. A fairly large white object slowly tumbles end over end as if it's tripping over itself trying to get away from the expanding fireball. A bunch of smaller dark objects on the opposite side of the fireball fly away in tight formation from this little erupting supernova.

The expanding fireball outruns the smaller objects and consumes them before they hit the ground. The destruction forms a path along the ground in the direction the jet was headed before it impacted Earth. A home sits in that path, and I pray that the fireball doesn't reach it. Clothes fly off clotheslines in the backyard as the fireball's progression stops before reaching the home but not before windows are blown out of the house. My own descent to Earth is being matched in the opposite direction by an ominous rising column of black smoke, some of which is coming from the roof of the home.

*Quick! Feet and knees together. Eyes on the horizon!* I think as my training kicks in and I see the ground rushing up to meet me. Apparently, my brain has released the slow-mo button and I'm back to normal time. My perception of the rate of descent slows down as my gaze shifts to a group of trees off in the distance. In rapid succession, I hit the ground with my feet, thighs, shoulder, and head—in that order. I lie on the ground for a few moments to assess if I sense any injury. Fairly confident that I'm OK, I rise to my feet and squeeze together the fittings that attach me to my parachute harness, which releases me from it. But my parachute itself and every-thing attached to it landed in a small tree and my weight, unbeknownst to me, was holding the tree near the ground. So, seconds ago, as I released myself from my harness, every-thing, including my survival radio, shot up into the air and just beyond reach.

With a little effort, I pull my survival gear out of the tree and retrieve my handheld emergency radio, tuning it to our emergency guard frequency. I transmit, "Spad Four," referring to Number Four in our formation, "this is Three, on guard. How copy?"

"Shit, Agent! What the hell happened?" replies my wingman, Tom "Gumby" Carr, who is holding overhead the crash site. Gumby was on takeoff roll, fifteen seconds behind me, and had a front row seat to the entire drama.

"Let's move over to ops freq, Gumby," I say.

Once we are on a discrete frequency, I explain to Gumby that I lost my engine on takeoff.

"Copy that, Agent. Emergency vehicles are en route to you and the crash site now," Gumby replies.

I'm gathering my things when I notice that my kneeboard and the paper cards that were affixed to my right thigh are all still in place. *That must have been an incredibly low-speed ejection,* I think. Just then, a local bakery delivery van pulls up to me from a dirt road a few yards away. A burly guy with a long beard leans over to an open sliding door and yells in a strong Southern drawl, "Hey, man, I saw you parachuting down to the ground. You need any help?"

"Yeah! Thanks. Can you give me a ride back to the base?"

The man says yes, but just as I'm about to climb in among the donuts and cinnamon rolls, base emergency vehicles show up and I jump into one of them, a small blue Air Force pickup truck. "Is anyone hurt on the ground?" I ask the driver.

"No word yet, sir, but emergency vehicles are on the scene battling the fire. Are you OK?"

"Yes," I reply as he drives me straight to the base hospital for evaluation, where my flight commander, Captain Bill "Kanga" Rew, meets me in the emergency room. At least he was my flight commander up until about three hours ago. Kanga is a fit, highly self-disciplined officer with incredible integrity. He is soft-spoken, always choosing his words with precision and purpose, seemingly in service to a higher calling. I respect him greatly.

Before taking off on this doomed practice sortie today, I had said goodbye to Kanga. A little while later, he was driving his car out through the front gate of the base, looking back in fondness at the Shaw Air Force Base sign as he left for a new assignment in Las Vegas, when he saw a pilot eject from an F-16 and a fire-ball ensue. He called into the squadron, and when he found out that one of his old "boys" ejected, he immediately turned around and headed back to base.

Kanga had been a great mentor to me when I first arrived at Shaw from Germany, and he oversaw my ascent up the pilot ranks. In addition, Kanga was the squadron weapons officer, a highly respected and sought-after position that requires that one graduate from the US Air Force Fighter Weapons School. Every year, a base will send 1 to 2 percent of its pilots, the best of the best, to attend the six-month intensive air combat school and fewer still make it to graduation.

Graduates, or "Patch Wearers" as they're called, with their coveted "Fighter Weapons School Graduate" patch on their left flight suit sleeves, are sent to fighter squadrons around the world to become the resident warfighting experts. Patch Wearers ensure that their squadrons are ready to go to war when called. Kanga not only attended this highly distinguished and exclusive program, he was asked to come back to the school and serve as an instructor pilot there, an even more exclusive club identifying him as the best of the best of the best. But his trip out to Nellis Air Force Base in Nevada will have to wait. He first needed to check on one of his own.

✦

Doctors have ruled that I suffered no injuries, and the investigation has ruled out fuel contamination as a cause of my aircraft mishap yesterday. Consequently, the base has resumed flight operations. In the spirit of getting back on the horse, my squadron commander has agreed to let me fly today. Taxiing out to the arming area of Runway Zero-Four, I realize that since the wind has shifted and we will be taking off to the northeast, we won't fly over the crash site. *That's well enough.*

Today, I'm leading a formation of four F-16s on a training mission. I pull onto the downwind side of the runway with the rest of the formation in trail, then I signal for everyone to push up their engines to 80 percent power. Holding the brakes, I feel a sense of *déjà vu* as my jet pitches down toward the runway. Since ejecting yesterday, I have spent countless hours answering questions about my aircraft's gauge indications before, during, and after the explosion. I spend a little extra time assessing each gauge in the hope that it might spur some more memories and extract some critical data.

All looks good, and I release the brakes and slam the throttle to full afterburner. In spite of yesterday's events and the fact that I've had thousands of takeoffs, I still love the invigoration of hurtling myself down the runway. I love the feel of the gentle hand of acceleration pushing me back into my seat as 24,000 pounds of thrust is ejected in the opposite direction of travel. Thank you, Sir Isaac Newton!

Once safely airborne and I've retracted my landing gear, I retard the throttle out of afterburner and hear a "pop." *I bet it's always done that and I'm only now noticing it because I'm being hypersensitive and aware,* I think. But just as I succeed in convincing myself that nothing is wrong, the unmistakable high-pitched wail of the low speed warning alarm sounds, indicating I have another engine malfunction! Something has caused me to lose thrust, and my airspeed is decreasing rapidly.

I'm a little higher and faster than I was yesterday, and there's no rush hour traffic underneath me. There's nothing in my path but wide-open fields. I push the emergency stores jettison button and feel a *kathunk* as tons of stores drop from underneath the aircraft's wings. The jet yaws to the right and is now harder to control. "Guys, you're not going to fucking believe this. It happened again!" I transmit to my formation as Number Two is beginning his rejoin to my wing, Number Three is just getting airborne behind me, and Number Four has just released his brakes to start his takeoff roll.

"Two, continue straight ahead. Shaw Tower, Spad One declaring an emergency. I will be landing opposite direction on Runway Two-Two," I transmit to the tower as adrenaline surges through my veins. I begin a right turn back toward the runway I just lifted off from as I trade altitude for airspeed. The nose of the aircraft starts yawing left and right, and I find it's taking all of my concentration to keep it heading back toward the runway.

In spite of the confusing aircraft handling, I know that the ensuing mishap investigation board is going to ask me what each of the aircraft gauges read. I carefully scan each gauge, committing the readings to memory. Everything looks fine until I spot the "nozzle position" gauge. The nozzle is wide open, and at this throttle setting it should be closed. Because it won't close, the aircraft does not have enough thrust to maintain altitude. Fortunately, I am able to wrestle the jet to the ground and land just after Number Four gets airborne.

I bring the aircraft to a stop on the runway and immediately shut the engine down, open the canopy, unstrap from the ejection seat, and quickly climb out. You never know when an engine malfunction can turn into an engine fire. I am met almost immediately by emergency vehicles, including a pickup truck driven by the supervisor of flying, who we call "the SOF," the pilot charged with ensuring that flight operations run smoothly and safely.

"Why didn't you punch off your stores?" the SOF asks me.

"I did!" I answer as I turn around to see a huge fuel tank and three 500-pound inert practice bombs underneath my right wing. *What? I know I punched off the stores. I even felt the kathunk,* I think as I try to figure out what happened. Then I look at the left wing and see that everything is gone from it— and that's when I understand what transpired. When I pushed the emergency stores jettison button, unbeknownst to me, the aircraft malfunctioned again and only the stores on the left wing were jettisoned, leaving my jet in an asymmetric condition that was not certified for flight. That's why it handled strangely.

On the ride back to the squadron in the SOF's truck, I feel different than I did after my incident yesterday. Even though I was able to bring the jet back and no one was hurt and nothing was damaged, everything feels extraordinarily surreal. I'm hit in the gut by the sobering fact that after thousands of uneventful takeoffs, I've now had two that almost killed me back to back. *Is this a wakeup call that I hit the snooze button on yesterday?*

Returning to the squadron, the guys are eyeing me much differently than they did yesterday. Their looks of concern and relief are replaced with suspicion. I can't say that I blame them. I would be somewhat suspicious of someone who had two extremely rare, life-threatening emergencies in two days. That just doesn't happen.

After several hours of interrogation over today's incident and several more follow-up questions regarding yesterday's, I am finally released to go home to the one-story ranch house, not far from the base, that I share with Carmel. For the first time in my flying career, I realize in an undeniably concrete way that I am not fully in control of everything that happens to me in the air. Even though I have, already, in my short career, lost squadron mates and friends to aircraft mishaps and though I understand that there has never been any guarantee that I will come out of the Air Force alive, I had suppressed that reality out of my consciousness. Up until today, getting killed in a jet was something that happened to other guys, not me.

After the second mishap four days ago, my squadron commander took me off the flight schedule. Even though the incident did not result in a crash, the Air Force has initiated a separate full-blown mishap investigation, or as we call it in Air Force speak, a Class A investigation. Presently, officials are conducting two Class A investigations on me. This could be a new one for the record books. The intense scrutiny and my own second-guessing have gotten me really down. A lot of the joy of flying is drifting away.

Just as I'm feeling that things couldn't get any worse, I receive news that William Smith, a gentleman who was injured running into his burning home at the first crash site, has died. With this news, I feel like a part of me dies along with him. I know that I did everything I could to avoid hurting anyone on the ground, but that awareness doesn't relieve the pain or the second-guessing of what I could have done to try to avoid the crash. Despite the fact that the multiple avoidance scenarios I have run through my head still result in destruction and more people getting hurt or killed, I feel myself descending into an even deeper chasm of despair. I feel an impending doom as if a sorrowful wave is rippling out through the universe, as if all is not quite right. I start shrinking under a heavy blanket of sorrow. I spend some time in deep prayer for the soul of William Smith and his family. I will keep him in my thoughts and prayers for the rest of my life.

At home, I inform Carmel of all of this news, and she and I embrace in a way that only soul mates can. "We're going to get through this," she says with calm confidence. I drift into the comfort and warmth of Carmel's heart and feel as if I can stay there forever. Our embrace provides me a momentary secure foothold amidst the disorienting anguish that is swirling all around me. Then suddenly, banging on our roof jars me from Carmel's loving sanctuary and I go outside to investigate. On our roof, about five squadron mates are jumping up and down. Many cars are parked down the street, while other squadron mates approach the house.

Apparently, Carmel and I are victims of an age-old Air Force tradition called "roof stomping." In a roof stomp, squadron mates jump on an unsuspecting squadron member's roof until said squadron member lets everyone in for an impromptu party. Normally, "victims" are graded on how long it takes before roof stompers are in their house, beer in hand. *Not now, guys,* I say to myself. *This couldn't come at a worse time.* But then the real reason for the roof stomp dawns on me. This is a sign of solidarity. This is the guys' way of saying, "We're with you. We're going to get through this together." Within minutes, Carmel and I open our door and usher in more than twenty squadron mates and their spouses. Hours later, as the party ends and everyone says goodbye, I realize that I really needed that. I truly appreciate the gesture and the momentary respite from the dark times that have befallen me.

In addition to this brief moment of solidarity and Carmel's love, our squadron chaplain, Father Robert Sable, has extended me emotional support. "Father Bob" has performed pre-canon marriage counseling for me and Carmel and has felt the need to counsel me through this situation. Initially, I didn't think I required his assistance, but the more I reflected on everything that happened, the more I realized I could use all the help I could get. For the first time in my life, I am confronted with death in a dramatically real way—death that could come to others through my actions and my own death. Death has elevated itself above the background noise of my everyday life.

More than a month later, in early November, both Air Force mishap investigations have ended just in time for me to head out of town for my wedding. I was exonerated in both incidents.

In the first event, a definitive understanding of what exactly transpired in the engine was never fully determined. The evidence seemed to indicate that the computer that controls fuel flow to the engine sensed an overspeed and forced the nozzle to close. This is likely what I felt as a "pop." Then, because the afterburner was still ignited, a massive overpressure developed in the exhaust nozzle, which rapidly built and culminated in an explosion. The computer controlling fuel flow reacted to this by rolling back the engine speed to sub-idle. The result of all this is that shortly after my landing gear lifted off the ground, there was no longer enough thrust coming out the back end of the aircraft to keep it in the air.

The flight data recorder indicated that I ejected 4.3 seconds before the jet impacted the ground and less than a second before I would have been outside of the ejection envelope. If I had stayed with the jet just one second longer, I would not have survived the ejection. On a more somber note, the report also stated that in addition to the fatal injury that Mr. Smith sustained, several other people in the vicinity of the crash were hurt. The news of other injuries adds to the weight being impressed upon my soul.

In the report for the second incident, several recommendations were made for things I could have done to remedy the aircraft malfunction. But it also acknowledged that my successful recovery of the jet in spite of multiple compounding malfunctions should be commended. I have since been returned to full-flight status and will fly one last sortie today before heading out on leave for my wedding this week.

It's a beautiful morning on November 5th, 1988, in Scranton, Pennsylvania. I feel some butterflies in my stomach as I ponder all that will unfold. Today, my love and I will be forever joined as one. To calm my nerves, I jog through the neighborhood of the Hill Section of Scranton. A cold crisp to the air feels even more noticeable in comparison to the warm sun on my face. As I head up a particularly steep hill, the certainty that Carmel and I were meant for each other hits me. I'm really excited to see what this next chapter of our lives will reveal. I also ponder the realization that it's not just two people being joined as one, but two clans. The Garan clan and the Courtney clan are about to be forever linked, and my circle of care and concern is about to be doubled. The catalyst for this expansion is love.

As I notice the few leaves remaining on the deep-rooted Hill Section hardwoods, it dawns on me that love is a powerful perspective-expanding tool that can unite us in ways that seem impossible. By opening up to love, the possibilities become endless. As I fall deeper in thought, I am abruptly brought back into the here and now by the realization that I shouldn't overdo this jog or expose myself to a twisted ankle or pulled muscle on the day that I will walk down the aisle arm in arm with my new bride.

Not long afterward, I trade running shorts for my white Air Force mess dress uniform and am standing at the altar of the

Holy Rosary Church. The image of two clans joining as one is reinforced as I look out and see all of my family, friends, and loved ones on one side of the church and all of Carmel's on the other. The scene fills my heart with warmth.

The heavenly sound of an organist and violinist playing Johann Pachelbel's "Canon in D Major" surrounds us as Carmel arrives through what is now a downpour outside and starts down the aisle toward me on her father's arm. Her white wedding dress perfectly accentuates her tall, beautiful figure. She is the embodiment of beauty, grace, and joy. Her father, Joe Courtney, symbolically presents Carmel to me, and together, along with my brother John and Carmel's sister Colette, we make our way to the altar and the priest who will marry us.

I look into the eyes of my soul mate as we exchange our vows, and Carmel's smile melts my heart as I realize this is one of the rare defining moments of life. I try to savor it but find my mind drifting toward thoughts of the possibilities of our future together. "I now pronounce you man and wife" snaps me back to the moment, and I feel profound spiritual love welling up inside me.

Moments later, Carmel and I, now married, begin our walk back up the aisle. My fighter pilot buddies, in their service dress uniforms, stand face-to-face in two rows on either side of us. On command, they all raise their sabers into a high arch, with tips almost touching and blades facing up and away from us. "Ladies and gentlemen, it is my honor to present to you Captain and Mrs. Garan," announces one of the sword bearers.

As Carmel and I walk under the saber arch, I'm suspicious of the grin on the face of the last sword bearer, Gumby Carr. As we pass Gumby, he lowers his sword and swats Carmel on the butt. Neither Carmel nor I are surprised, so we don't raise a ruckus, though maybe we suppress a snicker. This swatting is part of the tradition. Usually, the sword swatter will add, "Welcome to the Air Force, ma'am," but since Carmel has served in the Air

*Captain and Mrs. Ronald J. Garan Jr. in the back of a limousine after their wedding at Holy Rosary Church in Scranton, Pennsylvania, 1988.*
Credit: Ron and Carmel Garan

Force, Gumby doesn't say that last part. However, I don't think the responsibilities, sacrifice, and periodic heartache of being a military spouse is lost on either Carmel or me. We both have at least an inkling of what Carmel is signing up for.

Several months after our wedding, Carmel and I are completely settled in our ranch home near Shaw Air Force Base. Carmel is now a civilian and works as a nurse at the VA hospital in Columbia, South Carolina, and I am back to flying my butt off with my squadron. I really feel that I am ready to take my flying to the next level and have applied for consideration to attend the USAF Fighter Weapons School. It's a long shot, but I have the support of my wing leadership, which has strongly recommended me for the program, and I'm ready to "up my game."

I've noticed that I am a slightly different pilot after my two incidents back in September. I wouldn't say that I was a daredevil before them, but I now look at risk in a new light. I see it as the price to pay for a benefit. I feel an emerging appreciation for the concept of risk/benefit tradeoff developing.

Now, instead of just blindly throwing myself into risky situations, I first assess the location of the safe exit from a situation in case everything goes south. But before I put myself into a position where I might need an exit strategy, I ask whether the potential benefit of stepping into it is worth the risk. I have a feeling that if I stay in this chosen profession long enough, there will come times when the potential benefit will be so great and/or the cost of not taking action so high that I will have to enter situations knowing that there's no way out if everything goes wrong. I hope and pray that those situations remain rare. All of this new calculus has probably made me slightly less capable in the air—less capable but more survivable. I'm hoping that increased experience can help bridge the gap in my new flight philosophy.

I land on Nellis Air Force Base Runway Two-One Right. As I brake my F-16 to taxi speed, I see the Las Vegas Strip off in the distance to the south. After turning off the runway, I head north on Nellis's main ramp past rows and rows of fighter jets from different countries and services. On this early July day in 1989, all are in town to participate in a massive graduation exercise for the present Fighter Weapons School class.

Toward the north end of the ramp, I see the designated parking area for the F-16 Division. I spot the crew chief who is marshalling me to my designated parking spot, and I also see a group of pilots in their flight suits standing around a parked

F-16. *This must be the graduating class taking a class photo.* Among the group, I spot a conspicuously attractive woman also dressed in a flight suit that is most certainly not her own. I taxi past the group, and the woman looks at me, smiles, and unzips her flight suit and drops it to her waist to expose her naked, exceptionally well-endowed breasts. *Welcome to Nellis, "Home of the Fighter Pilot." This is going to be an interesting six months,* I think.

A few weeks earlier, I received word that I was selected to attend the Fighter Weapons School. I'll be here for the next half year in the most intensive flight training program on the planet, the one that my old flight commander Bill "Kanga" Rew came through. Some say this is the most dangerous flying outside of combat. Others say it's the most dangerous, including combat. The training will take place in the Nellis Range Complex, aka the Nevada Test and Training Range, NTTR for short. NTTR is more than a thousand square miles of airfields, defense systems, and other things that we get to blow up. At NTTR, we are permitted to fly as low as 100 feet off the ground through the canyons and over the mountainous terrain, all while dodging simulated missiles and adversary aircraft. I can't wait.

After I graduate, I will return to the 17th Tactical Fighter Squadron and take on an assignment as the squadron weapons officer. When I do, it will be my responsibility to ensure that the squadron is ready to go to war should we be called. This is not a responsibility I take lightly. I will give this training my all.

Through my canopy, I watch above me as the refueling boom of a KC-135 Stratotanker—a military version of the Boeing 707—gently rocks from side to side and forward and back, funneling fuel into my F-16 at a rate fast enough to fill an average swimming pool in less than five minutes. When my fuel tanks are all topped off, I detach from the refueling boom—what we call "dropping off"—gently back away, and drift out to the left underneath a wing of the KC-135 and near three other F-16s flying next to the aircraft. Then I rise, establishing my position as the fourth F-16 next to the other three jets. Across the formation fly four additional F-16s on the opposite wing, perfectly framed above Utah's Pine Valley Mountains off in the distance to the east. Each of our jets is carrying six live 500-pound bombs. Although this is a training mission, these are real bombs—the real McCoys. This training is serious business.

As I wait for the rest of the formation to get their fuel on a mid-December day at NTTR, I have a chance to continue coordinating the massive airstrike that is about to be unleashed on Southern Nevada. I am leading a strike force of thirty-six aircraft from the various Fighter Weapons School divisions against targets defended by a myriad of surface-to-air defenses and adversary aircraft primarily from the US Navy. This is all part of the mission employment phase of Fighter Weapons School, which will culminate with graduation later this week.

Three other tankers are on our side of the range complex, and four more are on the adversary side. All in all, over seventy aircraft are topping off their fuel tanks in preparation for our mock battle. Some of the "good guy" aircraft are tasked with bombing targets, some with taking out enemy defenses, some with jamming enemy radar and communications, and some with reconnaissance and battle damage assessment. All the aircraft on the other side have the same mission: stop us from achieving ours.

At the predetermined time, I pull away from the tanker and head east. In the other seven jets in my formation are an assortment of Fighter Weapons School students and our instructors. My wingman and instructor is Kanga. I can think of no one else I'd rather fly my last training sortie with as a Fighter Weapons School student than him. Of course, this will be my last sortie only if Kanga passes me.

As we spread out into attack formation and accelerate at near supersonic speed toward the simulated border of an imaginary hostile nation, I think back over the past six months—the twelve- to eighteen-hour days, the intense scrutiny of every maneuver and tactic, six months living on the ragged edge of performance and danger where a disastrous fiery death was always mere seconds away. I think back to the camaraderie that I experienced with my F-16 classmates and classmates flying other aircraft, to that cocky inexperienced pilot that I used to be who thought he knew everything when in fact he knew just enough to be dangerous.

But now, as I'm nearing the end of my time here, I feel like I'm on top of my game. I know enough to know that war is never something to hope for, but I feel if it ever does come to combat, I will never be more ready than I am right now. I feel like I've been training for the Super Bowl, a contest that may never happen, but a small part of me hopes it does. A small part of me wants to be tested in combat, wants to undergo that baptism by fire and prove myself worthy. I'm not sure where that part of me comes from. Is it genetics passed down from some distant warrior ancestor or just testosterone-fueled stupidity? Whatever it is, I'm about to tap into it to incite some high-speed jousting on modern steeds.

Eight contrails—streaks of water vapor—are marking the sky as we press toward the "enemy territory." Normally, flying at an altitude that induces contrails would be a rookie mistake, but today my eight-ship of F-16s is purposely out in front of the large strike package announcing our presence. Today, in addition to eventually blowing the shit out of some desert airfield and associated plywood aircraft, we are acting as decoys.

Over my radio I transmit that I see an adversary formation on my radar, which indicates that the adversaries are thirty miles away at an altitude of 48,000 feet above sea level. My radar warning receiver lights up like a Christmas tree, indicating that at least one adversary aircraft has also locked its radar onto my sweet ride. At the predetermined distance from the high-altitude adversary aircraft, which have likely launched simulated long-range missiles in our direction, I roll my jet inverted and pull toward the ground. The other seven jets in the formation do the same. All of us are heading straight toward the earth, creating roughly a ninety-degree angle between "us and them."

Shortly before we run out of atmosphere between us and the ground, I turn ninety degrees away from the bad guys and start to level out. Three jets in the formation follow me to the north while the other four head to the south. At a hundred feet above the rugged terrain, we turn tail onto the adversaries and rejoin the strike package.

Meanwhile, eight F-15s that trailed us have all called their long-range shots against our would-be attackers. They follow this up with various "kill calls" in rapid succession on the common exercise frequency. Instructors are monitoring the entire "war" in a computer simulation control room that will later serve as our debrief venue. If the instructors give you the dreaded "You're dead" call, your aircraft has been assessed to have been destroyed and your fun is over; you must return to base immediately.

Our formation temporarily breaks our eight-ship into two four-ships to establish the dual role of escorting less maneuver-able aircraft while setting up for our own attacks. My four-ship is out front with the second four-ship about ten miles in trail. Desert dry washes and vegetation whiz by as we continue toward our targets barely a hundred feet off the ground. Our attention cycles between hugging the terrain while not hitting the ground, to monitoring our position in the formation, to searching the sky for adversaries with our eyes and radar. We are purposely taking a path that puts us in the most rugged terrain possible, with a goal of putting terrain between us and the adversaries.

About ten miles out in front of us looms a rocky grey mountain range that rises steeply almost a mile above the desert floor. We are flying just above cactus height straight for the center of it. Our target, an airfield complex, is on the other side of the mountain range, presently hidden from our view. We continue toward the base of the mountains until the last possible moment. When continuing straight ahead is no longer an option without blasting four new caves into the side of the mountain, I pull four g's and climb my aircraft steeply up it. The rest of the formation follows in unison. A few seconds later, approaching the ridgeline, I roll inverted and pull across the summit. Still inverted, now past the ridge, I spot my target, a series of mock aircraft aligned on a taxiway. I pull down toward the targets to establish a thirty-degree dive at the earth.

As I roll back to wings level, the electronic heralding of my radar warning receiver announces that surface-to-air missiles have locked onto my aircraft. I start defensive maneuvers as smoke trails from simulated missiles rise from the desert floor. *Thank God this is just a drill.*

Convinced I eluded the missiles, I continue the attack. In my HUD, I line up green projected symbology over the top of the target. Included in the symbology is the continuously computed impact point, what we call the "death dot." This dot, a small circle with a dot in the middle, rises in my field of view toward the plywood aircraft. When it reaches the center of the parked formation, I depress a small red button—what we call "the pickle button"—on the top of my control stick, which is followed by a series of rapid *kathunks* as six 500-pound bombs release from under my aircraft's wings. I immediately pull up and back toward the ridge from whence we came.

Three other aircraft, all with their bombs hurtling toward their respective targets, follow me toward the ridge. Over my left shoulder, I see a series of fireballs engulfing the airfield complex as a sense of satisfaction and excitement washes over me—satisfaction for a job well done, excitement that now, with our bombs gone, we will transition to full-up air-to-air fighters. We still have to fight our way out of enemy territory, and I'm really looking forward to some turning and burning.

After experiencing a disappointing lack of adversary aircraft to engage on our egress from the target area, I line up my eight-ship with Nellis Air Force Base Runway Two-One Right. We have found a spot in the recovery sequence. Seventy jets, all returning to the airfield at the same time, is always a sight to behold. As we pass the runway threshold at 1,500 feet above the runway, I start a five-g turn to the right, away from the formation, and continue the turn while descending to landing. One by one, each of the jets follow me through landing and taxi back to our parking area.

I pull into my parking spot and realize that in all likelihood, this was my last flight as a Fighter Weapons School student. I still need to lead the massive debrief in the computer simulation facility, but I've done this countless times before and it shouldn't be an issue.

Later, after the debrief and all the lessons have been gleaned from the computer-generated recreation of the battle, I'm at the Nellis Air Force Base officers' club for "Patch Night." I've been looking forward to this since the day I arrived for training. One by one, our instructors call us to the front of the group. Each instructor shares some stories, good and bad, about their students, which culminates with a newly minted Fighter Weapons School Graduate patch slapped onto each student's left flight suit arm. When my turn comes, Kanga does the honor of slapping my arm into the small community of "Patch Wearers."

Pride wells up inside me as I savor the end of this challenging journey. I also feel the gravity of the responsibility I am taking on—the responsibility of ensuring that my squadron is ready to go to war if called. I feel up to the challenge.

# CHAPTER 3

# A Third of an Orbit

✦ Kicker Billy Rhodes lifts his leg, which is my signal to start sprinting behind the aligned Roosevelt High School kickoff team. I glance over to our sideline as famed high school football coach Tony DeMatteo nods at me. The message is clear: "You know what to do." As I get within a few yards of Billy, he starts toward the ball. I roll in and trail him as I accelerate to full speed.

I catch up to Billy just as his foot impacts the ball, which commences a highly contentious grudge match against our rival, Lincoln High School. My job is to sprint as fast as I can directly to the football. As the Lincoln players align in front of the ball carrier to form a blocking wedge, I am supposed to dive through the air and smash into as many blockers as possible to dismantle the wedge formation. As the "wedge breaker," I am to sacrifice my body in order to take out the enemy defenses. My selection for this kamikaze mission was due to my coaches' perception that, despite my relatively small frame of about five foot nine inches and 160 pounds, I had an optimum combination of aggressiveness, lack of respect for those bigger and stronger than me, and stupidity.

As the wedge forms, Lincoln players turn their backs, which gives me an avenue for the surprise attack. The two forward-most players are lined up perfectly as I push off my right leg and launch myself into the air. Flying across the ground horizontally, I stretch out as much as I can to increase my planform and make myself as lethal as possible. My right shoulder impacts the lead blocker below his chin strap just as he turns to find his target. My forward motion slows only slightly as I pick up the Lincoln High School barnacle. We both fall at the knees of the second blocker and tumble into a pile of red and purple uniforms as mayhem unfolds all around us, just beyond our perception.

I often find myself thinking back to such days when I competed on the football field. Those years played a key role in shaping who I would become. I love the camaraderie of military life. I know that my squadron mates would risk their lives to protect mine, and I would do the same for them. We are all brothers-in-arms. Playing football was a primitive archetype of a similar camaraderie that I now experience serving in the military. In high school, I traded my boxing gloves for a football helmet and expanded a me-against-him battle to an us-against-them battle. Initially, I tried to both box and play football but soon found the need to gain weight for football and the need to keep weight as low as possible for boxing untenable.

That matchup with our rival Lincoln High School was more of a war than a game. In the week leading up to the contest, Roosevelt High School was vandalized and an effigy of our star running back, George Bellino, was found on campus hanging from a noose among a great deal of hateful graffiti. This was discovered after George, who had many college scholarship offers, experienced a season-ending and potentially career-ending knee injury. Bad feelings ran high, as did an us-versus-them attitude. Sportsmanship went out the window as the contest went from sport to a desire to punish the enemy.

Thinking back on that game and many of the other contests we had my senior year, I can't remember a time that I felt more alive than when I was on the gridiron. The intense focus, concentration, and digging deep when I felt I couldn't take another step was otherworldly. I absolutely loved playing football, everything about it—the excitement in the locker room on game day, playing in front of the crowd, and the rush of inflicting a big hit. But as much as I enjoyed the sport, football was also an escape from a world that seemed to be crumbling all around me.

A year earlier, I, along with my younger brothers, John and Danny, were caught in the middle of the emotionally destructive divorce of our parents. At fifteen years old, I found myself moving from a loving, nurturing family situation to one where I had virtually no adult supervision. My parents were and are good people whom I love very much. They just got caught up in a marriage that wasn't working, and we were all entangled in its inevitable toxicity. I found myself adrift, and football was the rock I clung to. Football seemed to me to be the most important thing in my life, the only thing that made sense.

I began fantasizing about becoming a Division I college football player. But soon that dream would crash down around me too as a series of injuries and probably a lack of talent foiled that plan. I again found myself with no clue about what I wanted to do with my life. Even my childhood dream of becoming an astronaut seemed ridiculous. At the time, the Skylab program had already ended, and the Space Shuttle Program had not yet begun. To me, it didn't make any sense to pursue becoming an astronaut if we didn't have a space program.

"Dudes! We're stopping for lunch!" declares Jan "Tav" Tavrytzky, which snaps me out of my daydream. I unplaster my head from the passenger window of the government van I'm sitting in the back of on this August day in 1990 near Savannah, Georgia. Tav, an athletic and energetic Air Force Academy grad and former football player, loved by the ladies, likes to use the word "dude" a little too much and has been blasting Depeche Mode for the last two hours. He was "selected" for driver duty on this trip from Shaw to the Florida Panhandle, trading his normal ride, a candy-apple-red Porsche convertible, for a clunky government-issue van affectionately known as a "Blue-Steely." I'm still reeling over the decision to send us to Eglin Air Force Base for an air-to-surface missile training deployment when we should be preparing to go into actual combat.

As the recently minted weapons officer of the 17th Tactical Fighter Squadron, a squadron that has been designated as a rapid deployment unit to counter aggression worldwide, it is my job to ensure the squadron is ready to go to war. In all likelihood, we are on the verge of going into combat, and there's much to do. Adding to my displeasure is the long drive I'm enduring from South Carolina to Florida as one of the guys that drew the short straw and is traveling by van instead of an F-16 since we have more pilots going on the trip than jets.

A few days ago, on August 2 at 0200 Kuwaiti time, units from the Iraqi Republican Guard rolled into Kuwait. Supporting the operation were helicopter gunships and attack aircraft. The surprised and vastly outnumbered Kuwaiti defense forces were no match for the Iraqi onslaught. During one of the attacks, the brother of the Kuwaiti emir was shot and killed. His body was then placed in front of an Iraqi tank and run over. News media covering the invasion reported many other barbaric atrocities, including summary executions of women and children.

With all this going on, it makes no sense that we are deploying to Florida only, I suspect, to be recalled and then scrambled to the Middle East. I would prefer to have less scrambling in the scramble. We are on the hook to stop these bastards, and I'd prefer to get on with it. The big concern right now is whether Saddam Hussein will continue his roll into Saudi Arabia. In any case, this aggression cannot stand. At every stop along the way, I call from a pay phone back to the base to see if we've been recalled. Each time, I get the same answer: "Not yet, Agent. Continue on to Eglin."

As I suspected, not long after we arrive at Eglin, we receive word to return to Shaw because we are to deploy to the Middle East. I jump into one of our four deployed F-16s and take off in formation back to South Carolina. In the air, I feel myself going into *mission mode*. One by one, I begin to place things that I need to do into compartments in my mind. I think of all the things I will need to accomplish in the few hours remaining, and I start formulating long-range plans for when we arrive in theater.

A little less than an hour after takeoff, we arrive back at Shaw. The squadron is a buzz of activity. Personnel are packing mission-planning equipment and classified documents into large containers. Out on the flight line, our maintenance troops are outfitting twenty-four F-16s with live air-to-air missiles and long-range fuel tanks. As I observe this monumental under-taking, I notice the interesting demeanor of everyone in the squadron. All seem highly focused on what they're doing and very serious, but at the same time, excitement charges the air. We have been called on to right a wrong, to overturn an aggres-sion, and to come to the aid of an ally. We've been called on to put to use years of training and preparation.

"Agent, head home and be back here in eight hours for the deployment brief," says Hooter squadron commander Lieu-tenant Colonel Billy Diehl, who is a little shorter than me but has the physique of a bodybuilder and looks like he could bench press a Cadillac.

"Yes, sir!" I respond with a slight grin. *How lucky I am not only to be going into combat, but to being going into combat led by Lieu-tenant Colonel Billy Diehl*, I think. Our squadron commander, who amongst ourselves we all simply call "Billy" out of affec-tion, is a natural leader and a straight shooter. Everyone respects him and would follow him to the gates of hell. He's one of those amazing, completely transparent leaders. You know exactly what he's thinking because he has no hidden agendas and is laser-focused on completing the mission, protecting those under his command, and leading by example. It doesn't hurt that he already has combat experience and even a MiG kill in Vietnam.

On the way home, I see massive lines forming at the mobility center as cargo aircraft are arriving and being loaded with personnel and equipment. It puzzles me when I see what appears to be couples being married while in the line—one person in battle fatigues and the other in civilian clothes with a third seemingly presiding over a ceremony. I think it's probably my imagination until I see one of the couples embrace and kiss while others in the line applaud. All that was missing was the shotgun.

On the way home, some of us in the squadron, including me, stop at a local gun store to buy 9mm Berettas to replace our government-issue .38 Special handguns. We all figure we will probably need a little more than six shots in a gunfight. This is probably an overreaction, but we all got the "Kuwait invasion" discount. The frenzied activity is not confined to the base. The roads are abuzz with cars and trucks, and excited conversation punches the air. Sensing all the energy, I have goosebumps. I'm channeling that vibe to accomplish all I need to do before we ship off.

The next day at Shaw, by the time all our mission planning is complete and our jets are loaded, the sun is starting to get low in the sky. The wind on the flight line is eerily calm, and there's a slight coolness to the air. My mind drifts thousands of miles away, pondering what's going on at this moment in Kuwait, on the Iraqi southern border, and what's waiting for us. I ponder all of this as I conduct my aircraft preflight check in the unseasonably cool but humid South Carolina calm before the storm.

I climb up the aircraft ladder and start building my nest in the cockpit. Carefully, I place as many objects as I can into every nook and cranny between the ejection seat and aircraft fuselage—a couple of sandwiches, two liters of water, my Walkman, a med kit from the flight surgeons, "go" pills for when I get tired, and some "no go" pills to sleep when we arrive at our destination.

I have no idea what the pills are made of, and I hope I don't have to use them.

Also wedged between the seat and the aircraft are a few "piddle packs," plastic urine collection bags. With the F-16 ejection seat reclined thirty degrees, it takes a certain level of skill to use a piddle pack without peeing all over yourself like a two-year-old. If there's more business beyond taking a leak on what is likely to be a more than seventeen-hour-flight, we're *shit* out of luck. At the moment, we don't know exactly where we're going. All we know is we are to take off and head east over the Atlantic.

At the predetermined time, without making any radio call, each of our deploying F-16s taxis toward the active runway in four waves of six jets each. I line up as Number Three of the second six-ship and am reminded of another trip down this same runway nearly two years ago—a trip that ended with me on my ass in a South Carolina field. I wonder which takeoff will lead to more danger and destruction.

After releasing the brakes and picking up some speed, I see a small group gathered on the grass next to the runway. It's Carmel and two friends holding up signs. I have no idea what their signs say, but I'm sure they're awesome. The sun has set, and I follow the bright flame of the afterburners of the preceding jets in front of me, a trail of breadcrumbs against the burnt amber dusk. *Red at night, sailors delight, or some shit like that.*

After all our guys rejoin into our formation and as the last remnants of amber fade to pitch-black, a distressful sorrow takes hold of me. I think back to Carmel and our goodbye at home this morning, our last embrace, last kiss, last moment when our eyes met. We held each other as tight as we could in an attempt to overcome the separation being forced on us by a lunatic nearly 7,000 miles away. I may never see her face again or hold her. There's no guarantee that we will get to build a life together or raise a family together. Of course, there's never a guarantee of another day, but this is the first time in our lives together where we have had to say goodbye, not knowing when or if I will return.

All that I really know is that I'm heading toward danger along with twenty-three of my friends. Heading toward a violent conflict where blood is being shed. Heading into a situation where we have to be willing to fight, take lives, and possibly sacrifice our own. We are heading into serious shit. The stakes are the highest they have ever been in my life. The gravity of that is starting to become real.

As we head out over the Atlantic, the pitch-black blanket of night is cut by a beautiful full moon rising from the imperceptible curved line separating the blackness of the ocean from the blackness of space. The lights from the nearby coastal cities start to fade into a dark grey mist as Billy Diehl calls out, "Hooter One is diverting to Langley with zero oh-two pressure. Two, come with me." For some reason, the oxygen gauge in Billy's jet is indicating zero liters of $O_2$. It's not a good idea to head out over the ocean at high altitude in a single-seat fighter with no oxygen—*we need that to breathe.*

Billy and his wingman, Gary "Coops" Cooper, are diverting to Langley Air Force Base on the Virginia coast, where hopefully Billy can get his jet fixed and then join up with a subsequent deployment formation.

Just as I'm thinking about how hard it must be for Billy to relinquish command of this historic squadron deployment, he gets back on the radio and transmits, "Hooter One is rejoining the flight."

"What's up, Boss?" Coops asks over the mission frequency.

Billy explains that his cabin altimeter reads "12,000," and as long as he doesn't lose cabin pressure, he should be good to go. I had a feeling that nothing was going to stop Billy from leading his boys into the unknown, but I wonder if he's making a good decision.

Meanwhile, the moon has ascended to its throne high in the sky as billions upon billions of other luminous, heavenly bodies follow it upward from behind Earth. With my eyes fully adjusted to the clear night sky, I gasp as I see the Milky Way rise above the ocean. I have never seen our galaxy so bright. So many stars all appear as one bright, cosmic mist.

On my radar I see a contact directly in front of us. I lock my radar onto it. In my HUD, a green box appears that is centered on the brightest star in the milky cosmic mist—a star that's heading right for us loaded with fuel for our gas-starved Vipers.

At the predetermined distance from our formation, the target turns away from us as we close rapidly on the aircraft. We close within a mile as it rolls out on our easterly heading. We then begin one of ten or eleven aerial refuelings that will take place over the next seventeen hours. As I'm about to take my turn on the boom to get gas, a bright shooting star appears off in the distance. I watch as the meteor fireball changes from yellow to light green to red and then vanishes as the rock from space burns up in our planet's atmosphere. This is the third meteor I've seen since leaving Shaw not even two hours ago. I think I'll start counting them to pass the time.

The other three six-ships have each joined up on their own tanker. We hang with the tankers for a little over an hour, taking every last ounce of fuel they'll give us. Just as unceremoniously as they arrived, they peel off into the dark night without a word. Shortly after joining with the tankers, Billy Diehl and the 363rd Fighter Wing Operations Group commander, Colonel Rob Van Sice—Billy's boss—report that each of their aircraft's temperature control systems have failed to the full cold position. In other words, they're both sitting in the equivalent of meat freezers. Unfortunately, there's nothing either of them can do about this until we get near a base where they can land in Europe.

My neck is starting to hurt. Flying on the right side of the formation means I have to keep my head fixed, looking to the left. Losing concentration even for just a few moments can lead to a midair collision in which the best-case scenario would have me ending up in a raft in the middle of the Atlantic. As I attempt to work out some neck kinks by rotating my head, I notice that the Milky Way in all its glory has risen to directly above us. To put it more accurately, as we have traveled east across the ocean these past few hours, Earth has also rotated to the east in relation to the sun, the rest of the Milky Way, and the universe. This thousand-mile-per-hour rotation has dragged the atmosphere and us along with it toward our destination, a destination that unfortunately is receding away from us also at a thousand miles per hour.

The universe feels close. Somehow, it feels to be a part of me and me a part of it. As I look out at the thousands of stars, I realize that this vast sea of lights is but an infinitesimal fraction of the known universe. What I see is a small part of the thousands of millions of galaxies, each containing thousands of millions of stars. But what I find even harder to understand than the sheer number of stars is the incomprehensible vastness of the still, quiet nothingness between the stars. *What is space? I wonder. What is this emptiness that contains the vast majesty of the physical universe?*

There appears to be something much larger at work here, something just beyond the veil of reality. I'm not sure what. I feel as if I'm looking over a cliff of a tremendous chasm of understanding. As we fly toward danger with live weapons strapped to our aircraft, the great mystery gnaws at me again. *Why are we even here? How is it that a species that has evolved to the point where it can ponder the universe and ponder infinity still preoccupy itself with the animal instincts that no longer serve it?*

At some point during the evolution of humanity, I imagine that we came to recognize the miraculous nature of creation. This must have been the spark that set us apart from animals. *How is it that somewhere along the way in the development from childhood to adulthood, we learn to unlearn, or at least suppress, this fundamental realization?* I remember the awe and terror I felt as my awareness started to transition from the magical world of Santa Claus and the Tooth Fairy to one of the Big Bang, supernovas, and the apparent finality of death.

*Why is it that to function in society with strength and efficiency, we need to ignore the incomprehensible miracles that surround us constantly? Why is it that to function in the world, we must take on an oblivious self-confidence by placing ourselves in a tiny world, a small and limited subset of reality? Why is it that we abandon awe and limit ourselves to the prison that is right in front of our noses, guided primarily by our animal instincts, while ignoring our full perception of the world? We have the capability to project our conscious thought backward or forward billions of years yet act as if all that matters is the past and/or immediate future.*

The disconnect I'm experiencing comes from the realization that we don't just live on a tiny piece of ground or a country or even just a planet. We live in a universe that's billions of light-years across and contains an incomprehensible number of solar systems. Right now, however, I am hurling myself toward a microscopically small point on a microscopically small planet. Despite the utter insignificance from a cosmic scale of what we're heading toward, where I'm going is, to date, the biggest thing I have ever had to face.

"Hooter One, radio check! Hooter One, radio check!" Coops calls out on the mission frequency. Ahead, I see the lights of two Vipers turning sharply away and diving through the darkness toward the water below. "Billy! Go hundred percent oxygen! Go hundred percent oxygen!" Coops yells, as he suspects that Billy must have gone hypoxic and might have passed out. Coops is still flying close formation on Billy's wing and is being dragged through nighttime aerobatics as he attempts to help our squadron commander regain conscious reality. Then Colonel Van Sice calls out, "Billy, pull your green apple," referring to the knob that activates our emergency oxygen system. Just as we are all about to call out, "Eject, eject, eject!" Billy groggily responds, "Hey, guys, I'm back with you. I guess my cabin pressure failed." Normally, this would not be a big deal while wearing an oxygen mask, but the decision not to divert to Langley when Billy's oxygen fell to zero is coming back to haunt us. An oxygen mask doesn't do much good if there's no oxygen flowing through it.

Billy regains his cabin pressurization and starts climbing back up toward the jets that remained at high altitude. He still can't get his temperature control off full cold, however. Both he and Colonel Van Sice are still sitting in meat freezers, and the cold can be heard in their voices whenever they key the mic. Billy and Coops rejoin us just as my shooting star count increases to twenty-seven.

+

Three tanker cells have come and gone, and now it's almost midnight South Carolina time. I have no idea what time it is in our current location since I have no idea what time zone we're in. Five hours of staring at nothing but darkness and the green and red formation lights of our jets is starting to hypnotize me. I've occasionally listened to music on my Walkman. The tunes that seem to keep me awake the most are James Brown's. Feeling that everyone might be starting to get a little loopy, I unhook my rubber oxygen mask and place my small headphone set inside it. I then key my aircraft's microphone and hit play. *"Whoa! I feel good, I knew that I would, now. I feel good, I knew that I would, now. So good, so good, I got you . . ."*

It looks like the green and red formation lights are rocking back and forth to the beat. I think of the countless species of marine life in the ocean of water below our ocean of air that are oblivious to the melodic crooning of *the hardest working man in show business, the Godfather of Soul* himself, a mere six miles above their gills.

A little over nine hours into the flight, we see the first evidence that the sun that dipped below the horizon behind us has raced around Earth and is positioning itself in front of us. The slightest hint of an impending sunrise is enough to awaken me from a green-and-red-formation-light-induced hypnotic state. It's been a long dark night of sheer boredom interspersed with periodic terror. The Milky Way has long dissolved away, leaving only a few handfuls of discrete points of light. One by one, the stars too dissolve into a pastel-yellow to blue-gradient glow rising up from the now-visible horizon laced with miniscule silhouettes of distant thunderstorms. *Looks like the final shooting star count will be forty-eight.*

"Hooter Six is dropping down to low altitude for a few" I hear over the mission frequency. *Shit! Not again.* Throughout the night, some of the guys' wing fuel tank valves froze due to long-duration exposure to the frigid high-altitude temperature trapping the fuel in the tanks. We thawed out the valves by descending to a low altitude. This at times was a little sporty when guys had to descend down through thunderstorms at night. That's enough to keep you awake.

Just as the sun peeks above the horizon, I make out a landmass up ahead. Actually, I see two landmasses in close proximity. The Strait of Gibraltar, where Africa meets Europe, welcomes us to a new part of the world and signals the end of the transatlantic leg of our journey. We are now within range of multiple airfields where Billy or Colonel Van Sice could divert. I start plugging in various divert options into my flight computer to see which would be best.

About thirty minutes later, after we've flown by multiple potential divert bases, I realize that no one is diverting today. I wonder why Billy and Colonel Van Sice would continue on in what is probably a state of hypothermia, risking frostbite as well. I do not believe it is because of ego or a quest for glory. Both of these men are in leadership positions and knowing them, I suspect that they refuse to see those in their charge head to potential combat without them, if possible. At the moment, they believe it's still possible for them to make it. I'm sure they're taking this course of action out of concern for those they have been tasked to lead. Though I wish they would divert, I respect what I believe is the motivation for their decision not to.

Ten tanker cells have now come and gone and out up ahead lies the fertile Nile River Valley. The green snaking vegetation stands in stark contrast to the flat, dull tan of the rest of the region. Off to the left is Cairo and the deep blue Mediterranean Sea, with Israel a little farther up the coast. Ahead is the Sinai Peninsula and the Red Sea. My eyes travel up the Red Sea from the south to the north, where I see the Gulf of Suez and Gulf of Aqaba, which remind me of the bunny ears of a giant rabbit. In spite of the striking scenery, the fatigue brought on by the long sleepless night and previous day is really catching up. I'm finding it harder and harder to stay awake, so I dig into the med kit wedged next to my seat to grab and take a go pill.

The pill really works. Very quickly, I'm not jittery at all, just more awake. *All right, science!* Like clockwork, another tanker cell shows up in front of us for what I believe will be our last inflight refueling. A little while ago, we received the coordinates for our landing base. I'm not at liberty to say where it's located, but I was happy to learn it's in a country that has not outlawed booze. So, we got that going for us.

After we are all convinced that we have enough fuel to make it across Saudi Arabia and all the way to our deployment base, we drop off the tankers and head directly to the base. The vastness of the desert dunes of Saudi Arabia amazes me. What's more amazing is that after flying over nothing but sand for hundreds of miles, all of a sudden, I see one guy walking with a camel.

*Where did he come from? Where is he going?* In every direction as far as the eye can see, there's nothing but sand.

The sun yet again starts to get low on the horizon behind us as we descend to lower altitude. Our destination is less than a hundred miles away when Billy announces our presence on the local approach control frequency, which seems to take the controller off guard. Apparently, the coordination to land at this base was made with the national government, but no one bothered to coordinate it with the local base. Basically, twenty-four fully armed F-16s are showing up unannounced. As we get within range of base defenses, all of our radar warning receivers light up, indicating they have their weapon systems locked onto us. *This is a nice welcome.*

We all land without incident, but somehow, we beat all of our logistic support here. No one's here to park and service the jets.

As I pull into a parking spot, I get the signal to shut down my aircraft from one of the pilots that landed before us. I retard the throttle into the off position. For the first time in more than seventeen hours, fuel stops flowing to the engine. The whine of the slowing turbine blades sounds like the jet is exhaling a sigh of relief. She has served me well on this long journey. I open the canopy and a wave of hot, humid, salty air hits me. Slowly, I climb out of the jet. My legs twinge with pain and tightness after sitting in the same position all this time. Once completely out, I, along with everyone else available, work to park the other jets.

After the last six-ship pulls into parking, our surprised and bewildered hosts meet us. A local commander says they have nowhere for all our twenty-four pilots to stay. They have arranged for a bus to take us into town, where they have booked a hotel. Before boarding the bus, Colonel Van Sice, who will stay on this base tonight, stresses that we all need to be back here by 0600 to begin sitting close air support alert—being at the ready in case we are needed to take off to fight the Iraqis.

We are presently the only US Air Force response to a potential Iraqi incursion into Saudi Arabia. Colonel Van Sice also issues a stern warning: "I'm told that there's a bar in the hotel that you're going to. I want you all to check in and head straight to your rooms. No drinking tonight!"

As the bus pulls up to the hotel, a slightly frostbitten Billy Diehl stands up and announces, "OK, gents, the first round is on me." Minutes later, we are all sitting in the hotel bar, icy cold German beers in hand, listening to a live Filipino band perform country music. On the long journey here, a lot of possible scenarios ran through my head about our first night in theater. This was not one of them. It's not lost on anyone that this will probably be our last night to enjoy ourselves.

# CHAPTER 4
# The Slog Before the Storm

✦ Ever since our arrival more than a month ago in August, cargo aircraft have been landing and taking off around the clock. We were told that whatever supplies, facilities, and equipment we still need that haven't been airlifted over will be built or bought. This is not a good sign. This is a sign that we could be here for a really long time. Nothing has happened yet, and it would be better if something kicked off soon; the sooner it does, the sooner we can go home.

The locals are not exactly thrilled that the Americans have invaded their base, but they're scared shitless of Iraq, so, I guess it all cancels out. Most of the local guys we've talked to think Saddam is a lunatic and is liable to do anything. Fortunately, our operating base has an elaborate air defense system that would be pretty hard to break through and even if the Iraqis did, we'd be waiting for them. As an added plus, all of our jets are being stored in huge modern TAB-VEEs made up of more than thirty feet of reinforced concrete and embedded state-of-the-art chemical weapons protection equipment.

During the first few weeks after arriving on base, hundreds of our personnel were lodged in aircraft hangars and sleeping on the floor with no air-conditioning. The hundred-plus degree heat and hundred percent humidity got old fast. We fragile pilot folk were issued air-conditioned rooms, with three or four of us in each. The lucky ones had cots. The rest slept on the floor. All in all, this was resortlike living compared to what those in the field were experiencing.

But then teams started working around the clock to construct a tent city out in the desert, about fifteen miles from our base. At the moment, about 1,900 Americans occupy a tent city that we affectionately call "Shawbu Dhabi," a nod to our home, Shaw Air Force Base. The city was built adjacent to old trailers that construction crews lived in during the base construction. All of the pilots are housed in the trailers. I'm sharing a room in one of them with Tav, the Air Force Academy grad who drove us to the Florida Panhandle right before we were called back to deploy to the Gulf—the one who likes to call everyone "dude."

Tav is one of those people whom everybody likes, at least those who can put up with his high energy and ever-present optimism. I'm one of those people. I prefer to hang out with positive, upbeat guys versus the mad-at-the-world types. Tav, being Tav, made quick friends with some of the civil engineering troops here, which resulted in them constructing a patio deck in front of our trailer, complete with benches, a bar, and a sign that reads, "Ron & Tav's Excellent Hooch." Our place truly is excellent!

Most of the folks here are supporting the forty-eight jets that we currently have available for close air support alert. The jets are loaded with bombs and air-to-ground and air-to-air missiles. If Iraqi soldiers step across the Saudi border, we'll blow the shit out of them. Our primary targets will be Iraqi tanks that we will take out with Maverick missiles.

On an early October day, I'm deep in thought as I walk from the chow hall back to Ron & Tav's Excellent Hooch. In front of me looms a big yellow sun hugging the distant horizon above rows and rows of tents. The sound of heavy equipment pushing dirt to form defensive berms pierces the background noise of hundreds

*Captain Ron "Agent" Garan and Captain Jan "Tav" Tavrytzky stand*
*outside their trailer inside the military tent city known as "Shawbu Dhabi"*
*in 1990 during Operation Desert Shield.* Credit: Jan Tavrytzky

of simultaneous conversations. I feel a warm, moist breeze on my face. I can smell and taste the sea salt as it completes its journey on a river of air from the Persian Gulf to my nostrils and taste buds. To my right stands a perimeter guard fortification. Wedged behind five-foot-high mounds of sand and beneath camouflage netting sits a military vehicle painted the same color as the sand.

The helmeted head and shoulders of one of the three military police officers on duty at this sentry post protrudes through the roof of the vehicle, his hands clutching a machine gun pointed out into the desert. His fatigues, goggles, and scarf wrapped around his face make him look like a character right out of the movie *Mad Max*. I'm glad these guys, and all the other guys manning sentry posts around the tent city, are here, although sometimes this place really feels like a prison and I wonder if they are here to keep the bad guys out or us in.

Dust storms to the west are contributing to an exquisite sunset of neon orange, red, and pink. The sky appears to be on fire. The outline of the tents of our camp are accentuated by the tents' westward-facing fabric bathed in golden light while the eastward-facing fabric is in shadow. Even the tents are reflecting the beauty of this never-to-be-seen-again sunset. This moment makes me long for Carmel even more.

About two weeks after we arrived here, I got ahold of Carmel on the base pay phone after several attempts. To call home, we have to wait in line, sometimes for hours and sometimes only to find that the number is busy or no one is home. We also have to really watch what we say. Rumor has it that folks in the vicinity of the phones can tune into their frequency on transistor radios and listen in. During our call, Carmel informed me that we are pregnant. I have no words to describe the joy I felt and still feel. But right behind the joy came the realization that I can't be there for her. I can't be there to share in this experience. I have no idea how long I'll be here, if I'll make it home for the birth, or if I'll make it home at all. The weight of this situation and the weight of our separation became much heavier once I heard the joyous news.

Now, I wonder how she's doing and how the pregnancy is going. The incredible busyness during the time we've been here at Shawbu Dhabi has helped me keep my mind off things. It's the rare quiet moments like this when the separation and impending danger bubble up to the surface though.

Most of my time over the past two months has been filled with traveling around the theater coordinating a plan for the first three days of the war. An exception occurred one day when I attended a camel race out in the middle of the desert, at the invitation of some local pilots. I, along with a few other guys from base, watched from inside a moving Mercedes S-Class sedan as the camels took off with jockeys no older than eight to ten.

That day, we learned that sheiks spend millions of dollars on these races in which the jockeys are "imported" from Pakistan, sent over by their parents because they can make enough money in a couple of years for their families to start a business or buy land to farm. In addition to this, I learned more about camels than I thought possible, including the fact that the ones we saw were genetically modified just to win races. Ever since, two burning questions have bothered me: How in a region with so much destitute poverty and so many other problems can the sheiks justify spending millions upon millions of dollars on such a frivolous pastime that is enjoyed by so few? And what kind of hardship must those jockeys' families be enduring to send them off so far from home to engage in such a dangerous activity?

Besides the camel racing experience, I've visited bases in Saudi Arabia, Qatar, Bahrain, Oman, and the United Arab Emirates. These trips have all been part of our preparation for what's likely to come—I am one of about five people on base who have been briefed on a secret war plan called "Operation Desert Storm." Our job is to design, coordinate, and, if necessary, execute a plan to enter a very heavily defended target area and completely and utterly annihilate the Iraqis' air defense system and ability to conduct offensive warfare. This will not be a pinprick. The destructive force we will throw at the Iraqis will be truly overwhelming.

I've really enjoyed traveling around to all the different units in theater, collectively figuring out how to combine all the aircraft assets we have into the most lethal force possible. I have also spent a good deal of my time on the road trying to convince units to abandon the Cold War tactics that we have all been taught and mastered. The common perception has been that to survive an attack into a heavily defended target area, we need to enter and exit it at an extremely low altitude, using the terrain to hide the attack from enemy radars. Well, that doesn't work very well in a flat desert. There are many reasons to favor a tactic that enters and exits the target area at medium altitude, somewhere between 20,000 and 30,000 feet above the ground. One of the main reasons is that this altitude would keep us above most of the enemies' antiaircraft artillery. But, for some reason, a significant number of units are clinging to the old way of doing things.

On one of my coordination trips, I met a Kuwaiti squadron commander at an airstrip in central Saudi Arabia. He shared with me some stories from the invasion and how they were able to get their jets out just in time. He thanked me for being willing to join them in taking the fight back to the Iraqis to reclaim his country. This reminded me that in every country I've ever traveled to, when I meet a fighter pilot, the notion that a fighter pilot is a fighter pilot is reinforced—it doesn't matter where you're from. The fighter pilot values of camaraderie and service shine through. The love and pride in our chosen profession knows no national boundaries. After some time talking about the situation, the squadron commander and I walked out to the flight line and took a photo together in front of his aircraft, a Kuwaiti A-4 Skyhawk with the words "FREE KUWAIT" emblazoned across the fuselage. I posted that photo on the wall of my hooch, a constant reminder of why we're here.

Since we've arrived, our tent city population has increased substantially. The city is near completion with the construction of chow halls, exercise facilities, movie tents, and beer tents. There's a two-beer-a-day ration, but luckily for me, Tav doesn't drink. That means, for me, it's a four-beer-a-day limit. We've even constructed a makeshift officers' club, nicknamed The Vipers' Pit, in a Quonset hut, a prefabricated metal shelter. A sign at its entrance depicts a somewhat inebriated snake with its tongue in a mug of beer. To add a little class to the joint, a marquee was installed above the club entrance. It incorporates

*Ron Garan stands next to an unidentified Kuwaiti Air Force squadron*
*commander at an undisclosed location in central Saudi Arabia*
*before the start of Operation Desert Storm.* Credit: US Air Force

the shattered carcass of an ejected F-16 canopy that a couple of Hooter pilots "borrowed" from a base in Oman.

Inside the O Club, there's a bar, TV, and a pool table. We don't play pool on the pool table though. We play an old fighter pilot game known as "crud." Think of full contact pool with no cue sticks. TVs in the club blast nonstop CNN so we can keep track of our standings in the polls. A few weeks ago, we were joined by a squadron of Italian pilots and their Tornado aircraft. Tav and I make a point to go over to the Italians' chow hall whenever we can. It might have something to do with them serving real food and, of course, wine with dinner. If you have to go to war, this is not a bad way to do it.

Since our arrival, there has been constant tension in the air, so the O Club is an important outlet to help us unwind. We are always potentially moments away from going into combat. I always imagined that being in a combat environment meant that all the "Mickey Mouse" bullshit associated with a peacetime military would go out the window. Initially that was true, but it didn't take long for all the bureaucracy and pointless regulations to catch up with us.

It's also interesting to observe how the stress of impending combat affects people. Some, like Billy Diehl, have risen to the challenge and see this as an opportunity to become a servant leader and lead by example. Others see this situation as their ticket to becoming a general officer. Some are tripping over each other's egos to put themselves in positions that could potentially lead to promotions when this is all over. Worse yet, people are being put into combat leadership positions in the air not because of their ability, experience, or even certification, but solely because of their rank.

In the Air Force, typically junior officers lead more senior officers in flight. When a captain is the flight lead, his wingmen follow him even if they are colonels. I've always admired this about the Air Force. Your rank doesn't matter. What matters is how capable you are in the air to lead. But now, as a shooting war fast approaches, senior officers are jockeying to be on the point, to be the one leading into battle—not necessarily out of heroism or a sense of service but because it's a good career move. What's remarkable is that they're using false bravery to mask their own cowardice. They have no issue with putting their lives on the line to advance their careers, but they won't put their careers on the line and take a back seat for a higher cause.

Meanwhile, I'm getting the impression that things are heating up here. I don't know what's going to happen, but I feel that we're as ready as we'll ever be. We've been conducting a lot of great training sorties. If things kick off, the missions will be dangerous, there's no denying that, but I'm confident that we'll all do our job. I'm only a little worried, but that's natural and healthy. I feel a lot more confident than nervous. At one point, I really hoped that a diplomatic solution could be found, but I think it's too late for that. Almost on a daily basis, we receive reports of the atrocities that are occurring in Kuwait. We need to stop the Iraqis here and now.

I have *no* moral reservations about going into combat. Innocent people are dying in Kuwait every day, and more will die. But the longer we wait, the worse things will get. I'm not saying war is inevitable—it's not. What I'm saying is that this is a very bad situation.

The good news is that the whole world, except for Iraq, of course, is on our side. I find it completely unbelievable that Saddam would even think of challenging us now. We have enormous capability that, if employed, will completely destroy Iraq's military. *He has to know that. How stupid or arrogant can he be? How could someone have such a total disregard for his own people?*

Arriving at my hooch, I lie down on my cot and pop in a cassette tape from Carmel. Shortly after I arrived here, Carmel and I started recording audio messages that we mail to each other. Although they are usually a few weeks old when I get them, it's always wonderful to hear Carmel's melodic, soothing voice. Regardless of her actual words, the underlying frequency that carries those words to my heart always whispers, "I love you. I care about you. You are important to me." I normally wait until I'm ready for sleep before I listen to a cassette. I always want Carmel's voice to be the last thing I hear, and I usually fall asleep to it.

Now, as I listen to Carmel, I am transported through space and time to her arms, which brings me to a place of warmth, love, and comfort. As I pass into the demilitarized zone between wakefulness and sleep, I reach out to God. I think I've probably always been a believer, but I've never prayed to God as much as I have in recent months.

"God, please let the world be at peace. Let there be no more war, violence, disease, hardship, crime, or terrorism, and let all the people of the world live in harmony and happiness with each other. God, please let me do the very best I can in my training and become the best pilot I can be. Please protect me and all my friends who fly. And God, please never let me do what I've been trained to do. But if I must, I pray that you grant me the knowledge and courage to do the right things and make the right decisions."

It's October 8, but it feels more like February 2, Groundhog Day, as I'm in the base operations center planning yet another large strike-training mission. I'm coordinating and choreographing the tactics and routes for tomorrow's operation, which will include forty F-16s, eight tankers, eight F-15 Eagles, twelve F-4Gs, several RF-4s, and a couple of EF-111s—a combination of fighter, reconnaissance, and electronic warfare aircraft. All but the F-16s and RF-4s will be coming from other bases. I would much rather be flying in the training mission happening today, but I also enjoy developing the tactics and putting everything together.

Just as we're finishing up the planning, we get word that one of the RF-4s from the Birmingham Alabama Air National Guard, which has also been stationed here, went down during today's training mission. Things get chaotic as contradictory reports come in. First, we're told there were chutes spotted, and then no chutes. Finally, we receive definitive word that both crew members, Major Barry Henderson and Major Stephen Schramm, were killed on impact. The weight of that news starts to sink in. As crews from the mission begin to arrive, we ask what happened. "They just flew into the ground" is the only response we get. Training mission fatalities happen all the time, and they always seem senseless and preventable. Being this close to going into combat, though, makes it feel even more senseless.

Everyone is pretty shaken up, so we head to the O Club to gather in solidarity. It's a somber scene as I and a few of the other Shaw pilots walk through the Quonset hut door. At the bar sit some of the Alabama Air National Guard guys as CNN comes across the TV, as it does every night. They report that the UN Security Council has again authorized the use of force to stop Iraqi tankers in the Gulf. But we're not here to watch the news. We're here to toast our fallen comrades.

Tonight, there's no two-beer limit, and guys are passing bottles of smuggled Jeremiah Weed bourbon whiskey around. Fighter pilots are normally hypercompetitive. We are competitive amongst ourselves as individuals, competitive with other squadrons, and competitive with pilots who fly different aircraft and are in different services. Tonight, all that competitiveness melts away and what's left is unity. After about an hour into the somber gathering, someone turns off the TV and plays Lynyrd Skynyrd's "Sweet Home Alabama" on the O Club boom box. Everyone joins in song and tribute. Tonight, everyone is from Alabama.

A couple of months have passed since the crash. It's Christmas Eve, and Tav and I head over to a tent that has been converted into a chapel for Mass. As I pass through its flaps, a wave of incense hits me. It's as if we just passed between two atmospheres—one diesel- and dust-filled atmosphere of the machine of war and one incense-laden spiritual atmosphere. We find our way to some empty spots on benches, and a calm descends upon me. It's almost as if this camouflaged fabric chapel is an island of peace, tranquility, and clarity within an ocean of surreal, bustling preparation for violence.

I try to pay attention to the chaplain, but I keep thinking about *home. What is Carmel doing right now?* I wonder. I imagine all my family and friends going about their Christmas celebrations, and I feel a deep longing for the peace of *home* and *family*. Not being home for Christmas feels like the exclamation point on the sentence, "It's been a long four-month slog in the desert!"

At any rate, to say I'm not an avid churchgoer is an understatement. I attend church services no more than a few times a year, but Christmas has always been a magically special time for me. I have always marveled at how everyone seems to get a little bit nicer as the holiday approaches. I love Jesus's messages of *Love thy neighbor* and *Turn the other cheek*. But how does that apply to our current situation? How can we turn the other cheek when people are dying every day at the hands of the Hussein regime? Is there such a thing as a righteous war?

The chaplain's words pull me back into the Mass: "Offer each other a sign of peace." We all turn to one another, shake hands, and say, "Peace be with you." For the first time, the sign of peace has taken on a new, more literal meaning as I clasp the hands of my fellow service members.

Tav and I leave the chapel and head back to our hooch under an incredibly bright moon. I feel a slight desert nighttime chill on my face as I think back to a Christmas Eve twenty-two years ago when America sent the first crewed spacecraft there. Frank Borman, Jim Lovell, and Bill Anders were also separated from their families on a dangerous operation that holy night.

During the *Apollo 8* mission, the crew transmitted a televised address to the world. That address was the highlight of 1968, a year that saw massive unrest in the streets of America and most everywhere else on the planet. Heart-wrenching political assassinations occurred in 1968, and the Vietnam War was ripping America apart. I believe that *Apollo 8's* address from the moon and the mission itself served as a beacon of hope in an otherwise extremely tumultuous and sorrowful time.

Bill Anders started off the address by saying, "We are now approaching lunar sunrise, and for all the people on Earth, the crew of *Apollo 8* has a message that we would like to send you. 'In the beginning God created the heaven and the earth. And the earth was without form, and void; and darkness was upon the face of the deep. And the Spirit of God moved upon the face of the waters. And God said, Let there be light: and there was light. And God saw the light, that it was good: and God divided the light from the darkness.'"

Then Jim Lovell took over. "'And God called the light Day, and the darkness he called Night. And the evening and the morning were the first day. And God said, Let there be a firmament in the midst of the waters, and let it divide the waters from the waters. And God made the firmament, and divided the waters which were under the firmament from the waters which were above the firmament: and it was so. And God called the firmament Heaven. And the evening and the morning were the second day.'"

Commander Frank Borman concluded with, "'And God said, Let the waters under the heaven be gathered together unto one place, and let the dry land appear: and it was so. And God called the dry land Earth; and the gathering together of the waters He called the Seas: and God saw that it was good. And from the crew of *Apollo 8*, we close with good night, good luck, a Merry Christmas—and God bless all of you, all of you on the good Earth.'"

*God bless all of you, all of you on the good Earth.* If that's not the perfect summation of the spirit of Christmas, I don't know what is.

It's nearly mid-January, and we've undergone a grueling few weeks of preparation. Now, I have, for the first time in a long time, had a chance to rest and relax. I'm taking a few hours in my hooch to quietly reflect on all that has happened and all that may happen very soon. In a sign that things are really heating up, we've recently had a ton of visits from our senior leadership, including General Norman Schwarzkopf, the commander of the allied forces in the Gulf; General Tony McPeak, the Air Force chief of staff; Lieutenant General Chuck Horner, the commander of all coalition air power; and Brigadier General Buster Glosson, the chief air planner.

General McPeak got us all fired up when he declared our unit, the 363rd Tactical Fighter Wing, the most combat capable unit in theater; I bet he says that to all the units. Brigadier General Glosson said we should all be very confident in our abilities. He also stressed that if it comes to combat, we will be going into the most heavily defended target areas in the history of aerial warfare and we could expect to lose 10 percent of our pilots on every mission. Other estimates put it at 25 percent. That's a sobering thought. I hope it doesn't come to that, and I hope it doesn't come to war.

I truly believe that war is man's most tragic endeavor. I think all the guys, including me, however, are handling the possibility of going into combat remarkably well. We are confident in our abilities and capabilities. We feel that this is a just cause and one that will hopefully make the world safer and more stable. I pray that this is true. I am prepared to do whatever I must.

The fact is, the world has its problems, and one of them is a man named Saddam Hussein—a man who I think can accurately be compared to Hitler. If people like this didn't exist, I probably wouldn't have a job, which would be nice. I am a fighter pilot, that's what I do. My country needs me to do a job, and I intend to do it right. But I'd be lying if I said I wasn't nervous and a little scared.

Shortly after Christmas, we were joined by one more squadron of F-16s. Pilots from all three squadrons at Hahn were combined into a single unit to help us in the war effort. Since I am intimately familiar with those guys' tactics, having flown at Hahn for two years, I spent a couple of weeks helping them get up to speed with the medium-altitude techniques we're planning to use.

At first, it was a little difficult convincing them to abandon the low-altitude Cold War tactics that they are so comfortable with, but eventually they came around. I'm really happy they're with us. We need all the help we can get, and it is great seeing some of the guys I knew back at Hahn. Right now, I can say that they are fully integrated into our operations here at Shawbu Dhabi.

My happiness about the Hahn guys, however, is tempered by my concern for what's going on back at home. Yesterday, after a marathon wait in the telephone line to reach Carmel, I heard worry in her voice as she explained that she was measuring too big for this point in her pregnancy. This means one of two things: Either we are having twins or there is a serious problem with our child and he or she may not survive and if they do, they could be profoundly disabled.

Carmel told me that she was going to have an ultrasound in a few days, which would get to the bottom of things. Not being there for her during this stressful and scary time is killing me. What really worries me is not so much what will happen to me but what will happen to Carmel if something happens to me. This uncertainty is weighing on me heavily. I feel completely helpless.

I walk through camp to clear my mind. I am deep in thought and prayer. I beg God to protect our baby or babies. After about a half hour of wrestling and pleading with God, I ask Him for a sign. I beg Him for something to ease my mind. Just then, I find myself at the O Club. I walk through the door to see the gang sitting around the TV watching the movie *Twins* with Arnold Schwarzenegger and Danny DeVito.

I'm floored. This is the first thing other than CNN that I remember ever seeing on the O Club TV.

"Hey, guys, what are you watching this for?" I ask.

"We got tired of watching CNN every fucking day!" someone shouts. I take this as a sign not only that God is out there and that everything is going to be OK, but that He has a sense of humor too.

✦

A few days later, I get word that Colonel Van Sice wants to see me. I suspect what this might be about. I hustle over to his office.

Once I arrive, the colonel looks at me for a moment with a gaze I don't think I'll ever forget. I can only describe it as a look of intense, determined solemnity.

"Agent, Desert Storm has been executed. Go get some sleep."

The amount of data transmitted in those ten words is staggering. I have spent the last five months planning for this moment. The magnitude of those words washes over me as I excuse myself and start heading back to the tent city. The countdown timer to the start of hostilities has begun. All of a sudden, the world seems surreal. I think of the hundreds of combat aircraft that, in a few hours, will take off from bases on all sides of Iraq and head toward dozens and dozens of key targets. I think of all the destruction that has just been unleashed. I have about six hours before I will have to head back to base and begin briefing the first daylight raid of Baghdad.

Back in the hooch, as I lie in my cot, I run through all the choreography of the mission in my head—which aircraft will be where. I review the visual identification points on the ground that will lead us to our target. I imagine my bombing run, hurtling my aircraft toward my designated target and releasing my bombs. I wonder what kind of defenses we will face. *Will they be able to send up MiGs to meet us? Will their surface-to-air missile sites still be operational?* I feel my heartbeat slowly increasing in a strangely familiar way and realize that I used to lie in bed the night before a big football game and run through all the plays in my head.

I know that tomorrow may be my last day alive. As heavy as that thought is, thinking about Carmel and what she must be going through right now tortures me even more. There's a pretty good chance I will never see her again and never meet my child—or children. I am willing to take this risk because I believe in something bigger than myself. I love my country, and my country is asking this of me. It is my duty to respond to this call. I believe that what we're doing here will benefit our nation. I also take courage in the fact that I'm not alone. Everyone else here understands what's at stake. So far, every person has answered the call.

As my body and mind start to prepare for sleep, I am somehow transported a few hours in time for a glimpse into the future. I imagine all the aircraft taking off toward their targets in the darkness of night. The first few waves have the task to take out as much of the Iraqi air defenses as they can. I hope those guys all get the job done, otherwise we are going to have a rough time tomorrow when we head downtown in broad daylight.

## CHAPTER 5

# The Storm

✦ I feel like I have just closed my eyes when my alarm goes off early on the morning of January 17. It's still pitch-black outside. As I shake off the last remnants of the borderless dream world, the enormity of this day crashes back into my full awareness. *How is Desert Storm going so far? Is everything going according to plan? How much of the Iraqi air defense system remains?*

Before I'm even out of my cot, a squadron of butterflies takes flight deep in my gut. I experience a strange mixture of nervousness and excitement. After a quick shower, I ride the squadron bus into base, where I see that the operations center is abuzz with surreal activity.

"How's it going?" I ask some intel folks as I enter the building.

"So far so good. We'll give you the rest in the brief," replies the chief intel officer.

I help hand out the mission packets to the thirty-two gathered F-16 pilots. "This should look real familiar," I say. Even though only a handful of us knew it, we have been practicing for this specific mission for months. We had carefully designed our training sorties to mimic the actual operation as close as possible. Billy Diehl enters the room, and everyone snaps to attention. Billy is going to lead this historic strike mission. Our target is an Iraqi MiG base on the outskirts of Baghdad. Our job is to prevent the Iraqis from using the airfield to launch an attack against coalition forces.

After the mission brief, as we're all in our life-support shop suiting up with our harnesses, G-suits, and trusty Berettas, it really does feel like suiting up in a locker room on game day. This time though, the stakes are much higher, and we're not blasting Led Zeppelin like we used to do in high school before big football games. We ride the bus out to each of our respective TAB-VEEs. One by one, pilots get out and walk to their jets. I get out in front of an F-16 with a painting on the jet's nose of the cartoon character the Tasmanian Devil holding a missile. My name, Capt. Ron "Agent" Garan, appears on the canopy.

Suspended under each wing is an external fuel tank and a 2,000-pound bomb designed to penetrate through thick concrete before exploding. Attached to rails on each wingtip, a Sidewinder heat-seeking air-to-air missile is cocked and ready. Under the centerline of the aircraft hangs an electronic counter-measures pod designed to jam enemy radars.

After checking over all the weapons and the aircraft, I climb up the ladder and into the cockpit like I've done over a thousand times before. This time it's different. This time it's for real. My crew chief helps me strap into my ejection seat, then he smacks me on the shoulder and says, "Go kick some ass, sir! We'll be here when you get back."

"Thanks," I say, and shake his hand.

After starting the engine and running through all the systems checks, at the predetermined time, and without saying a word on the radio, everyone starts taxiing from their respective TAB-VEEs. In a finely choreographed march, all thirty-two F-16s line up in the proper order to take the runway. This armada of fully locked and loaded jets aligned against the morning desert sun is an amazing sight. Inside each of the bubble canopies sits a friend, a brother-in-arms, a patriot who has answered the call to right a wrong.

Four by four, the arming crew arms up each of the formations. When it's my four-ship's turn, a tightness spreads rapidly in all directions throughout my body. I drift into anxious prayer. *Please,*

*Lord, protect everyone on this mission today. Please protect Carmel and our baby—or babies—and please bring everyone home safely.*

Suddenly, the tenseness that moments ago gripped my entire body releases as I sink deeply into my ejection seat. I feel calm. I sense that I am being protected and nothing will happen to me. I must have just somehow talked myself into this positive mindset. For the life of me though, I can't figure out how I could have done that in an instant. How could I go from being anxious, and if I swallow my pride and admit it, maybe scared, to being instantly calm with waves of peaceful certainty washing over me? I don't know if I will ever be able to fully explain what just happened. The crew signals that my bombs and missiles are armed, and I head toward the runway.

Four-ship by four-ship, we take off from our desert airstrip and join in formation with Billy Diehl on the point. The plan: to launch two waves of attack with sixteen F-16s in each wave. I'm Number Three in the first four-ship of the second wave with Captain Mark "Nick" Nichols on my wing. Nick is a very capable, no-nonsense pilot. Coincidently, his wife, Kari, is also pregnant and about as far along as Carmel.

Our first objective is to head to aerial refueling tracks south of the Iraqi border in Saudi Arabia. At this moment, we're checking in with the airborne early warning and control system controller on board an E-3 aircraft, another military version of the Boeing 707. The controller, from an orbit somewhere in Saudi Arabia, begins to vector us to the tankers. We are about two hours away from crossing the border into Iraq.

En route, I think back to April 12, 1981, the day I started on the road that led me here, strapped to an F-16 on my way to my first taste of combat. On that date, the first space shuttle launched. As a sophomore at the State University of New York at Oneonta, I vividly remember watching John Young, who had walked on the moon years before, and Bob Crippen launch to orbit on space shuttle *Columbia*.

That evening, I stared out the window of my dorm room into a starry upstate New York sky wondering what Young and Crippen, orbiting our planet, must be thinking and experiencing. I felt a deep longing to be there with them.

That event led to an abrupt course correction to my life's trajectory. Two years earlier, as graduation from high school had approached, I felt lost. I had no idea what I wanted to do with my life. My childhood dream of becoming an astronaut was ridiculous since we didn't have a space program, or at least I thought we didn't. Besides, becoming an astronaut was for smart people with great grades. My grades were mediocre at best. I shipped off to the only college that accepted me and enrolled in the most practical program I could think of: business. But, when I heard the TV announcer say in 1981, "And we have liftoff, liftoff of America's first space shuttle. And the shuttle has cleared the tower," I again felt like I was floating on a sea of possibility. I received a second calling—a calling just like the one I felt on July 20, 1969, when I heard, "Houston, Tranquility Base here. The Eagle has landed."

Now, my plan was clear: I was going to take as many math and science courses as I could, learn to fly, and then join the military and become a fighter pilot and then test pilot. I would then follow the path of all the early astronauts, including John Young, to NASA.

The day after that first space shuttle launch, I asked my academic advisor how I could take nothing but math and science courses for the remainder of my electives. A few months later, I started taking flying lessons at the nearby Oneonta Municipal Airport. Now, I find it comical that the first time in my life that I ever flew in an airplane, I sat in the pilot seat, at the controls, flying the aircraft. I took an introductory flying lesson to see if I would like it. That first flight hooked me. I discovered a yearning for the freedom of flight. The experience also made me feel slightly less at home on the ground. I often found myself walking through my day-to-day life wishing I was in the air.

I will never forget my first solo flight. It was a beautiful summer evening on the Oneonta Airport, perched on the summit of one of the many hilltops dotting the New York Adirondacks. My flight instructor somehow convinced himself I was ready to fly solo and threw me the keys to a Cessna 150. "Put 'er on the ground before the last bit of sun dips behind the mountains" was all he said to me.

Pushing the power up, releasing the brakes, and rolling down the runway, I wondered if my flight instructor knew what he was doing. *Should I be trusted not to kill myself?* The moment I lifted off into that crystal-clear summer evening, however, a wondrous exhilaration surged through me. Climbing the aircraft up a few thousand feet, I could see what appeared to be a never-ending series of green ridgelines extending to the distant horizon. A little while later, I watched as long shadows appeared throughout the landscape as I imagined crickets and fireflies preparing to start their nocturnal work shift. I was completely lost in the moment. I imagined what it would be like to pilot a fighter or the shuttle. Soon, my instructor's warning surfaced in my consciousness—*before the last bit of sun dips behind the mountains*—and I brought the aircraft home. Not long after I rolled to a stop on that Oneonta hilltop, the certainty that I had just found my life's calling hit me.

As college graduation approached, I took out a $5,000 loan to continue my education and pursue a second bachelor's degree, this one in aerospace engineering. After graduating in December 1982 with a degree in business economics, and with my private pilot license in hand, I loaded up my broken-down Fiat Spider convertible and headed to Florida for Embry-Riddle Aeronautical University in Daytona Beach for that aerospace engineering degree. It was a long journey in a vehicle I affectionately called the "Flintstonemobile" because I could see the road through the rusted-out floorboard.

I planned to study at Embry-Riddle until I either got accepted into the Air Force pilot training program or I ran out of money. Luckily for me, both things happened at the same time during my second semester. I left the university before I could finish that second bachelor's degree and headed to San Antonio, Texas, for Officer Training School, a program that led to my commissioning in the Air Force. This was followed by pilot training in Enid, Oklahoma, and fighter lead-in training in Alamogordo, New Mexico. I did well enough in those courses that about a year and a half after all of that training began, I wound up in Phoenix, Arizona, where I spent six months learning how to fly the F-16 Viper. Right now, the Viper I'm strapped to drops off the tanker as the additional jets in our sixty-aircraft formation all join up for the push into Iraq.

Radio communications on our frequency-hopping radios are kept to a minimum as the F-15s, F-4Gs, and EF-111s join our F-16 mass gaggle. The plan is to have eight F-15Cs sweep out ahead of our route to draw in any Iraqi aircraft launched to intercept us. Behind the sweep will be the two waves of the main formation, four F-15Cs out front, followed by eight F-4G surface-to-air missile killers, aka SAM killers or "Wild Weasels." A distance behind that front group are the first and second waves of sixteen F-16s. Wedged between the two waves are four radar-jamming EF-111s and an additional four F-15Cs.

As we approach the Iraqi border in broad daylight at 21,000 feet above mean sea level, my pulse quickens and adrenaline pumps into my bloodstream, commanded by some ancient biological algorithm. Looking out over this massive formation, the sky filled in all directions with jets, I imagine that my great uncle Sonny Cater must have been a part of a similar scene before he was killed in the skies over Germany during the Second World War.

We cross the border, and I arm all my weapons and defensive systems, turn off my external lights, and turn the volume of my radar warning receiver way up. I look at the stark landscape below and wonder what's going on down there. *Are there people just going about their business, bedouins tending their goats, folks fetching water from wells? How many of those folks would like to kill me right now?*

On my right knee rests my attack map with time, distance, and heading carefully marked out between all our navigation points. Circles indicate waypoints where we will update our heading. A square indicates our initial point or IP, where we will start our bombing run. A triangle designates our target airfield. Also on the map are the planned orbits of all our support aircraft—the F-15Cs, F-4Gs, and EF-111s. However, numerous red concentric arcs—depicting the maximum range of all the known surface-to-air missile and antiaircraft artillery sites—are the most ominous designations on the map. I don't remember ever seeing anything so heavily defended in my Fighter Weapons School training missions.

"Bulldog is tracking two MiG-29s orbiting bullseye two-seven-en-zero, twenty-five," announces the controller to our formation. Bullseye is an arbitrary reference point that we mark on our maps. I plot out a 270-degree bearing on my map from the point and mark an "X" at twenty-five miles. *Shit! That's right over our IP.* "Bandits are cold and have not made radar contact yet," announces the controller, indicating that the MiG-29s are on the leg of their orbit that has put them tail onto us. The controller then transmits, "Bandits turning hot," followed shortly by, "Bandits have radar locks and have targeted the formation—cleared to kill."

As much as I wish I was up front with an opportunity to engage these MiGs, our job today is not to blow a couple of MiGs out of the sky. Our job is to keep all of the jets at our target airfield from ever taking off. I'm not worried about the

MiGs being a threat to our part of the formation. The part of the formation that I'm in is still more than fifty miles away from the MiGs. The price we pay for this initial insulation from the threat is that we're the "Tail-end Charlies," an affectionate term to designate the guys who usually get shot down over the target area—the ones at the back of the formation who get the brunt of the surface-to-air munitions thrown at them once the element of surprise is blown by the huge explosions on the ground caused by the guys up front.

Two calls come over the radio in rapid succession indicating that the F-15C sweep just fired two long-range missiles at the MiGs. I strain to see the missile trails, but I guess I'm too far away. After what seems like an eternity, the call we've all been waiting to hear comes across: "Bulldog confirms two kills—no joy on any other bandits." This indicates that the Iraqi Air Force has two fewer fighter jets and the coast is clear, at least from air threats. At hearing the news, I yell, "Yes!" and punch my fist in the air. I imagine most everyone else in the formation just did something similar.

I wonder if there are two Iraqi pilots floating back down to Earth in parachutes or if they got vaporized by a direct hit. Both of those scenarios are presently quite likely in my own immediate future. Only one of those scenarios, however, would result in me having any control over my survival. The thought of potentially riding a parachute down into a heavily populated area of people who would like to tear my limbs off has me thinking back to my Air Force survival training. I quickly run through all the things I would do on the way down in the chute, ways I could try to evade capture, and what I would do if captured. If I was somehow able to survive to the point where I ended up in an Iraqi prison, I could make use of my prisoner-of-war training as well. That training taught me that surviving, in the end, comes down to a matter of perspective.

Thinking back to my simulated POW experience, it absolutely amazed me how fast people could lose perspective and turn into sheep to be herded. Even in that short, simulated event, some people lost hope. At the time, I thought, *What's wrong with these people? They have airline tickets that will fly them out of this in a few days. They know how this ends.*

If somehow this day ends with my body in an Iraqi prison cell, I will do my best to keep my mind free and outside the walls. I will do my best not to limit my perspective to a prison cell or to the pain I may experience inside those four walls.

Right on cue, the F-15Cs, F-4Gs, and EF-111s peel off out of formation to set up their orbits outside of the threat rings in support of our attack. From this point on, it's just our thirty-two F-16s heading into the target area. Behind us lie hundreds of miles of open desert. In front of us looms the cradle of civilization, an area where countless empires and kingdoms rose and fell. This war is only the latest beat in the endless violent rhythmic heartbeat announcing humans' presence on this planet. My heads-up display indicates six minutes to the target.

Six thousand miles away, Carmel, who has not yet had her ultrasound, is listening from our home in South Carolina to a televised address from our commander in chief, President George H.W. Bush.

*"Just two hours ago, allied air forces began an attack on military targets in Iraq and Kuwait. These attacks continue as I speak. . . . This conflict started August second when the dictator of Iraq invaded a small and helpless neighbor. Kuwait, a member of the Arab League and a member of the United Nations, was crushed, its people brutalized. Five months ago, Saddam Hussein started this cruel war against Kuwait. Tonight, the battle has been joined. This military action, taken in accord with United Nations resolutions and with the consent of the United States Congress, follows months of constant and*

*virtually endless diplomatic activity on the part of the United Nations, the United States, and many, many other countries. Arab leaders sought what became known as an Arab solution, only to conclude that Saddam Hussein was unwilling to leave Kuwait. . . . This past weekend, in a last-ditch effort, the secretary general of the United Nations went to the Middle East with peace in his heart, his second such mission, and he came back from Baghdad with no progress at all in getting Saddam Hussein to withdraw from Kuwait."*

Up ahead of us, standing out like a dark beacon against the endless desert sands, lies the water of Lake Habbaniyah, west of Baghdad. We are heading right for the western tip of the lake. That is our IP, the point from which we will all funnel out toward our individual targets. My target is a runway-taxiway intersection at a MiG base on the eastern shore of the lake, not far to the west of the town of Al-Fallūjah. A quick scan of the formation confirms that everyone is exactly where they're supposed to be.

Six thousand miles away, my mother and stepfather are listening from their home in Florida to a televised address from President Bush. My HUD indicates that the target is five minutes away.

*"Now, the twenty-eight countries with forces in the Gulf area have exhausted all reasonable efforts to reach a peaceful resolution—[we] have no choice but to drive Saddam from Kuwait by force. We will not fail. As I report to you, air attacks are underway against military targets in Iraq. We are determined to knock out Saddam Hussein's nuclear bomb potential. We will also destroy his chemical weapons facilities. Much of Saddam's artillery and tanks will be destroyed. Our operations are designed to best protect the lives of all the coalition forces by targeting Saddam's vast military arsenal. Initial reports from General Schwarzkopf are that our operations are proceeding*

*according to plan. Our objectives are clear: Saddam Hussein's forces will leave Kuwait, the legitimate government of Kuwait will be restored to its rightful place, and Kuwait will once again be free. Iraq will eventually comply with all relevant United Nations resolutions and then when peace is restored, it is our hope that Iraq will live as a peaceful and cooperative member of the family of nations, thus enhancing the security and stability of the Gulf. Some may ask, 'Why act now? Why not wait?' The answer is clear: The world could wait no longer. Sanctions, though having some effect, showed no signs of accomplishing their objective. Sanctions were tried for well over five months, and we and our allies concluded that sanctions alone would not force Saddam from Kuwait."*

We pass within the first threat ring. It is eerily quiet. My senses are heightened. I run through my attack over and over in my mind as other thoughts creep in. *How many warriors throughout the millennia likewise mentally prepared for their attack on this area? How many countless attacks were planned from or toward this area during the Babylonian Empire? Is pride in the history of once having the most powerful empire on Earth clouding Saddam's judgment? Does he imagine a Hussein empire?* Six thousand miles away, my father is listening from his home in New York to a televised address from President Bush. My HUD indicates that the target is four minutes away.

*"While the world waited, Saddam Hussein systematically raped, pillaged, and plundered a tiny nation no threat to his own. He subjected the people of Kuwait to unspeakable atrocities, and among those maimed and murdered, innocent children. While the world waited, Saddam Hussein sought to add to the chemical weapons arsenal he now possesses, an infinitely more dangerous weapon of mass destruction, a nuclear weapon. And while the world waited, while the world talked peace and*

*withdrawal, Saddam Hussein dug in and moved massive forces into Kuwait. While the world waited, while Saddam stalled, more damage was being done to the fragile economies of the third world, the emerging democracies of Eastern Europe, to the entire world, including to our own economy. The United States, together with the United Nations, exhausted every means at our disposal to bring this crisis to a peaceful end. However, Saddam clearly felt that by stalling and threatening and defying the United Nations, he could weaken the forces arrayed against him. While the world waited, Saddam Hussein met every overture of peace with open contempt. While the world prayed for peace, Saddam prepared for war. . . . Saddam was warned over and over again to comply with the will of the United Nations: Leave Kuwait, or be driven out. Saddam has arrogantly rejected all warnings. Instead, he tried to make this a dispute between Iraq and the United States of America. Well, he failed. Tonight, twenty-eight nations—countries from five continents, Europe and Asia, Africa, and the Arab League— have forces in the Gulf area standing shoulder to shoulder against Saddam Hussein. These countries had hoped the use of force could be avoided. Regrettably, we now believe that only force will make him leave."*

We are almost over the IP. I see the target airfield due east. To the north of the airfield snakes the Euphrates River. I hear not a word on the radio. Silent determination fills us as we approach the lion's den, what was once Mesopotamia, the fertile nursery that gave rise to man and started thousands of years of innovation and refinement. It's likely that the wheel was invented here, as well as mathematics, astronomy, and agriculture, which all led to the technology to send people to the moon and place me in a supersonic fighter carrying 4,000 pounds of highly explosive bombs. Six thousand miles away, our entire nation is listening to a televised address from President Bush. My HUD indicates that the target is three minutes away.

*"This is an historic moment. We have in this past year made great progress in ending the long era of conflict and cold war. We have before us the opportunity to forge for ourselves and for future generations a new world order—a world where the rule of law, not the law of the jungle, governs the conduct of nations. When we are successful—and we will be—we have a real chance at this new world order, an order in which a credible United Nations can use its peacekeeping role to fulfill the promise and vision of the UN's founders. We have no argument with the people of Iraq. Indeed, for the innocents caught in this conflict, I pray for their safety. Our goal is not the conquest of Iraq. It is the liberation of Kuwait. It is my hope that somehow the Iraqi people can, even now, convince their dictator that he must lay down his arms, leave Kuwait, and let Iraq itself rejoin the family of peace-loving nations. Thomas Paine wrote many years ago, 'These are the times that try men's souls.' Those well-known words are so very true today. But even as planes of the multinational forces attack Iraq, I prefer to think of peace, not war. I am convinced not only that we will prevail but that out of the horror of combat will come the recognition that no nation can stand against a world united, no nation will be permitted to brutally assault its neighbor. No president can easily commit our sons and daughters to war. They are the nation's finest. Ours is an all-volunteer force, magnificently trained, highly motivated. . . . Tonight, America and the world are deeply grateful to them and to their families. . . . Tonight, as our forces fight, they and their families are in our prayers. May God bless each and every one of them and the coalition forces at our side in the Gulf, and may He continue to bless our nation, the United States of America."*

The time to target clicks down to one minute, forty-five seconds. I pass over the IP as my radar warning receiver starts chirping and beeping, announcing that they see me. The quiet on the radio is periodically interrupted by targeting calls from the Wild Weasels, the F-4G SAM killers. I expect missiles to fly in both directions any second. We head toward a distinctive bend in the river that will position us for the roll-in to our dive-bomb attack.

It's a beautiful sunny day without a cloud in the sky except for directly over our target area. But as I see more and more clouds forming, I realize that they are not clouds at all. They are exploding antiaircraft artillery shells. The first wave has already begun its attack. Between the aircraft sequentially rolling in and diving toward their target and the airfield, I see what looks like grey popcorn popping. All those guys up front who are presently hurtling themselves toward the ground will fly right into all that shrapnel, and our turn is coming up fast.

Since we are carrying dumb bombs, not precision-guided munitions, our bombs will hit our targets only if each of us dives at the ground and flies through the most lethal part of the enemy's air defenses on a precise trajectory. We must then release our weapons at the exact moment and under precise conditions, taking into account our speed, the wind, and dozens of other factors. Basically, for the first part of the attack we are, in effect, the precision-guided munition, only in our case the guidance computer (us and our aircraft) will only guide our weapons to the point of release. After release, we will let Newtonian physics take the bombs the rest of the way.

As we approach our roll-in point over the Euphrates, I notice explosions from the first wave's bombs. Most are centered on the runway, but we are also targeting fuel and munitions storage areas and I see massive secondary explosions as those incendiary targets are hit. The moment of truth is upon us. It is our four-ship's turn to roll in. In unison, all four of us slice our aircraft to the right toward the target. The horizon spins left, placing more sky below my feet than over my head. I look to my left to check on Nick, who is in formation tucked in close to my left wing. I experience a surreal sensation of imbalance. Sights, sounds, and emotions that seem otherworldly bombard me. The foundation of my concept of reality is being challenged by a life-and-death here and now. Everything seems out of place. I'm leaving the familiar behind and pressing into a dangerous unknown.

As I roll out wings level in a forty-five-degree dive toward the earth, the concentration required for the task at hand provides an escape from my existential discomfort. Everything in the universe melts away, and all that is left is my assigned target. In my HUD, I fine-tune the aircraft's dive to place my flight path marker just beyond my target runway-taxiway intersection. The flight path marker is the onboard computer's estimate of where the jet is heading. If I do nothing from this point on, the jet will impact the ground just long of the target, on the spot where my flight path marker is presently sitting.

I fly to keep a line connecting the flight path marker to the death dot tracking through the target. I watch as the death dot slowly walks up toward it. Here's where an effort to pull the dot up to the target in a rush to get through the attack will lead to throwing the bombs long of the target. I fight the urge to pull back on the stick to get this over with and get the hell out of here. The next five seconds are for Uncle Sam. Up ahead, I see the grey popcorn bursting, but luckily it's not obstructing my view of the target.

The death dot reaches the target, and I gently depress the pickle button on my control stick and feel a familiar *kathunk* as two 2,000-pound bombs separate from my aircraft. My job is done. Now, I can get the hell out of here. I quickly confirm that Nick's bombs are gone too and that he's still with me. I then pull about five g's away from the target as I mash a button on the left side of the canopy rail, which releases flares in case any heat-seeking missiles are tracking me. Simultaneously, it also releases chaff, the metal foil that when released, blossoms into a radar return bigger than my aircraft's to confuse any incoming radar-guided missiles.

I look over my left shoulder, and just as I lock my eyes onto my target runway-taxiway intersection, I see it engulfed in the blast of two 2,000 pounders that probably buried themselves a good ten feet in the ground before exploding. I also see explosions taking place on all the other runway-taxiway intersections as well as down the length of both runways. All of us need to hit our targets if we want to deny the use of the base to the Iraqis. We can't leave even a single path to the runway.

To start a climb back up to our egress altitude, I light my afterburner. The periodic chirping and beeping of my radar warning receiver transitions to a loud squeal. I've been locked onto by a high-altitude SAM. I strain to look back over my left shoulder in the direction of the SAM site to check for a possible white smoke trail rising up from the ground to meet me. Nothing yet. I start developing a plan for my evasive maneuvers in preparation for when they do launch on me. Just then, two F-4Gs, about eight miles out, are flying toward me.

A weapons system officer in one of the F-4Gs announces over the radio that he's just launched a HARM—a high-speed anti-radiation missile—to destroy the surface-to-air missile site that is presently targeting me. As I fly my aircraft directly away from the SAM site in full afterburner, a white smoke trail from the HARM streaks out and up from the F-4, climbing very steeply. Then I get an indication that a high-altitude SAM has been launched on me as the white smoke trail of the HARM reaches its apex and tips over to establish a trajectory toward the ground.

Shortly after tipping over, the HARM's motor burns out and I lose sight of it once the smoke stops. My focus now shifts toward the location of the SAM site. I crane my neck and twist my torso to the left, straining against the parachute harness designed to keep me centered in the seat. I have to find and keep

*US Air Force F-16C Fighting Falcon fighter aircraft from the 363rd Tactical Fighter Wing, Shaw Air Force Base, SC, are refueled by US Air Force KC-135 Stratotanker aircraft in preparation for the first daylight attack on Baghdad during Operation Desert Storm. January 17, 1991.*
Credit: US Air Force

my eyes on the missile to defeat it. I can't avoid what I don't see. As I continue to search for it, I mentally extrapolate an estimate for how long the HARM would take to reach the ground based on how fast it appeared to be traveling when I lost sight of it. At the exact moment when I think, *That HARM should hit right . . . about . . . now,* the loud squeal of my radar warning receiver abruptly goes quiet. *Man, I owe those guys a beer (or two).* I never saw the missile coming at me.

We all make a mad dash across the border back into Saudi and converge to join in formation with the refueling tankers so that, one by one, each of us will get enough gas to make it home. Everyone is low on fuel. As we rejoin with the tankers, we safe up our systems, take a roll call, and do battle damage assessments on one another. Everyone is accounted for, and no one in the formation reports damage.

Pride wells up inside me. You never know how you're going to deal with combat until you're in it. I'm proud of how everyone, including me, handled ourselves in our first combat mission and how we got the job done. I'm especially proud that the mission I helped plan and coordinate over the last five months went off like clockwork with apparently every aircraft returning. As the adrenaline wears off and the fatigue of a long, stressful day makes itself known, we head back to our base for what I'm sure will be a warm welcome.

Day four of the war is over. I've worked the last twenty-four hours straight, planning some important missions directed by the White House. They went great, and the guys destroyed three Scud missile sites pointed at Israel. Saddam is lashing out indiscriminately with Scuds, ballistic missiles intended to destroy ground targets, wreaking havoc in Israel and Saudi Arabia. After getting some rest, I'm off on what we call a "road recce" mission—road reconnaissance. Today, I'm leading a two-ship. My wingman Nick and I were given a kill box. Our mission is to attack anything that moves within the grid on our map that defines the kill box. We are patrolling in Southern Iraq. The Kuwaiti border is not far away, to the east.

Shortly after arriving on station, I see a vehicle moving down a road in the kill box. This is the first time I've seen anything moving on the ground. Excitedly, I set up my weapon system to drop two 500-pound bombs and I start a dive toward the vehicle. I line everything up, and as the death dot reaches just in front of the moving vehicle, I release the bombs. As I pull up to recover from the dive, to my disappointment I see the bombs explode long of the target. This is the first time I've missed so far in the war. Then I have a different thought: *There are no military markings on this vehicle.* Even though I am cleared to attack anything in this grid, I have received no intel that this is a military target.

I have no idea who is in this vehicle. It could be Saddam Hussein, or it could be a Kuwaiti family trying to escape to Saudi Arabia or someone in the Kuwaiti resistance. I decide to let this one go and find some tank revetments to attack. Regardless of who is in the vehicle, I'm glad I missed and didn't try to attack again. Indiscriminate bombing is not the best way to win a war.

The next day, bad weather is making our job tougher; but every day we take out more and more of the Iraqi air defenses, making it easier to do our job.

Watching how everyone has been handling combat is interesting. I think all of us understand that making it out alive is not a guarantee, and different people react to this fact differently. Some guys just quietly get the job done. There's little complaining and little bravado. Others are much more vocal and aggressive. Some seem to have retained their respect for life—all life, not just American life—while others have demoted our enemy to something less than human—something to be wiped out.

It's late January, and I finally get a phone line to call Carmel. Billy Diehl has agreed to let me use his satellite phone, probably breaking a few rules. Over these past nine days of combat, I have done my best to compartmentalize and try to keep the uncertainty of what's going on at home from affecting my ability to fly and fight, but the not knowing is still killing me. No matter what's going on with Carmel's pregnancy, it will be better if I know once and for all and can start dealing with it. Carmel should have already had her ultrasound. I just need to know the results.

When Carmel answers the phone, I'm transported to a higher dimension. Hearing her voice for the first time since the war started beautifully jolts me out of the narrow world of combat and reminds me that there's a bigger world out there. I have a home and a wife and people who love me. There's a normal life out there evidenced by this beautiful voice.

After our greeting, three words leave Carmel's lips, travel to a geosynchronous satellite orbiting 22,236 miles directly overhead Brazil, then to another satellite, and then to me on the sat phone in my commander's hooch: "We're having twins!"

Relief makes me weak. I have to sit down. A tremendous weight lifts off me, and intense gratitude wells up inside. "Oh, sweetheart, I'm so happy. I miss you so much."

We use this rare opportunity to speak to catch up as best we can and express our love for each other. It's tough hanging up, not knowing if I'll ever hear Carmel's beautiful voice again or if I will ever get to meet my children. But I have to believe I will. I believe that God has special plans for us and our little family.

I head to the O Club to tell all there the great news. Maybe it's time to break out some more smuggled Jeremiah Weed. A bunch of the guys' wives are pregnant or have had babies while we've been here, so I encounter a sympathetic crowd. As I share the news, CNN is reporting that the Iraqis shot some more Scuds at Israel today. *Saddam is such a dickweed! I wish someone would just blow him away.*

About a month of war passes before I get a day off. To date, I've flown twenty-three combat missions and have seventy-five hours of combat time. I've flown forty-five hours this month alone, and today's only February 13. To put that in perspective, a normal full month of flying back at Shaw is usually less than twenty-five hours. I have no idea how long this is going to last.

I can't imagine those poor bastards in Kuwait and Southern Iraq hanging in there much longer. We have been pounding the shit out of them day and night. I feel sorry for the troops on the front line because if they try to surrender, they get shot by an execution squad; and if they don't surrender, they continue to get bombed twenty-four hours a day—not to mention we've cut off all their supplies. We've been concentrating mostly on the Iraqi Republican Guard units though. I don't feel sorry for those shit-heads. They must not be loving life.

For some reason, Saddam has decided to start blowing up Kuwaiti oil wells and is dumping millions of barrels of oil into the Gulf. This is causing unimaginable environmental damage from the countless oil fires and the intentional oil spill. It's as if he's a spoiled bully who's not getting his way, so he's going to light a match and watch the world burn.

Eight days later, February 21, I have now flown twenty-seven combat sorties, and all have gone great. My wingman Nick and I just dropped off the tanker, and we're heading north to hit some Republican Guard targets northwest of Kuwait. I think the ground war is about to start. I have mixed feelings about it. On the one hand, it means the beginning of the end, and I know we'll do great. But on the other hand, I know it's going to come with a cost in US lives. Unfortunately, I think that is inevitable and necessary. We've come this far. We can't let these bastards off the hook.

Shortly after crossing the border into Iraq, a controller on the airborne early warning and control system makes a call directly to us. We're "cleared to engage, cleared to kill!" This is the first time since the first day of the war that I've been anywhere near an Iraqi aircraft, and this time it's ours. I lock my radar onto the threat and call to Nick, "I'm contact nose twenty miles, painting bandit," referencing an enemy aircraft that my onboard system confirms. If I were carrying long-range radar-guided missiles, I would have already fired off shots. All I have today though are two close-range heat-seeking Sidewinder missiles. My heart races as I center the target in my HUD.

My radar warning receiver is quiet, leading me to believe that the threat doesn't see me. That initial comfort vanishes as the aircraft turns in my direction. I depress a button on my throttle, which uncages a Sidewinder seeker head. A loud squeal in my headset confirms that the missile is locked on and can be fired.

Just as I'm about to let it go, I think, *You've come this far, you might as well visually identify before firing.* I hold my shot and pass the jet canopy to canopy. Across the fuselage of the desert-camouflaged aircraft I see "FREE KUWAIT" emblazoned. *It's a Kuwaiti A-4!* It could even possibly be the jet in the picture that's been hanging on the wall of my hooch for the past several months. I quickly make a radio call back to the controller: "ID friendly, ID friendly! Previously reported bandit is a Kuwaiti A-4. I repeat, previously reported bandit is an A-4!"

The controller responds simply, "Bulldog copies." No one says another word, and Nick and I proceed to our date with the Republican Guard. I have no idea why the controller and my onboard system identified the aircraft as an enemy. I'm really thankful that I chose to confirm its identity with my own eyes.

Did the memory of my encounter with an unknown vehicle in a kill box a few weeks ago have anything to do with my precautions? I wonder.

# CHAPTER 6

# The Ground War

✦ Today's mission brief is filled with a level of tension that I haven't felt since the start of the war. Attendees are strictly controlled and instructed that nothing we say here can leave the room. When the intelligence part of the brief starts, we learn that in three hours, the American and allied ground forces will roll north into Iraq to attack the entrenched Iraqi forces, signaling the start of the long-awaited ground war. Our number one job now is to support the ground forces.

Up until this point, the message from the generals above was that no target is worth dying for. Today, February 24, that calculus has changed. Every effort, no matter how risky, must be employed to increase the probability of a swift victory on the ground. Every aviator must make that happen. Secrecy is critical in order to maintain the element of surprise.

We are all sworn to secrecy with the admonishment that the only reason they are telling us any of this is because we could get retasked from our interdiction missions to close air support missions. I guess somewhere along the line, the secret got out because as we leave our life-support shop for our jets, CNN is blaring from a TV, "This just in: Reliable sources are reporting that the ground war is scheduled to begin in a matter of hours."

✦

*Left to right: Captain Mark "Nick" Nichols, Captain Jan "Tav" Tavrytzky, Captain Ron "Agent" Garan, and Captain John "Buck" Burgess stand in front of CBU-87 cluster munitions during a break in Desert Storm combat operations in 1991.* Credit: US Air Force

Three days later, it's been a long day as I find a place to sit my butt in a poorly lit Quonset hut at King Khalid Military City, KKMC for short, in Saudi Arabia. Over the past few days, we have been flying three missions a day in support of the ground war. We take off from Shawbu Dhabi, air refuel, hit targets in Iraq or Kuwait in support of ground objectives, land at KKMC, get more bombs and fuel, hit more targets, get more fuel and bombs at KKMC, hit more targets, and then go to the tankers to get enough gas to make it home. Unfortunately, at the moment, massive thunderstorms have grounded us, so we're all waiting for a break in the weather so we can get back to work.

I find a spot next to an old Hahn buddy, Bill "Psycho" Andrews. Tall, soft-spoken Psycho, who bears a resemblance to a young Jimmy Stewart, is a great guy and a strong flight lead. He is also waiting with his four-ship for the weather to break. At this point in the war, we are starting to see a potential end to the hostilities. Things have been going very well, and now, with the ground war well underway, it's only a matter of time before this whole thing is over and we'll be heading home.

Like warriors everywhere, when we have some idle time on our hands, we talk about home and all the things we can't wait to do when we get back there. I share with Psycho my desire to make it home before Carmel gives birth to our twins, to which Psycho notes that his wingman Joey Booher is the only one in his four-ship whose wife is not pregnant or just had a kid.

Psycho also shares with me some details of a "danger close" mission he flew a few days earlier—a close air support mission where bombs had to be dropped so close to friendly troops that their survival couldn't be guaranteed. Psycho, along with a four-ship led by Billy Diehl, rescued an eight-man US Army Special Forces unit that had been surrounded by hundreds of Iraqi troops deep in Iraq. Due to Psycho's and Billy's effort and the effort of their wingmen, all the soldiers made it out alive. Psycho says he felt a special bond with those guys on the ground, a bond between countrymen and warriors. He had never been in as tight a spot as when he was helping those guys, he says.

As Psycho and I chat, we agree that there's no place else we'd rather be than right here. We also reflect on the intense focusing of operations. We have thousands of aircraft, tanks, and artillery, which all up until a few weeks ago were being deployed across an entire vast country. Now, all of those assets are being employed in an extremely small and still-shrinking area. Until recently, to avoid midair collisions, we could employ the big sky theory—basically the idea that the sky is so big that the odds of randomly running aircraft into each other is very slim. This is rapidly becoming a false and especially dangerous theory.

The same thing is happening on the ground as all the armored divisions are collapsing on themselves as more of the Iraqi war machine is destroyed. This is a good problem to have. I would much rather be on this side of that chaos than the other. But that doesn't alleviate the feeling that things are getting considerably more dangerous. If we are not careful, this concentration of destructive power could blow up in our faces. There may still be hell to pay before this is all over. Throughout our conversation, the unspoken knowledge of the increasing danger is written on Psycho's face. I imagine he can read the same thing on mine.

After almost two hours, the weather breaks just enough for us to get the OK to get off the ground. Both my four-ship and Psycho's will be heading to the front lines to attack Republican Guard elements that are engaging the US Army's 7th Corps. Our flights are equipped with CBU-87 cluster bombs, which, after deployment from an aircraft, will release multiple bomblets that can take out hard targets, such as tanks, and soft targets, such as troops. We will be hitting the Medina and Hammurabi divisions of the Iraqi Republican Guard, the latter division named after the sixth king of the first Babylonian Dynasty. I also heard that he might have made up some laws. I find it ironic that the Code of Hammurabi was one of the first sets of laws that put an emphasis not on compensating the victims of crime but on punishing the perpetrators, and here we are about to go inflict some serious punishment on some heavily fortified perps.

Almost immediately after takeoff, as all three of my wingmen have joined up in close formation, I lead us in a climb into thick, dark clouds. I contact our assigned forward air controller, whom we call "the FAC," and he informs me that he is in an A-10 and our target is a column of Iraqi tanks that are exchanging shots with the US Army's 7th Corps near the Kuwaiti-Iraqi border.

When my inertial navigation system indicates that we are approaching the target area, I descend to get below the weather.

Looking to my left, I can see Nick tucked in tight on my left wing. To the right, I see my Number Three, but the clouds are so thick and dark that I can barely make out a silhouette of my Number Four jet on Number Three's right wing.

Breaking out through the bottom of the cloud deck, it seems like we've descended into Dante's Inferno. Two-thousand-foot-thick dense black smoke from numerous oil rig fires lit by the Iraqis hugs the desert like a blanket of death. Somewhere in this black fog our targets lurk. If I took a four-ship into a situation like this when I was a student at Fighter Weapons School, I would have undoubtedly failed the sortie. We are working in a small slice of the atmosphere, just a few thousand feet between the bottom of the cloud deck and the top of the smoke. We are being highlighted against the bottom of the cloud deck above us. The enemy almost certainly sees us while the smoke completely hides them. This is not good. There's no way out if everything goes south.

The FAC attempts to talk our eyes onto the target, but all I can see is smoke. "No joy on the target," I call out as the FAC starts a bombing run to help us find them. I see the A-10 roll in and disappear in the smoke, and as he pulls out of it, I see the flashes of his cluster bombs exploding on the dark desert below. "Spot One-One hit five hundred meters south of my marks," radios the FAC. I direct "Three" and "Four" to stay high. "One and Two are in," I radio.

I dive my F-16 just south of where I saw the A-10's bombs hit. As I approach the smoke, tracers—artillery rounds that trail bright exhaust—fly past my canopy. Nick is tucked in right where he's supposed to be. I approach the minimum drop altitude and still don't see the tanks. I pull out without dropping any bombs. My eyes sting, and I can smell the smoke from the oil fires. "Three" and "Four" roll in, also with no success.

Meanwhile, about thirty miles to the northeast, Psycho's four-ship is starting to run out of fuel after difficulties getting ahold of their FAC. Making matters worse, Psycho's wingman Joey loses sight of Psycho as they both continue their descent through the weather to the desert. When Psycho and Joey break out of the weather, they start talking about landmarks on the ground in an effort to get back together. Joey's jet is almost immediately engulfed in a cloud of antiaircraft artillery fire and takes evasive action, climbing back into the clouds.

Initially, the tactic doesn't work. Even while in the clouds, flack explodes all around Joey's jet. Not until he pops out of the top of the clouds does the antiaircraft artillery fire subside. In all this, no one has heard a word from Psycho. Everyone in the flight begins making radio calls to "Mutt Four-One," Psycho's call sign, but he doesn't respond. A chill descends upon the guys as they try to figure out where he is.

I am oblivious to what's going on with Psycho's flight as I'm dealing with my own mess. I roll in for my third attempt to locate the targets. We used up a lot of gas as I tried to deconflict our attacks with incoming artillery shells from the 7th Corps. It doesn't take long before I abandon my attempts to deconflict and revert back to the big sky theory to keep us from getting hit from our own incoming artillery. Again, I can't see the targets through the thick smoke. This time, as I pull off, the hair stands up on the back of my neck and I break as hard as I can away from Nick and put out chaff and flares. Just as I do, a missile passes about 200 feet behind me and sails off into the clouds. *That was a little too close.*

I inform the FAC that we have enough gas for one last pass. I roll in with Nick tucked in tight. This feels really stupid. The guys on the ground have our number. They know exactly where we are and where we're going. *But,* I think, *if the FAC has the balls to be here in an A-10 traveling at two hundred and fifty knots, then we can be here in F-16s traveling at four hundred and fifty knots.* As we dive at the dark desert below, I laser-focus on the spot where I think the targets are located, but out of my peripheral vision, I see sparkling flashes of light.

Taking my gaze off the desert floor, I realize that flack is exploding and tracer rounds are whizzing by all around us. The tracers are made even more prominent against the dark backdrop of the overcast, smoke-filled atmosphere. If I can see them, then the gunner can see them, making his job easier to adjust the rounds to intercept our presently predictable flight path. I press just a little bit below the minimum allowable altitude, and as I do, a line of black rectangular objects emerges from the dark, smoky background.

I hit the pickle button, and in rapid succession, four canisters of CBU-87 bombs drop from my wings. Nick, seeing my bombs come off, releases his own, and we both pull as hard as we can away from the ground while pumping out chaff and flares.

A few seconds after release, all eight of our dropped bomb canisters spin up to a predetermined rate as they dive toward the tanks below. Inside each of the CBU-87 canisters are 202 BLU-97/B bomblets. At the predetermined height above the ground, the spinning canisters open, spewing the bomblets throughout the target area, each being slowed to the most lethal speed by its own small parachute. The bomblets that hit something hard fire a shaped charge, a heavy metal-lined explosive, that penetrates through armor. For softer targets, each bomblet also has a scored fragmentation case that flings frag in all directions at supersonic speeds and a zirconium ring for incendiary effects. These are extraordinarily nasty weapons that get the job done.

I look back at the target area to spot the missiles that are undoubtedly heading our way when I see the sparkle of our BLU-97/Bs engulfing an area the size of many football fields. Inside this inferno is the line of black rectangular shapes that are now engulfed in the sparkling fireworks. The concentration of projectiles overwhelming the tanks provides near statistical certainty that some of them are finding their targets. As bomblets impact the exterior armor of the tanks, they explode in a precisely designed way to propel an armor-piercing molten slug through the tank like butter.

After passing through the tank's exterior, the high-speed slug enters into its interior, ricocheting off interior walls and ripping through and igniting anything in its deafening path. Within a few seconds, the tank's interior is destroyed, along with anyone in it. Smoke billows up from the tanks, joining the thick blanket of smoke from the oil fires set by the Iraqis. In comparison to the oil fires, this smoke is like the smoke from a candle rising up to meet the smoke of a room engulfed in flames.

"Great bombs!" yells the FAC. "Shack! Put the rest of them right there!" As Nick and I continue our climb, Number Three and Number Four roll in and drop on the area where our bombs hit. After they pull off target, they rejoin on my aircraft as I climb us back toward the clouds. Just before entering the cloud deck, we get a call from the FAC that the targets have all been destroyed and the 7th Corps units are moving north.

Laced with the feeling of accomplishment for a job well done is the somber awareness of the gravity of war and the lives it destroys. Inside those tanks were enemy soldiers who were engaged in battle and actively attacking American forces. They were part of a regime that has been systematically butchering innocent people. This is the regime that ripped babies from incubators in Kuwait City and ran over innocent people with tanks. It must be stopped.

But deep within me, I also know that not all members of the Iraqi military are monsters.

In those tanks were also men who will never again be seen by their mothers, children, wives, brothers, fathers, and friends. In those tanks were probably men who were just doing what they thought was their duty, men no different than Psycho, Billy Diehl, or me. I'm sure others were there only because they were forced to be, in some way or another. In those tanks were men that in other circumstances, it is quite possible, I could have become friends with.

On the one hand, I and the others in my command are probably responsible for saving American lives today, but we are responsible for causing suffering and death to others too. A common way to suppress the horror of our actions is to simply ignore the fact that all Iraqis are not monsters, to double down on the us-versus-them mentality. To take on the mindset, "Fuck those assholes! The more we kill, the faster they'll surrender and the faster we can get the hell out of here." To take on a mindset that somehow our enemy is something less than human. But taking that approach requires that we ignore reality and live in a self-constructed fantasyland. I'm not willing to deceive myself for false comfort, and I'm not willing to don the false mask of external indifference. It sucks that we're here fighting this war. *What a stupid human endeavor! What a waste! I wish I lived in a world where sadistic tyrants didn't invade other countries.* A deep sadness descends upon me as I brush aside these thoughts. I don't have the luxury for this self-reflection right now. I have to get my guys to the tanker to get enough fuel to get back to base and get ready to do it all again.

Thirty miles to the northeast, still separated from his wingman, Psycho looks over the left canopy rail for Iraqi targets on the desert floor below. Suddenly, he feels a massive force behind him, which knocks him forward. It's as if someone just hit him with a giant sledgehammer. A missile that Psycho never saw coming impacted his aircraft just behind his cockpit, exploding on contact. The nose of his jet pitches over violently, throwing Psycho's head and arms up into the canopy, and the negative g-force pins him against it. The jet begins to violently roll and yaw.

Psycho quickly realizes that his only hope for survival is to eject. He fights with all his strength to pull his arms down from the canopy and reaches toward the ejection handle between his legs. He pulls the handle, and in that instant, everything in the world changes for him. In a flash, he is transported from a world of activity, action, and technology to a different type of conflict. No longer is he in his own protected world separated from the enemy by speed and altitude. No longer is the battlefield a place where he visits briefly a few times a day to attack the enemy from a distance. He has been thrust headfirst into the reality of the ground war.

Psycho is jolted as his parachute opens. He sees that he is heading right down into the midst of the Republican Guards as the smell of the burning oil stings his eyes and the sound of small arms and antiaircraft artillery crackles over the background sound of the air rustling past his descending parachute. He tries to steer the parachute away from the troops, but they are everywhere. They completely surround him.

His flight mates have no idea what has just happened to him, and his Number Three, Captain Evan "Ivan" Thomas, is automatically elevated to flight lead since there's still no contact with Psycho. Ivan develops a sick feeling deep in his gut reminiscent of the many times he, as most fighter pilots, has experienced a comrade going missing. Suddenly, he hears a familiar voice on the radio. It's Psycho, but something sounds different. His voice is obviously not being isolated and channeled by an oxygen mask into a sterile transmission. Instead, it sounds low and muffled, as if he's communicating via walkie-talkie on a windy day. "I'm in my chute," radios Psycho.

He had pulled out his emergency radio from his survival vest in an attempt to contact his flight. As Ivan responds to Psycho's calls, Psycho sees tracer rounds whizzing by him at close range. He looks over his left shoulder and sees that the Iraqis are shooting at him with antiaircraft artillery.

Ivan starts to coordinate what he hopes will be a rescue operation. He contacts the controller for the airborne early warning and control system and attempts to pass on his best guess about

Psycho's location when he hears a radio call that changes his game plan. "They're shooting at me! They're shooting at me in my chute!" Psycho can be heard saying.

*Screw this*, thinks Ivan as he starts a dive into the clouds, pointing directly at Psycho's last known location. Ivan's wingman, Captain Pete "Abner" McCaffrey, is about 6,000 feet line abreast on Ivan's right wing and dives into the clouds with him fully aware he will lose sight of his lead—big sky theory at work.

Ivan and Abner leave the sunny bright blue world above the clouds behind as they plunge into the white nothingness of the thick cloud deck. Lower and lower they dive. Outside their canopies, the white clouds transition to brownish-black. Finally, they pop out of the bottom of the clouds into a world of smoky gloom with a surface torn by the black smudges of the many bomb impacts of the past few weeks and columns of black smoke rising from various fires throughout the alien landscape. Once underneath the weather, Ivan and Abner frantically try to locate Psycho, but every time they get close to his last known location, they're met with a barrage of antiaircraft artillery and missiles unleashed from the desert floor.

They both put out chaff and flares and climb into the weather. As Ivan pops back out into the sunny blue sky on top, he notes that it looks like any other day flying F-16s except that now the beautiful blue sky is laced with the crisscrossing smoke trails from missiles as they too pop out of the clouds, targetless projectiles looking for their prey.

The ground rushes up to meet Psycho as he descends into the middle of a whole bunch of very pissed-off Iraqi Republican Guard infantrymen. As he hits the desert floor, his right tibia shatters on impact and the bone protrudes through his skin just above his boot. "My leg is broken. They're shooting at me, and my leg is broken!" yells Psycho over the radio. This revelation compels Ivan and Abner to make another dive into the darkness.

The Iraqi soldiers approach Psycho for a few steps, stop, take some shots at him, and then take some more steps toward him. The terrain around Psycho is as flat as a board, nothing to provide cover.

Just seconds later, a platoon of machine-gun-carrying soldiers surround Psycho. He assesses that trying to fight his way out of this with his 9mm Beretta will not end well. He drops his gun and radio and raises his hands in surrender as Ivan and Abner are now back under the weather circling overhead while Psycho's wingman Joey remains above the weather coordinating a possible rescue. As the soldiers close in a few yards from him, Psycho sees a missile launch heading right for Abner's jet. He quickly lowers his hands, grabs the radio, and yells, "Break left! Flares!" Rapid gunfire kicks up dirt all around Psycho as he throws the radio back to the ground.

Abner, hearing Psycho's call, defeats the missile. Both Ivan and Abner are out of gas, flares, and ideas and climb back through the weather to help coordinate a rescue. Repeated calls to Psycho on the radio go unanswered. Now a call is placed to ask if the Army can help. Words are passed to the Corps staff along with confirmation that Psycho was alive and communicating when he hit the ground. Army officials confirm that they will launch a rescue mission, but information about the area where Psycho went down is limited and the fog of war is settling in.

A short time later, three helicopters—one Blackhawk and two Apaches—fly toward Psycho's last known location. On board the Blackhawk, on the floor with her back against her medical gear, sits Army flight surgeon Major Rhonda Cornum. The trio of Army helicopters flies so low that Major Cornum can see, through the blowing sand and smoke, the faces of US soldiers on the march north, deeper into Iraq. As her helicopter and the other two approach the battlefield at 140 knots, the war-torn desert below the choppers erupts in crackling flashes. Tracer rounds streak by each of the open side doors of the Blackhawk.

From each of the Blackhawk's doors, a gunner returns fire. Rounds from Iraqi antiaircraft artillery penetrate through the fuselage toward the back of the helicopter as hot spent casings from the door gunners bounce off the floor. The smell of burning gunpowder permeates the inside of the Blackhawk as the pilot at the controls banks hard to the left, probably low enough to clip the top of a basketball hoop, to evade the fire.

While still in the left turn, a bang goes off as a direct hit blows off the tail boom of the Blackhawk, which is felt by all. One of the pilots calls out, "We're going in!" The nose of the chopper hits the sand and cartwheels while metal crushes in all around the crew. The twisted wreckage of the Blackhawk comes to rest in the middle of a complex of underground Iraqi Republican Guard bunkers.

Major Cornum slowly regains consciousness amidst the rubble of what's left of the Blackhawk's fuselage. She wonders if she has died and is having an out-of-body experience. As her vision comes into full focus, the appearance of five Iraqi soldiers pointing guns at her convinces her that she is still very much alive—alive but badly injured. Major Cornum was shot in the back during the crash and, on impact, broke her arms and dislocated her right leg. With the Blackhawk down, the rescue mission is called off. No one in the air or back in headquarters knows the status of either the Blackhawk crew or Psycho.

The remaining three aircraft of Psycho's four-ship make the long trek back to base in reflective silence. Each pilot runs countless "what if" scenarios through their head. What could they have done differently? What happened to Psycho? Things look very bleak. Ivan finds himself thinking of Psycho's wife, Stacey.

As Ivan suffers for her and Psycho, the same question runs through his mind over and over: *Is Psycho alive?*

Psycho is the third pilot from Shawbu Dhabi who has gone missing since the war started. Captain Scott Thomas had to eject over Iraq and evade capture on the ground until he was recovered in a daring rescue by US forces. Another pilot, Captain Dale Cormier, failed to return to base after his third combat mission of the day. We later found out that he was killed when his jet crashed short of the base runway because of an as-of-yet unknown reason.

As for Psycho, a day passes after he goes missing. On this February 28th morning, a somber blanket of gloom engulfs the mission brief. Losing Psycho, and the uncertainty of his status and the status of the chopper crew that was shot down trying to rescue him, weighs heavily on everyone. The mood lifts slightly when we hear that all combat operations have been suspended. The war is over! The Iraqis have asked for a cease-fire to negotiate the terms of surrender. The news is met with mixed feelings. Does this mean the Army will stop short of Psycho's crash site? Will we ever know what happened to him?

Before long, flyers are circulated throughout our tent city announcing the Mother of All Victory Parties, a nod to Saddam Hussein's claim that he would defeat his enemies in the Mother of All Battles. Prior to the festivities kicking off, Billy Diehl pulls Nick and me aside and says, "You need to be on the next cargo flight out of here so you guys can be with your wives. We don't know how long the cease-fire will hold, and I don't want you to miss this opportunity to be there for the deliveries." We thank Billy and agree that we will head back to the States ASAP.

Later, at the Mother of All Victory Parties that night, assorted booze flows like rain. Despite it all, everyone has Psycho in the back of their mind. I try to remain optimistic about his fate, but I know the odds are against him. It takes a great deal of alcohol to deaden that reality.

In an island of sober reflection in the Gulf of Alcohol, I think back over these past seven months of voluntary imprisonment—months of physical imprisonment inside the barbed wire and revetments of our tent city, but also a deeper level of imprisonment. Prison represents the cordoning off of a small part of reality, separating out the full richness of life and social inter-action for a specific purpose. Like Don Henley sang in "Hotel California," we're all prisoners "of our own device."

But, unlike prison, the purpose of our incarceration was not punishment but focused unity—unity forged from mutual self-sacrifice for a higher mission. Although I'm really looking forward to breaking out of this voluntary "prison" and returning to the "real world," I also reflect on the honor I feel to have been a part of this team—not just our squadron or wing, but the US military overall. The pressure of combat brought about a level of camaraderie that I never knew existed.

I would have laid down my life for my brothers-in-arms, and I believe they would have done the same for me. In all of this nightmare of death and destruction, what appears as the smoke disperses is love. I love these guys that I have fought shoulder to shoulder with, and I love my country.

I've never been prouder to be an American.

# PART 2

# INFLECTION: LEAVING THE CAVE

"As man advances in civilization, and small tribes are united into larger communities, the simplest reason would tell each individual that he ought to extend his social instincts and sympathies to all members of the same nation, though personally unknown to him. This point being once reached, there is only an artificial barrier to prevent his sympathies extending to the men of all nations and races."

— **Charles Darwin**, ***The Descent of Man***, 1871 AD

# CHAPTER 7
# The Top of the Mountain

✦ On a late August day in 1991, in the temporary living facility at Luke Air Force Base in Arizona, Carmel and I zigzag around our small studio apartment, each bouncing a crying four-month-old baby on our chests. Tomorrow, I will start a training course on the Air Force's newest version of the F-16, what we call "the Block 40." But tonight, our goal is to just get these peanuts to sleep.

Four and a half months ago, I made it back to Shaw just in time to see our twins, Ronnie and Joseph—each named after one of their grandfathers—come into this world. Since then, I have been assigned as an F-16 instructor pilot at the USAF Fighter Weapons School, an "impossible" dream come true.

Never did I think I would end up back at the Fighter Weapons School as an instructor. To me, I've arrived at the start of what I'm sure will be the summit of my professional career. The plan is to spend a few weeks here at Luke learning to employ the Block 40 before returning to Nellis Air Force Base in Las Vegas to start my instructor pilot tour. With its infrared targeting pod to steer laser-guided weapons, we will fly low and fast at night with the help of forward-looking infrared imagery and terrain-following radar.

After about thirty minutes of strolling, bouncing, and humming lullabies, Carmel and I get the boys to sleep. Just as we nestle them into their portable cribs, a knock rattles the door of our one-room home. Carmel and I trade the same exact look that screams, "Who the hell is that?" Seconds later, I open the door to see Bill "Psycho" Andrews standing on the steps with a grin and a six-pack of Budweiser in each hand.

"Hey, Agent, wanna hear a story?" Psycho's grin grows into a full smile. I walk out onto the front steps of our ground-level apartment, followed by Carmel, who walks out of the dark room into the heat of an Arizona summer evening and gives Psycho a "welcome home" hug. Then she quietly retreats back into Baby-land as Psycho and I park our butts on the steps.

Psycho recently arrived at Luke to begin a tour as an F-16 instructor pilot. We sit for a few moments, not saying a word, until the sound of two frosty cold cans of Budweiser snapping open in rapid succession pierce the silence.

"Man, it's good to see you, Psycho. We were really worried about you," I share as we both stare off in the direction of the Luke Air Force Base flight line. Psycho then proceeds to tell me his incredible story.

After his capture, the Iraqis loaded him onto a truck bound for the Iraqi city of Basra under the cover of darkness. En route, the vehicle had engine trouble, forcing the driver to pull off to the side of the road. Psycho recounts how moments later, he saw the silver and gold sparkles of cluster bombs sweeping across the road right in front of them. The deafening chainsawlike sound made Psycho wince. The bombs were no doubt dropped from an F-16 whose fire control computer had calculated a perfect lead point for their vehicle as it traveled down the road. Fortunately, the bombs exploded where their vehicle *would* have been if they hadn't stopped.

Psycho looks at me, smiles, and says, "I'm very thankful that I had a direct payoff from a bunch of prayers from a bunch of people."

"I was one of those many, many people," I share.

They never made it to Basra that night. They ended up back in the area where they started. After returning, they dragged Psycho into a bunker. One of the Iraqi soldiers made it clear that he wanted to help, and together Psycho and the soldier made a crude splint for his leg. The soldier's compassion seemed completely out of place when compared to the treatment Psycho had received so far. Throughout the night, Psycho heard rockets and artillery booming overhead—no doubt originating from the US Army. He hoped that the US 7th Corps would overrun his position and rescue him.

At one point during the night, probably in response to the US advance toward them, the Iraqis dragged Psycho out of the bunker and set him next to their vehicle as they hastily packed for their retreat. Apparently, because of Psycho's injuries, they deemed him to be no threat and quit watching him. Seeing an opportunity to escape, Psycho hid under a piece of canvas in the bunker. He heard a lot of yelling and screaming, and eventually the Iraqis drove off without him. Amazed that he had escaped, his plan was to just sit and wait for the US Army to sweep over him. He fashioned a white flag and waited.

Unfortunately, the next day the Iraqis reentered the area and found him. Again, he was on his way to Basra. After about an hour bouncing along the crater-pocked desert, each bump sending waves of pain radiating through his body, an Iraqi officer leaned over to Psycho and in near-perfect English said, "You know, the war ended a few hours ago." Psycho responded, "That's great! Do you mind dropping me off in Kuwait City?" But Kuwait City was not in Psycho's travel plans that day.

After a day in a jail cell in Basra, he was transported in a school bus to a prison in Baghdad. Also on board the bus for the long ride were three members of the Blackhawk crew that were shot down in the attempt to rescue him—Major Rhonda Cornum, Staff Sergeant Daniel Stamaris, and Sergeant Troy Dunlap. Psycho later found out that the five other members of the Blackhawk crew—Chief Warrant Officer Four Philip Garvey, Chief Warrant Officer Three Robert Godfrey, Sergeant First Class William Butts, Staff Sergeant Patbouvier Ortiz, and Sergeant Roger Brelinski—were all killed in the crash. The treatment in Baghdad was tough, especially during the interrogations, which Psycho described as "violent, ruthless, and harsh." The Iraqis made it clear that they weren't going to play by the rules and they would do whatever it would take to get their information.

Psycho shared one particular incident that he felt was a turning point in his treatment. At one juncture, two guards entered his cell. Psycho was sprawled out on the floor in a futile effort to find a position that would decrease the pain radiating from his leg. One of the guards, obviously very agitated, began yelling at Psycho in Arabic with the other translating. "He says that two of his children were killed by American bombs and he knows that you are a bomb dropper," translated the English-speaking guard.

Psycho responded compassionately, saying that he was sorry to hear about the loss of his children and that the war was so difficult for him. The Iraqi father and guard then lifted his boot over Psycho's broken leg. The message was clear: Payback was going to be a bitch. He was going to stomp Psycho's broken leg, and he was going to stomp it hard. Psycho leaned back, folded his arms, looked the guard in the eyes, and said, "Go ahead."

After a long stare down, the guard put his boot down and muttered something in Arabic. The other guard translated the muttering: "He says you are very brave." Then both guards walked out. Psycho's treatment improved after that incident. The episode also taught him a lesson.

"Agent, as a prisoner, there's a lot that you don't have control over, but what you do have control over is the way you feel and what's going on inside your head. You may be in a bad situation, but you can choose to stay positive and ride that positivity as long as you can."

Silence again descends upon us as we both slip into deep thought. I'm thinking back to that night of mixed feelings at the victory party in the Shawbu Dhabi O Club. The weight of not knowing what had happened to Psycho or what he might be going through overshadowed the end-of-the-war celebrations. I lean over and look Psycho in the eyes and say, "Bill, there's no doubt in my mind that you are a true American war hero." Psycho, in true Psycho style, brushes off my declaration with a look that says, *I just did what anyone would do.* But the truth is, he put others first in the most harrowing moment of his life.

Looking down the barrel of many Iraqi guns, with everything stacked against him, wounded, bloodied, and with no way out, Psycho elected to put his life on the line to radio a warning to his wingman overhead, no doubt saving him from a similar fate or worse, and his valor continued as a POW. Psycho's heroic actions earned him the Air Force Cross.

With quite a few frosty Budweisers under our belts, I savor how wonderful it is to see Psycho again. It is my honor to call him a friend. The courageous level of self-sacrifice that some are able to rise to never ceases to amaze me. Some people just have a natural predisposition to see something greater and more important than themselves. Psycho is one of those people, and he gives me hope for humanity.

As all but the last remnants of the blazing Arizona heat dissolve into the night, Psycho takes a swig of his beer and, while staring off toward the illuminated flight line, says, "You know, those guys did everything they could. I was just in an impossible situation." He was referring to his wingmen and the failed rescue attempt. After a long pause, he adds, "Didn't stop them from trying though. When I was the guy on the ground needing rescue, I felt that same bond, that same link between warriors, between countrymen."

That bond shone like a beacon of hope and unity. That unity was never more obvious than the moment he was repatriated, which Psycho explains was the moment he and the other POWs crossed the Iraqi border on their flight out of Baghdad after a prisoner exchange was negotiated with the Iraqis.

Psycho shares that all the soon-to-be repatriated POWs were reserved when they boarded a chartered airliner jet in Baghdad, took off, and headed toward the border. Anticipation built as the pilots started giving a countdown to the border: "Forty miles to the border, twenty, ten . . ." As they crossed it, US Air Force F-15s joined on their wing. Psycho thought he might have seen a couple of Royal Air Force Tornado jets in the formation too.

He remembers looking out the window and seeing F-15s moving into close formation to escort them back through friendly territory. His face lights up into a big smile as he describes it: "That's when everybody just bust loose. Everyone was cheering, shouting, and waving to the pilots." Also on board the flight and partaking in the jubilation were the three surviving members of the Blackhawk crew who attempted to rescue Psycho. In addition to other American repatriated prisoners of war, POWs from Italy, England, Kuwait, and Saudi Arabia on board cheered too. Psycho recounts, "There was an outpouring of emotion because then we knew we were back. The F-15 pilots caught our enthusiasm. They dropped their masks and were waving to us, rocking their wings and dropping flares. A lieutenant in an F-15 on the left wing moved out a little and did a big aileron roll beside the airliner. Everyone enjoyed the show."

He shares the warm welcome he received after returning home and how well he was treated aboard the Navy medical ship USS *Mercy* shortly after the Iraqis released him. He felt as if he were a baby back in his mother's arms when he got back with the "good guys."

I then share with him my homecoming. I describe landing in Newark Airport and seeing my father and other family members

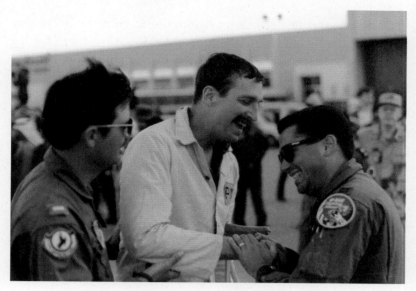

*Captain Bill "Psycho" Andrews is reunited with squadron mates*
*after being repatriated from Iraq in 1991.* Credit: US Air Force

at the gate for a brief reunion on my layover destined for South Carolina and reuniting with Carmel. As I recount this, a previously unacknowledged awareness bubbles up from somewhere deep inside me. For the first time, I realize how surreal the return to "normalcy" has been. If it's been surreal for me, it's probably completely overwhelmed Psycho after all he's been through.

For me, I've felt simultaneously overcome with joy to be back in the arms of my country and loved ones while somehow feeling out of place. Part of me wants to be back in the war, back in the action. I don't understand this disconnect. Even though I'm a warrior, I hate war. War is humanity's biggest failure. *Why do I miss it?*

Then the reason for the disconnect dawns on me. Even though there was a lot to complain about during the war, like stupid "Mickey Mouse" regulations and senior officers vying for career advancement opportunities, in the big scheme of the entire conflict, those things were outliers that barely rose above the background noise. I felt a belonging in combat unlike any I had ever experienced. I felt a primordial bond.

All of us in combat were inextricably dependent on each other for our very lives. We were not only fighting for our country, we were fighting for each other. Returning to the comfort of a "civilized" life seems mundane and trivial. Even though my reunion with Carmel, the love of my life, has been heaven on Earth and a prayer answered, I, on some level, feel generally disoriented. Something is missing. Worse yet, I've noticed things about my country I've never noticed before.

In spite of the jubilation over winning the war and being on the receiving end of a public desire to do better by the Gulf War vets than the country did for our Vietnam vets, I have noticed, in a profound way, the deep divisions in America. Tuning in to the news and seeing political pundits spewing contempt for others simply for having a different opinion is now repugnant to me. I've heard rampant us-versus-them sound bites coming from all directions. I know that part of what I was fighting for was the freedom we all cherish so dearly, including freedom of speech, but this is different. Having the right to free speech does not mean you have a right to your own facts or your own truth. Having free speech is not a free pass to spew hatred or to abandon civil discourse.

Watching the news, I've seen that disproportionate attention is being put on perceived differences leading to divisions between rich and poor, black and white, male and female, Democrat and Republican, urban and rural, educated and undereducated. Of course, I acknowledge that people put too much attention on these differences even before the war, but after emerging from the Iraqi conflict, I see the division in a new light. In the war, all of those perceived differences melted away into insignificance. All that mattered was *Are you fighting with us or against us? Are you part of our tribe or the enemy tribe?* For us, it wasn't even whether you were American. All you had to be was part of the coalition.

Now, back in the civilian world, it seems that most Americans have completely forgotten the bond we all share as countrymen. It seems we are no longer Americans first. It seems that what is of more importance than being Americans is our perceived differences. What is missing is the community we shared in combat, the camaraderie of being brothers- and sisters-in-arms, of being a part of something bigger and more important than ourselves, of being willing to die for each other simply because we are part of the same community.

During the war, it was as if each of us were all part of an overarching superbody. Each of the individual soldiers, sailors, airmen, and marines of the various nations aligned against Iraq were like neurons of a giant brain. The cerebral cortex of that brain directing the activities of the body was headquarters. Our aircraft, ships, and weapon systems were the muscles of the giant body. We were combined, aligned, and organized into an overarching structure with a mission more important than its parts. In this case, the function of this brain was to punish, destroy, and liberate. Although our national leadership seemed to do much better in this conflict than past conflicts, the analogy breaks down when you introduce Washington. Maybe the politicians are the amygdala, the reptilian brain responsible for fear, anxiety, and aggression.

It seems that I've come back to a world with the mantra *every man for himself*, a world of corporate and individual corrupt greed, a world ripe with selfish Wall Street con artists trying to find their next "sucker," a nation where it seems some politicians care more about themselves or their party than the country, a nation that has forgotten its motto, *"E pluribus unum," out of many, one*. This world is in sharp contrast to the one-for-all mindset of military combat that I just left. Even seeing something as seemingly trivial as someone littering makes my blood boil.

But whenever I'm with Carmel and the twins, this post-combat fog lifts. They remind me that I have a mission. I have others depending on me. I have a purpose. I have a tribe. The sound of two more frosty can openings snaps me out of my self-reflection. *How long did we just sit in silence?*

"Good to hang with you, my friend," I say shortly before my taste buds rejoice as the cold brew flows across my tongue on its way to my bloodstream.

It's another summer day, but not the same summer when I shot the breeze with Psycho at my temporary waystation home in Arizona. Three years have passed since then, and now my tour of duty instructing at the most intensive combat flight training program on the planet, at the Fighter Weapons School in Las Vegas, is coming to an end. Once again, I'm feeling self-reflective. My time here has been incredibly rewarding but also incredibly dangerous. Over the last few years teaching here, I've attended five memorial services for friends, squadron mates, and students who lost their lives during our training. Most people don't understand that the commitment and sacrifice of military members extends beyond combat. The sacrifices are real and exist twenty-four seven, regardless if we are in peacetime or war.

That said, I've appreciated my experience here and the many friends I've made, but lately I've been feeling as if I've reached the highest point I can summit in the fighter pilot business. I've developed a strong case of "what-do-I-do-now-itis." As the saying goes, "When you're at the top, it's all downhill from here." But is it? What if there is a higher mountain to soar over?

Today, that question repeats over and over in my mind. No wonder. It's July 20, 1994, the twenty-fifth anniversary of the first moon landing. As I have done so many times over the years, I am remembering that historic day in 1969 when I watched the monumental event with my extended family. I reflect on how I felt like I was floating on a sea of possibility. I remember the calling—the peculiar certainty that I should set out and follow in Neil's and Buzz's footsteps. Looking back on it now, I can describe it as a call to awe. That call then revisited me on April 12, 1981, when John Young and Bob Crippen blasted into space on board *Columbia*. That second calling motivated me to shake the dust off my feet from my hometown of Yonkers and set out on an adventure, one that so far has led me here, to Nellis. Above all else, I remember that I once had a burning desire to experience the awe and wonder of seeing our world from space.

I ignored that calling as I succumbed to the limiting idea that the goal to become an astronaut was impossible. But the calling has recently arrived back at my door. Initially, the door was slammed shut in a flurry of sobering facts and self-doubt—I didn't have the right education, never attended test pilot school, etc., etc. In spite of these seemingly compelling reasons to not waste my time pursuing an unachievable goal though, a thought keeps gnawing at me from my core.

I imagine myself elderly, at the twilight of my life, looking back. I see myself wondering what would have happened if I had decided to give my all to the goal of becoming an astronaut. The weight of that old man's self-doubt and self-disappointment is too much to bear. I don't want to be that old man. I don't expect to ever become an astronaut, but if I really do try my best to achieve that goal, I can look back on my life, no matter what happens, and feel content that I did all I could. I could be content in the notion that my failure to achieve the goal was beyond my control.

A few years ago while at Shaw, before Desert Storm, I did give it a try but I wouldn't classify it as giving my all. I applied to a videotaped master's in engineering program offered by the University of South Carolina. I was not accepted due to my lack of undergraduate engineering courses. At that time, I also looked into applying for test pilot school but was told that an engineering degree was a requirement and not to apply. The last thing I looked into was pursuing a master's degree through the Air Force Institute of Technology, but again I was told that I did not qualify.

At that point, I resigned myself to the fact that I would never become an astronaut and actually, I was enjoying being a fighter pilot so much that I convinced myself that I really didn't want to be an astronaut anymore. But thinking back over my time here at the Fighter Weapons School has me reconsidering all of that.

These past years have been a blessing to our little family. The twins are three years old and are absolutely adorable. They provide Carmel and me immense joy every day. I am filled with a love for those guys more powerful than I knew existed. I cannot imagine a force more powerful than the love I feel for them. We have also been blessed with another son on the way, due in late August to early September. We've decided to call him Jake. We're not really sure why. It just seems like that's his name.

Jake's impending arrival isn't the only change in my life. While teaching at the Fighter Weapons School, I also finished a master's degree in aeronautical science from Embry-Riddle University. I did this solely to increase the chance that I would get promoted to major, which I hope will happen before the end of the year.

And sometime during my tour here, probably around the time we found out that Carmel was pregnant again, I started feeling discontent with the amount of pay I receive from the Air Force. I started thinking about the kids' college tuition, my retirement, and dozens of other things that require money. I started looking for ways to supplement my income. I wanted to find a way to get a piece of the pie and my share of the American dream.

The answer came one day after I had been driving for more than forty-five minutes looking for a car wash. Living in a dusty desert city where it hardly ever rains, you'd think there'd be a car wash on every corner, but, for some reason, there were none in our part of town. It dawned on me that since our home is in the fastest-growing part of the fastest-growing city in America, if we could buy some land and build a car wash on it, the land appreciation alone would make it worthwhile. Since then, my brother John, his wife, Joi, and their infant son, Steven, have moved out to Vegas. Together, after taking out a small business loan, we built a car wash, emissions test station, and auto repair shop. The businesses are doing well.

Getting a master's degree while building several businesses, working twelve-plus hours a day in a high-stress military flight program, and living in a three-bedroom house with three toddlers and four adults has been busy, to say the least. But in spite of all that busyness, I have also started searching for something different. I, at times, have found myself thinking back to when I found calm in prayer before taking off on my first combat mission. I have found myself thinking back to the movie *Twins* on the TV at the O Club just when I had begged for a sign to lift me out of my despair over not knowing what was going on with Carmel's pregnancy.

I have found myself wondering, *Why did I survive Desert Storm? Why were one of those five memorial services here at Nellis not for me?* I have found myself searching for a higher meaning and a higher purpose.

If there is one thing I'm sure of, it's that there's infinitely more to reality than we experience through our senses. In some way, we are like Plato's prisoners chained in a cave, unable to turn our heads. We only see shadows on the cave wall. We are oblivious to the larger, more colorful, and more desirable world outside of the cave.

The realization that there is something bigger beyond our normal perception has been at the center of my thoughts. I feel a different calling now—a calling to seek truth, meaning, and understanding. I have begun searching for answers anywhere I can. Carmel fully supports me on this journey and I support her in hers, but in deference to her privacy, I will share my personal discoveries only. For the first time in my life, I've read the Bible from cover to cover. In recent years, I have attended various church services and Bible study groups, and it has all felt right. Things have started to make sense. I have begun to feel comfortable. I have to believe that I have been searching for God. I couldn't bring myself to believe that the beauty of the human experience and the majesty of the universe just happened randomly.

Now, when I say "God," I believe that the word is a human-made attempt to label what defies labeling. And when I use the masculine pronoun "He," I am not trying to assign gender to a creator who is infinitely beyond such material description. I simply do so out of convenience. My use of capitalization of the pronoun is my feeble attempt to make a mere word a less insufficient description of the indescribable.

I don't think of "God" as a man with a long grey beard and a crown, sitting on a cloud. I imagine something that is unimaginable, a presence and force that exists beyond the dimensions of space and time. A presence and force that exists beyond the narrow confines of any particular religious doctrine. A presence and force that somehow has communicated with me during various times—a communication that did not come through words or tablets of stone but through a direct imprinting on my being.

As I've pondered all of this, I've come to believe that what we call the universe was created. Since a creation cannot be more than its creator and since we have the capacity to love, the creator must also have the capacity to love. This, to me, means that the creator must know us all intimately enough to love us. I choose to call this creator "God." I didn't know where my search for God would lead, but I knew I wanted something more. I wasn't satisfied with the status quo. I started to wonder if religion could be a path for me to find God.

In my search, I've ruminated on the long-running battle between religion and science. Science, at times, has made every attempt to destroy God, citing the lack of evidence to support an intelligent designer while ignoring the lack of evidence to disprove one. As scientific discovery has unlocked the mysteries of the universe one by one, religiously derived explanations for the origins and workings of the universe have been replaced. Many times throughout history, religious leaders viewed the unseating of religious explanations as undermining foundational cornerstones of doctrine, and this provoked them to fight scientific advancement at almost every step. But religion and science need not be mutually exclusive. I believe that they are deeply intertwined and are, in reality, two sides of the same coin, both seeking to unlock the mysteries of the universe. There may well exist an aspect of reality that will forever remain unexplained by science, whatever the word "forever" might mean.

I used to believe that religion was counter to spirituality. But that may have been due to my own arrogance and ignorance. I am now open to the idea that deep spirituality can come through religious practice that is rooted in a deep and humble search for understanding and a path to worship. I'm starting to believe that religion could be a vehicle that points to the truth. I am blind to the other levels of reality that I suspect exist all around us. I consider these other realities the spiritual realm. When I close my eyes, I only see darkness. I only see what is visible to me through my eyes. But I know that there's more than what I can see. I seek a way to bring light to this darkness, to let that light in fully to illuminate the true universe, my darkness giving way to truth and understanding. I think where religion may go astray is when leaders and followers of a specific religious doctrine or tradition mistake the vehicle of religion for truth itself.

I'm starting to think that all religions could possibly point toward the truth or be a vehicle to help carry us toward it. But I also suspect that no religion is the truth, the whole truth, and nothing but the truth. How could we possibly encompass the infinite into a finite doctrine?

As these thoughts have gnawed at me, the dream of becoming an astronaut has also bubbled back up. *Are the two things connected in some way?*

✦

I am at a crossroads in my life and career, so I ask God for help. I believe that God knows that I feel compelled to pursue becoming an astronaut. I have decided to put it totally in His hands. I have no idea if God also wants me to be an astronaut or even why He would. But I will never know if I don't try. I need to finally answer the call and put all of myself into the pursuit of the goal that I've had almost my entire life. Most of what will happen will be out of my hands, out of my control. I will simply press ahead and accomplish all that I can, and if any doors shut in front of me and there is no honorable way around the obstacle, I will know that being an astronaut was not God's will, and that would be that, without any regrets.

A few days after I come to this conclusion, Carmel and I are dining outside at a restaurant, under the stars. Over our meal, I share with her that I desire to travel around the world every ninety minutes—that I truly want to go to space. She tells me to go for it. "You can achieve anything you set your heart on," she says. With those words, I feel supported and more confident to begin this quest.

The first step to becoming an astronaut is to attend a test pilot school. A while ago, a leader at the Air Force TPS, short-hand for US Air Force Test Pilot School, told me I had no chance of being accepted there because I don't have a degree in engineering or science and my time in military service exceeds the maximum allowable ten years. But on a phone call today, in late July, some friends who graduated from Air Force TPS tell me that the test squadron they are currently assigned to at Eglin Air Force Base in Florida—a potential gateway to test pilot school—has an opening for one non-TPS graduate. It's a slot for a Fighter Weapons School graduate. I'm definitely going to look into that.

About a week later, at Nellis, I speak to Bill "Kanga" Rew, my old friend and mentor, about my desire to become an astronaut.

Kanga, now a lieutenant colonel, has returned here to take over command of the F-16 Division of the Fighter Weapons School. In his office, I lay out my plan for what I hope to do, starting with heading to Eglin to join the 39th Flight Test Squadron.

Kanga shakes his head in disbelief. "Let's put this into perspective," he says. "First of all, you have not attended test pilot school. You have too many years in the Air Force to attend, and you don't even have the correct degree."

He says my Air Force career has set me up for even bigger things, and he thinks my astronaut dream is a reckless diversion that will probably permanently throw me off course. He raises several arguments.

It's not a formal requirement that an astronaut attend TPS, Kanga says, but for someone like me, a career military pilot, TPS is the only reasonable path. As for the degree, normally, astronauts have a technical degree in either science, technology, or engineering—at least a master's degree and in many cases, a PhD. My recent degree in aeronautical science from Embry-Riddle, he points out, does not count. When Kanga says this, I think ruefully of the fact that the most technical task I performed during that degree program was figuring out how to email my professor on the blossoming World Wide Web, an effort that earned me extra credit.

Despite the fact that I hear Kanga loud and clear, in response to each of his arguments, I have a plan.

"If I'm able to transfer to Eglin," I say, "I can apply to the aerospace engineering master's program at the University of Florida extension campus there. I know it's going to be extremely difficult to get accepted since I don't have an undergraduate degree in engineering, but I want to try."

Kanga tries to instill some "reality" in me by pointing out the biggest hurdle. "You're not medically qualified and would not pass a NASA physical. Really, they wouldn't even give you one."

Two years ago, I was diagnosed with gout, a condition that medically disqualifies me from astronaut duty. Ever since the diagnosis, I have been on medication and have required a waiver to continue flying. I explain to Kanga that the diagnosis was never definitive and I'm going to seek to have it re-evaluated.

After some more back-and-forth with Kanga, to my complete surprise, he seems to do a 180. He confides in me that he too dreamed of becoming an astronaut once, and even though he doesn't think it's a wise move, he supports my decision and wishes me "Godspeed." His statement shocks me, but I recover enough to thank him for his support and for all the support he has provided me throughout my career.

Later that day, I pass through the main gate at Nellis to head home. After making a turn west, in the distance, I see Mount Charleston, with its barren peak, its snowpack melted months ago by the summer desert sun. Somewhere in the foreground is the center of my universe, Carmel, approaching a due date for our third son, and two little knuckleheads who are probably up to all kinds of shenanigans.

Kanga's concern and realism start to weigh on me as I'm lost deep in thought at a red light. *Why should I abandon the career path that I'm on? Why should I pursue an impossible dream? Am I being reckless, selfish, foolish?* A few things become clear: At thirty-two years old, this is certainly the last chance I will get to head down a path toward NASA, and there is no way I will be able to achieve this goal alone. I'll encounter many things beyond my control. I truly believe that to be successful in this pursuit, miracles will have to occur. *What is my chance for success?* The answer comes just as someone in a hurry behind me beeps as the light turns green. *My chance of success is either 0 percent or 100 percent, depending on whether God wants me to do this.*

# PART 3

# EPOCH B: ASCENT

"As a result of a thousand million years of evolution, the universe is becoming conscious of itself . . ."
— Julian Huxley, *New Bottles for New Wine*, 1957 AD

# CHAPTER 8

# A Path in Miracles

✦ A few months ago, I requested a transfer to the 39th Flight Test Squadron at Eglin Air Force Base. The request was approved and a few weeks afterward, Jake was born, and not long after that, we packed up the family and moved to Florida. Since then, I've been flying with the test squadron at Eglin, and I'm enjoying it. It's a whole new type of flying. I've traded in my role as a tactician, where all that matters is accomplishing the mission, for a role that requires a much higher level of precision flying. Our job is to ensure that weapon systems are performing as advertised before they are deployed to the warfighters. Even though I haven't attended test pilot school, I'm permitted to fly many test missions.

I arrived at Eglin in a full sprint toward all the monumental obstacles arrayed in front of me on my quest to become an astronaut. First, I met with an internal medicine doctor who confirmed what I already knew: My gout diagnosis was not definitive but highly probable. I've gone off gout medication for a week, per her instructions, so she can run some tests to get a better idea of what I'm up against. To remain on flying status, I have to continue taking the medicine, which means I'm not flying this week.

I've also sent in an application to Air Force TPS, ignoring their instruction not to bother. If they don't want to admit me, that's their decision, but it's my decision whether to apply. Hopefully, they'll at least consider my application.

In the midst of all of this, I also met with the dean of the University of Florida Research and Engineering Education Facility to discuss the possibility of my acceptance into the aerospace engineering master's program there. I gave him all my transcripts, and he indicated that he'd look them over.

I'm at a crucial point. The biggest immediate hurdle? Passing the medical tests. The other hurdles? Being admitted to the University of Florida and getting my application to the TPS board for consideration.

I talked to a representative at Air Force TPS a few days ago, and she said that my application will not be allowed to compete at the selection board because I don't meet the academic requirements. This frustrates me because the selection committee based this decision solely on my transcripts. The committee members have no idea who I am, what my qualifications are, or what I have accomplished. They did not look at my application, resume, or recommendations. Honestly, I did not expect to be admitted to TPS, but I *did* expect to be allowed to compete.

This is a serious obstacle. I need to go to test pilot school to really even have a shot at becoming an astronaut. *Kanga was right*, I think. *Why am I pursuing a path with such a dismally low chance of success?* It seems everything is stacked against me and the obstacles are insurmountable.

A few weeks later, two days before Christmas 1994, I get some great news. My medical tests show that I have no sign of hyperuricemia, an inability to either break down uric acid or excrete it. My doctor says there's enough evidence to challenge the gout diagnosis and that my test results are enough to get rid of the flight waiver entirely. I'm eager to get the diagnosis overturned.

On top of this development, I've also convinced the University of Florida dean to allow me to take six credits—two courses—at the school without actually enrolling in the master's of aerospace engineering program there. If I do well on the Graduate Record Exam and ace both of the courses, then maybe, just maybe, Florida will let me enroll in the full aerospace engineering program. I've signed up for my first class, spacecraft navigation. *I know how to navigate an aircraft, so how hard could spacecraft navigation be?* I have a feeling those could be famous last words . . .

A month later, the results of the latest astronaut board come in. We learn that not a single pilot in my squadron made it. These guys are very sharp, some with double master's degrees and all with spectacular accomplishments. Most of them are understandably discouraged. Likely, each of them worked a good portion of their lives toward becoming an astronaut. I'm sure they made many sacrifices. I'm sure I'm not the only one who was floating on a sea of possibility back on July 20, 1969, not the only one who heard and felt a deep calling to follow in the footsteps of the *Apollo* astronauts. These guys all paid their dues and came up short. I'm not even at the point where I can begin to pay my dues. Truthfully, their rejections make my own quest seem even more out of reach.

The same month we received the astronaut board results, I'm sitting in a military-office-turned-classroom. At the front of the spacecraft navigation class stands Professor Chris D'Souza.

Although this class has an innocuous sounding title, it is actually an advanced astrodynamics course. Dr. D'Souza began our session telling us that our first few classes will be a review of material we should all thoroughly understand already. That is the last thing he's said over the past forty-five minutes that I have understood. Right now, he's spewing a litany of Greek letters and squiggly lines with, every now and then, a number plopped into the middle of the gibberish.

I literally don't comprehend a word Dr. D'Souza is saying. I'm afraid that the math is going to prove way over my head—math that I'm supposed to be intimately familiar with that I've never been taught. To get through the class, I will have to teach myself a considerable amount of advanced mathematics. I'm determined to do whatever it takes.

At the end of class, I exit the building into a breathtakingly beautiful night. A cool ocean breeze brushes my face. The sun has set, but enough of its photons are still bouncing around to allow the sky to retain some of its blue tint. Slowly and gradually, grey is replacing blue. A first quarter moon is racing toward the western horizon. I love this time of day. The moon appears as if it's popping out from the bluish grey blanket of sky. Light from the sun illuminates the moon in a way that makes it bright, but not so bright that its features are blurred. The craters, mountains, and "seas" seem to pop from the lunar canvas.

For as long as I can remember, I have found the moon hauntingly beautiful and I feel her gravitational attraction. My heart is drawn to her in a way that almost lifts me off the ground. I feel her in the center of my chest pulling me toward her. I have a deep, burning desire to see her up close someday, to walk on her surface and gaze back at Earth. This yearning is so powerful that it almost hurts. I guess the slight sensation of pain stems from the fact that in near certainty I will never get to fulfill my desire to explore her. But there she is almost every day, taunting me, or maybe beckoning me to come and say hi.

When I gaze at her, it's as if part of me is transported closer and closer but never fully reaches her. Even if I never make it to see her, I hope that her gravity will at least pull me into Earth's orbit. Of course, the first step will be to escape the gravitational pull of my spacecraft navigation course. At the moment, this seems highly unlikely.

I've been in the spacecraft navigation course for a week now and studying a great deal, but nothing seems to help. I always knew that this class was going to be challenging, but now that I'm in it, I'm not sure that I will be able to pass it. I figure all I can do is my best. I'm going to try as hard as I can, pray for God's help, and whatever happens *happens*.

The next month, in Fort Worth, Texas, the morning commute is starting to get busy as I drive my rental car from a Hampton Inn to a Lockheed Martin aircraft assembly plant on a grey, overcast day. I'm on day two of a very boring F-16 simulator test. As I round the corner of Lockheed Boulevard and head toward the plant, I think about my class. It's not going well at all.

I wish I had more time to study. I wish I was back in Florida attending class, not here participating in simulator testing. As much as I promised myself that I wouldn't let the course stress me out, it *has* affected me emotionally. Once again, I've proven to myself that things are usually much harder to accomplish than they seem. This course is where "the rubber meets the road" on this quest. Part of me realizes that doing what is necessary to achieve this goal has to be incredibly difficult or accomplishing it would seem somewhat less than miraculous.

At the simulator complex, a sim operator named Henry greets me. Out of the blue, Henry says, "Hey, Ron, I brought a few math books with me to work today. If you want, you can bring them into the simulator with you."

A little confused, I ask, "Why would you do that?"

"I just thought it might help pass the time during resets."

For vast periods of my daily eight hours sitting in the simulator, I'll just be waiting for an operator to reset the computers. Not satisfied with Henry's response to, "Why would you do that?" I press him further. He shares with me that he hasn't looked at the books in ten years but just felt the urge to bring them in and review them today. The strange thing is, I met Henry only once before and we've never said more than hello to each other. I thank him for thinking of me, and I bring the books with me into the simulator.

After several days of simulator tests, I've read one math book from cover to cover and most of another. The books deal with many of the subjects we're learning about in class, and I actually understand the math in them. I've xeroxed a great deal of the material to go over when I'm not in the sim. Unlike all the other books that people have given me, these books have unlocked my understanding by presenting things in a way that makes sense.

Now, I realize this story about Henry's books is hard to believe. I find it hard to believe myself, and it's happening to me! I've tried to figure out a logical explanation for why someone I don't know brought in the exact books I needed to unlock my understanding of a tough subject. Although I haven't come up with an explanation, this experience is encouraging me. Just when I was starting to feel low, an amazing "coincidence" lifted me up.

A few days later, I'm back in Florida, where I've been doing a lot of thinking. I often fantasize about what my life would be like if I was not trying to become an astronaut. I know that things would be a lot quieter, less stressful, and much more enjoyable. I've concluded, however, that if God has a plan for me and my family that includes that I pursue becoming an astronaut, then I no longer have the option to quit just because I think I won't be successful. If I quit, I would be going against God's will. The real question will continue to be, "Is it God's will that I become an astronaut?"

Every day, I pray that God grants me the wisdom to see His will and for faith and courage to accomplish His will. If it is God's will that I become an astronaut, I hope that becomes apparent by way of me surmounting obstacles. If it's not His will, I hope that becomes apparent by way of doors being slammed shut.

That said, I'm facing yet another significant obstacle. I'm not optimistic that I will succeed at being admitted to the University of Florida when I apply. Recently, I met a Purdue University–trained engineer with ten graduate credits from the University of Florida and straight A's whose admission to Florida was rejected! In addition, he did better than I did on the GRE. He was told that he did not get in because his undergraduate GPA of 2.9 was too low.

Despite this discouraging news about an applicant who is vastly more qualified than I am, I still plan to submit my application to Florida. I will leave it to God to show me if being an astronaut is in my future.

I exit through the Valparaiso gate of Eglin Air Force Base and head toward home in my bright green Dodge Caravan minivan. I'm thinking about what's sure to be a buzz of toddler and baby activity awaiting me in our little house, and I can't wait to dive into the middle of that. I also can't wait to tell Carmel the good news. Today, I learned that my old gout diagnosis has been overturned in my records and I no longer require a waiver. As of right now, I am completely medically qualified for astronaut duty. Miracle number one has occurred!

Most of the test pilots I work with are busily preparing to send in their NASA applications for the next selection board. Even though I'm no longer medically disqualified, there's no sense submitting an application at the moment since I do not meet the minimum academic requirements. The next board after this one should be in the spring of 1997. Currently, it's March 1995.

Despite receiving the great news about the overturning of the gout diagnosis, it's been a long and mentally draining day. Over the course of it, I studied for my spacecraft navigation midterm with a classmate. We primarily focused on the formulas and fascinating astrodynamics theories of Johannes Kepler. I always marvel at the workings of great minds.

It seems that all I've done these past few weeks is eat, sleep, work, and study. I have been giving it my all. A few weeks ago, I thought it impossible that I would even pass the class, but now, I am feeling more confident. This morning during a test review, things started to click to some extent. This is a very difficult course. Presently, besides me, only two other students are still in it. The rest dropped out.

As I continue to head home, the traffic is heavier than normal due to construction ahead on the Rocky Bayou Bridge. Lately, I have had so little time with the boys, and this delay is cutting into that precious time. To take my mind off the wait, I switch on a Christian radio station. Right as I do, the announcer introduces a program that is about to start: "Welcome to *Great Christians in History.* Today's episode is 'Study of the Heavens: The Johannes Kepler Story.'" *This is absolutely bizarre,* I think. Goose bumps pop up on my arms.

I listen intently as the program describes how the church harassed Kepler for his theories and how God helped him in his life. It explains how Kepler provided an entirely new perspective, one that completely changed the way we see the universe, the way we see reality. As the program concludes, I still can't believe that out of all the great people in the history of the world, this radio station aired a story about Kepler and aired it on the day before my exam on his theories at the exact time I was driving home and I just happened to tune in. Now, I'm looking forward to taking the test.

+

I got my midterm back yesterday. My grade? A.

The day before the exam, the instructor said he had good news and bad news. The bad news was that he wound up making the test harder than he initially intended, but the good news: He was giving us all weekend to work on it.

As I was taking the test, I might have come to some insight about God's will. Although things started to click while I prepared for the test, over the weekend, it seemed impossible to do. I ended up spending over twenty-two hours on it. It seemed as if God let me push myself to the limit of my intellectual ability before I was somehow "helped" on each problem.

In every case, seemingly insurmountable intellectual obstacles were abruptly removed probably within nanoseconds of my impending surrender. After hours and hours of working on a problem, just when I felt like there was no way I would be able to solve it, something would click. For example, on the last problem, which I spent well over ten hours trying to figure out, I hit a dead end and started to panic. But just when I thought, *There's no way I'm going to get this*, my instructor called me at home and gave me a hint that made everything make sense and then some.

As it turns out, on Friday, I had called his office looking for a chart that was missing in my notes and left a message on his machine. Subsequently, I found the chart and forgot about the phone call. On Saturday evening, he went to work, heard the message, and called me. In the course of our discussion, he nonchalantly said something that made a lightbulb pop over my head. Not only was I able to solve the problem the way he hinted at, I also solved it another way he hadn't thought of. I included both solutions on the test with a note describing the method I was using before he gave me the hint.

A little over a month later, I hand in my spacecraft navigation final exam. It was truly an experience, incredibly difficult. I learned a lot this weekend while I worked on this test—and not just about astrodynamics. When I first began it, I could not see a way that I could possibly arrive at the solutions, which discouraged me. But by the time I completed the test, I learned that the quest to become an astronaut may be more important than achieving the goal itself.

Now, a small, quiet premonition is developing deep within me. I feel that as I travel along this journey, God will continually push me to my limits. Each time He pushes me will be an opportunity for my faith to become stronger. I sense that He will also test me each time to see if I will try to cut corners or take the path of least resistance. Just like on my exams, when I thought I was not capable of putting in another hour of concentration, I believe that things will continue to click and fall together.

I can't explain what's happening. At this point, the best I can do is just record my experience. As for spacecraft navigation, what's remarkable is the suddenness and timing of how I began to understand the course. It reminds me of the sudden peace I experienced when I was getting ready to take off on my first combat mission. Just like then, when I went from being extremely anxious to calm and peaceful in an instant, during my studies, I went from feeling utterly lost with no possible way out to knowing exactly how to solve a problem in an instant—an instant that in some cases was twenty-plus hours in the making.

Over our time here in Florida, I have become closer to God. I feel a certainty that reality is based on an eternal universal unity. Somehow, a thread holds the entire universe together. Somehow, we are all part of that thread, and it leads to what I have chosen to call "God." I feel His presence and energy. I attribute a great deal of that closeness to our children. Over the course of our time caring for Ronnie, Joseph, and Jake, a deep love has developed. It is a love that finite words cannot fully express. A love I had never experienced before. A love stronger than I knew existed. I love our boys more than anything on Earth. I would do anything for them.

On this June night, as I tuck them into bed, I experience the insight that the love I feel for them is the same love that God feels for us. I mean literally. I think God uses that love to bond with us. If you have experienced that love and then believe that God has that same love for you, that's an immensely powerful force.

It's this love that is leading me to believe that God wants me to become an astronaut. It's not because I think I am somehow more special than everyone else or that I have some preordained divine calling to greatness. No, I believe it's simply because God knows that I deeply desire to achieve this goal and He knows my motivation is to serve Him through that calling. Just as my love for our boys will lead me to do things to help them achieve their hopes and dreams, I believe God too desires that we all become fulfilled.

I've also come to believe that God wants us to grow spiritually. Presently, I feel stronger than I have ever felt in my life. I know that as long as I trust God, I will always be free and no one or no *thing* will ever have control over me. Today, it is fashionable to blame everything that is wrong with your life on your past, childhood, or parents. I believe that we should only concern ourselves with things that we can control. We cannot change the past; the only thing that we truly can control is this moment in time. What we choose to do with this moment is all that really matters.

On an early August day, I am again in a state of panic. I'm sitting by myself in a mundane office in a nondescript building taking my midterm exam for a course in laser principles. I have only thirty minutes left of my allotted hour and a half and no idea how to do any of the three problems on the test or even where to start. In the astronomically small chance that there were mistakes on the test, I call my professor. After a brief conversation, it turns out that the test has several typos, but after clearing that up, I still can't figure the test out. At least he said I could have more time to take it.

Deep in concentration, I barely notice the office secretary entering the room.

"Ron, I will be leaving and locking up the building," she says. "When you're finished, please just place your test on the desk and when you leave the building the door will lock behind you."

I become aware of the time on the clock over the door. The secretary then hands me my textbook and notes and walks out.

*Well, this is a dilemma.* This is a closed-book test. I now have the opportunity to use my textbook and notes and work on the test here all night if I want to. I decide not to touch the textbook. I work on the test for about another hour, take my best guesses, and leave. I'm sure I will fail the exam, but cutting corners is not an option. I *have* cut corners before. At times, I *have* failed to take the higher moral ground. In fact, I have failed many times. But this is different. I know in my heart that there's no way I can become an astronaut on my own. It will only happen if it is in accordance with God's will.

This is a sacred quest. I will never know if it is truly God's will that I become an astronaut if I cheat and take shortcuts. At the moment, I suspect that the act of pursuing becoming an astronaut is part of the plan. Whether actually becoming one is also part of the plan is to be determined.

I received a 50 percent on my laser principles midterm exam. Everyone had problems with it. But the instructor graded it on a curve, which, weeks afterward, has enabled me to score an A overall in the course. I know I did not do it alone. But the big news to report is that I was accepted to the University of Florida's master's program in aerospace engineering with no restrictions. This is truly a miracle. It's bizarre enough that I got accepted, but to get accepted without restrictions is unthinkable.

One of the secretaries at the University of Florida can't believe it either. She said that even students with undergraduate degrees in another engineering field are usually accepted into the program with restrictions, which means they are required to take several undergraduate "articulation" courses designed to bring them up to speed in aerospace engineering. If I had to take any articulation courses, I would likely be unable to complete the master's program while I'm still stationed at Eglin.

Now, there is a lot that I still must accomplish, but it is all within my capabilities. Two of the miracles that had to occur before I could even consider submitting a package for NASA astronaut selection—not including attending TPS—were being medically qualified and being accepted into an engineering master's program. As of this moment, both of those miracles have happened. Now, the fun begins. I am signed up for seven credits this semester—one advanced differential equations class and one computer modeling class. My work is cut out for me.

On top of this, as for TPS, I just got back from a weeklong flight test at Edwards Air Force Base in Southern California, where I learned the route for gaining admittance to test pilot school is even more difficult than I thought. While I was there, I spoke to the folks that denied my TPS application from going to the selection board and learned that I had to be academically qualified *before* I could meet a board. To do that, I would have to have my master's degree completed. It's all a little discouraging, but like I've said all along, I'm going to keep trying to pass through doors until they get slammed shut and locked. I will reapply to TPS anyway this fall.

Days ago, my family and I evacuated the Florida Panhandle for Montgomery, Alabama, just before Hurricane Opal hit. While in Alabama, I studied for an advanced differential equations test that I knew would be waiting for me when we got back here. Upon arriving home, we found that our community was hit hard, but fortunately, our home did not sustain any damage. I thanked God for his mercy, and I got back to studying.

In all, I studied for more than forty hours for the exam and surmounted several challenges to my faith in the effort. First, one day I found myself alone in a classmate's office and spotted a copy of the test, which he had already taken, on his desk. If I were to just peek at it, I would have had a tremendous advantage. But I didn't glance at it even once.

The second challenge: A friend who had taken the test was on the verge of telling me about specific test problems. I stopped him and told him that I had not taken the test yet.

The last challenge: I had a chance to watch a videotape of a post-test review for another group of students who had taken the class. I did not bite into this tempting apple.

Shortly after all this happened, things started falling together in my studying. I felt as though I was being rewarded for doing the right thing.

But more lessons were to come.

To my horror, today when I was finally handed the test, I had no idea how to do two of its three problems. Worse, the one I knew how to do gave me tremendous trouble. I started to panic. After nearly an hour, the total allotted time for the exam, I hadn't written anything down. No one was timing me because it was after the workday and I was alone in the building. I worked on the test a little longer than an hour and made some progress on the question I had a clue about, but I simply wrote down in essay form what I had tried to do, but couldn't accomplish, on the other problems. Then I left the test for the secretary to pick up later and headed out of the building for home.

I worked longer on that test than I should have, but now as I reflect on the experience, I rationalize that that doesn't matter because I could have worked on it all night and not figured it out. As it is, I'm sure I'll have the lowest grade in the class.

Driving home now, I feel confused. *What does my performance, or lack thereof, on the test mean? Is this a reality check? An opportunity to really assess why I'm doing all this?* I wonder. If I'm doing it for me, then I should be very upset with my apparent failure. If I'm doing it because I think that's what's in accordance with God's plan for me, then all I need to know is that I put as much effort into the test as possible. If I still fall short after all that effort, then that is God's will and I must accept it—and I do. The good that has come from the test and the lesson that I've learned is that I'm really doing this for the right reasons.

✦

About two months later in my office, I see a blinking red light on my desk phone. It's a message from Lieutenant Colonel Weitzel at Wright Patterson Air Force Base asking me to give him a call. Lieutenant Colonel Weitzel is in charge of processing my request for a TPS waiver for time in service. *What could he possibly want?* Yesterday, I called him to see if anything was happening with my request, and he told me that it had been rejected, explaining that more than a hundred highly qualified applicants are competing for only about three slots. Because of that, there's no justification to grant any waivers. I thanked him for his time and said goodbye. I took the news hard, but then I reflected on my commitment to accept God's will and felt at peace with the waiver decision.

Now, I'm on hold, waiting for the lieutenant colonel's secretary to call him to the line. I wonder if he needs my military address to send me my rejection notice. As the minutes pass, I experience a strong sensation that seems like some sort of communication. It's a feeling that's saying, *Because you put your faith in God, watch what happens.* Just then, Lieutenant Colonel Weitzel picks up the phone and says, "Hi, Major Garan. I just want to let you know that there's been a reversal in our decision and you will be granted the waiver after all." He explains that when they presented the decision letter to his boss, his boss chose to grant the waiver.

I exceed the maximum time allowed in service by something like three years, so therefore I needed a three-year waiver. The longest waiver they had ever granted, according to TPS, was three months, and technically I am not even qualified to attend TPS since I don't yet have a technical degree. So, with this waiver in hand, I've experienced miracle number three.

The fact that the chance of being selected to attend TPS is still extremely remote is reinforced when Lieutenant Colonel Weitzel reminds me, "There's over a hundred applicants for three fighter slots." I am very happy just to get to compete based on my own merits. What I've gotten out of all this is that God is firmly in control and I am perfectly content to follow where He leads.

+

It's February 13, 1996, the day I find out whether I've been selected to attend TPS. All day, I've been waiting for the official orders to be published, which will include the list of those selected to attend the year-long course. Finally, I get the email announcing the board results. I open the scanned attachment containing the image of the selection letter and quickly look down the alphabetical list to the "G's." It's there! My name! But surprisingly, it states that I'll be attending the US Naval Test Pilot School at Naval Air Station Patuxent River, Maryland—"Pax River" not Air Force TPS!

I've been accepted into an exclusive exchange program. Every year, the Air Force sends a few of their TPS selectees to the Naval Test Pilot School in exchange for a few of the Navy's TPS selectees. I'm thrilled to get accepted to any TPS, but acceptance into the Naval Test Pilot School makes me want to high-five the first person I see. I think attending the school may really help me in my bid with the astronaut board. NASA probably views the Air Force and Naval test pilot schools equally, but maybe graduating from Pax River will put me in an even better position with NASA. I assume the Air Force members on NASA's astronaut selection committee will already understand and identify with my Air Force flight experience, but having some naval test flight experience may earn me some points with the Navy members of the committee.

Once I gather my thoughts and composure, I try to put everything into perspective. Everyone, including TPS, was telling me that because of the required time-in-service waiver and my lack of the required technical degree, my chances of getting selected hardly warranted sending in an application. Not only have I been selected, but I have been selected for the class that will allow me to finish my master's degree before my assignment at Eglin is complete. I will be qualified to submit an application to NASA for the next astronaut selection board!

I am one of two Air Force guys selected to attend Naval TPS. This is strong confirmation that this pursuit is in accordance with God's will. With absolute certainty, I know that I could not have possibly been selected solely on my own merits. I did not do this on my own.

After a few hours of jubilation, reality starts to settle back in. It will be almost a year before I head to Pax River, and I have a huge mountain to climb before I get there. Right now, I'm taking two particularly difficult courses and work has also become much more demanding. I was recently selected as my squadron's chief pilot, which has brought on a lot more responsibilities. Coupled with all this is a fairly busy travel schedule. I can't let everything get me too stressed out. I'm going to try as hard as I can. Beyond that, nothing much else matters.

By the end of February, things continue to be very hectic at work and school. Even when I'm home, I'm preoccupied with everything that's weighing on me. This is not fair to my family, especially to Carmel, who has been juggling life with a baby and two toddlers while continuing to work as a nurse and, more recently, on a master's degree in a related field. I'd figured that from now until the fall things were going to be really hard but that if I could just tough it out through the summer, things would be all right. This is the wrong attitude to take. I cherish Carmel and my time with my family, and I know that this stage in our children's lives is absolutely precious and should be savored. The boys won't always feel comfortable hugging and kissing me and showering me with affection. I'm going to miss this very much when it's gone, and I don't want to miss any of it while it's here.

I also realize that this time is so important to the boys that surely God would not want me to sacrifice it for school. Until now, I have spent as much time at home as I thought was possible without jeopardizing school. But now I believe I should spend as much time as I can at home even if it is at the expense of school. This realization liberates me. It lifts the weight of a great deal of stress off my shoulders.

A little over a week later, I'm attending a two-week mandatory military course at Defense Acquisition University in Huntsville, Alabama. This is the last place in the world I want to be, but I'm making the most of it. I'm just about to start the second week of another astrodynamics course and have devoted almost all of my available free time to the schoolwork that I brought with me.

I'm facing an academic wall again. No matter how many hours I devote to my present coursework, I still don't get it. I've become spoiled, and I keep waiting for God to bail me out like He always does. I'm very far behind in all aspects of school. I'm now concluding that there is no way in the world I would pursue becoming an astronaut if I didn't think that it was God's plan. Flying in space on its own merit can't possibly be worth this trouble.

Seeking motivation, I head over to the Marshall Space Flight Center here in Huntsville. I see sections of the International Space Station under construction, the neutral buoyancy tank where astronauts train for spacewalks, and the rocket test stands used to test the space shuttle, *Saturn V*, and *Redstone* rocket engines. All this impresses and inspires me, but then I feel something is wrong. *If I'm using all this for motivation, then*

*I'm looking at things from the wrong perspective,* I think. *The goal of serving God and doing His will should be more than enough of a motivator.*

To get through this present dip in the road, I'm going to keep the attitude that all I can do, and all God expects from me, is my best. Unfortunately, I've let this present situation become somewhat overwhelming, and I pray that God will give me the strength to see the path through it.

Nearly a year after my visit to the Marshall Space Flight Center, the master's program is finally over. I passed all of my courses. Looking back on my two years in the program, I am absolutely sure that I couldn't have made it through without God's help. While I was in it, not only was I my squadron's chief pilot, but I also finished up Air Command and Staff College. This is a requirement for promotion to lieutenant colonel, and I didn't want something that I did, or didn't do, to prevent me from receiving a promotion.

Now, it's February 1997, and my family and I are all settled here in Lexington Park, Maryland, as I've already begun the program at TPS. The twins have started soccer and are going to a private Catholic kindergarten and seem to love it. Jake is at a particularly cute age and is absolutely adorable. I love being with all of my boys more than I can describe. Meanwhile, TPS has been a lot of work, but so far, it's been manageable and there's a great bunch of guys in the class.

After a long day of flying and classroom work, I return home. I've been anxious to get back because I know there's a letter from the Air Force waiting for me. A few weeks ago, in May,

I was finally able to mail my NASA application to the United States Air Force Special Flying Programs Office. The Air Force first has a selection board to decide who among their applicants will be forwarded on to NASA for consideration.

I enter the house, and a rush of little men scurry to say "Hi" to their dad. I love coming home. After giving Carmel a hug and a kiss, I sit down at our kitchen table and open the letter. I'm a little nervous. I think I have a good chance of making it through the Air Force board, but as I begin to read the letter, my heart sinks.

> "The Air Force Astronaut Board reviewed your application for space shuttle duty. Unfortunately, you failed to meet the National Aeronautics and Space Administration (NASA) medical selection standards. Specifically, you were medically disqualified for a history of hyperuricemia (gout). This condition exceeds NASA's medical selection standards and there are no provisions for waivers. Thank you for your interest in the astronaut nomination program. We wish you continued success in your future endeavors."

What? I was really expecting a different answer. A member of the Air Force board had called me at work a few weeks back and said that the board members wanted to know why I was awarded the Distinguished Flying Cross. I faxed them the narrative for the award I received for the mission I led against Republican Guard tanks back in Desert Storm. I called the Air Force board member back, and he said that they received the fax and that my application was rescored. It all seemed promising, so the board's rejection letter is deflating.

The board's disqualification confuses me since the diagnosis of gout was overturned in my records. Specifically, a three-page typed internal medicine summary goes to great lengths to make it clear that I do not have gout. After the initial shock and disappointment subsides some, I look at this as an opportunity to show God that I have been truly working all this time to accomplish His will, which I have. If God wants me to be an astronaut, I still do as well. If He doesn't, then neither do I.

✦

This past weekend was a busy one spiritually. I spent much of it thinking about the possible end of the road to NASA, and in so doing, I experienced a wide variety of emotions. Intellectually, I totally submitted to whatever God's will is, but emotionally, I was confused and disappointed, and disappointed in myself for being disappointed. I was especially disappointed after I called a member of the Air Force astronaut selection board and learned that they'd selected me but the subsequent Air Force medical board had disqualified me. The board member encouraged me though when he said that they would review my records on Monday and ask the medical board to give them another look.

My encouragement was short-lived. I also called the test pilot school's flight surgeon for his advice. He told me that it's futile to try to have the disqualification overturned. What he said made perfect sense; there are so many highly qualified applicants for so few slots that NASA would not be willing to take a chance on anyone with a possible medical problem. He went on to say that conditions in space are conducive to dehydration and could lead to issues. He painted a pretty bleak picture.

The disappointing turn of events has inspired me to do some soul searching. Yet again, I am forcing myself to examine my true motivation for this quest. I know that there still exist ego-based motivations. A fear exists within me that I will live out my life in mediocrity. Part of me yearns for the exalted accolades that would come from adding the title "Astronaut" in front of my name. Intellectually, I abhor that desire. Emotionally, I'm sorry to report, I still cling to it.

Today, between classes and flight training, I search for the strength to accept whatever will be and to rid myself of ego-based desires. But before the day is over, I find out that the board has overturned the medical disqualification and is forwarding my application to NASA! The Air Force decided to let NASA choose if it wants to take the medical risk on me. Again, just as it looked as if I was at the end of the road, another miracle occurred.

In stifling heat and humidity on this late June 1997 day, I drive from the Astronaut Selection Office to the Flight Medicine Clinic on the sprawling Houston campus of the Johnson Space Center. Off in the distance, I see the space shuttle simulator building and Building Four-South, where all the astronauts have their offices. I'm visiting Houston to discuss my application with anyone who will listen. I've met briefly with the chief of the Astronaut Selection Office, Duane Ross, who explained the screening process and made it clear that it is extremely hard to get accepted. He was cordial and friendly, but I could also tell that he was very busy.

Now, I'm meeting with NASA flight surgeon Dr. Joe Dervay to discuss the gout diagnosis. In his office at the Flight Medicine Clinic, I see what appears to be a large medical textbook sitting open on his desk. Dr. Dervay seems like someone I could have been friends with back in my younger days. His New York accent and kind manner put me at ease immediately.

After our initial greeting, we take our seats and Dr. Dervay gets straight to the point. He flips the book on his desk around so that I can read the words on the opened page. They state in very clear terms that gout is a cut-and-dry automatic disqualification. I ask him to read the internal medicine summary that I brought with me that overturned the gout diagnosis.

He reads it, then he explains that without this summary, there would be no question that I would be medically disqualified. He tells me that during the medical screening process, there will be three piles of applicant medical records—a pile of records that have no issues and are put forward, a pile of records that are disqualified and will be rejected, and a third pile of questionable records. Based on what they presently have to go on, my record would probably end up in the medical disqualification pile, he says.

"Is there anything I can do to at least get my records in the 'questionable pile'?" I ask.

Dr. Dervay replies that getting a whole new series of specific tests run and a clean bill of health written by an endocrinologist would probably do the trick. I thank him for his time and advice.

As I make my way north on the Gulf Freeway toward George Bush Intercontinental Airport, I look at Dr. Dervay's sobering news in a positive light. If I didn't come to Houston to speak with him, I would have been blindsided by this. Dr. Dervay was specific about what I have to do and outlined the tests that need to be conducted. I will do all the tests when I get back to Pax River, but I know that even if everything comes out perfect, it is still unlikely that NASA will be willing to take the risk on me.

To a degree, I'm reveling in this uncertainty. I am now convinced that God wants me to be an astronaut for His purpose, and I know that all the tests are going to come back normal and that NASA will eventually select me to become an astronaut—if not this time then next time. Maybe that's just wishful thinking, but it feels real.

After undergoing all the suggested medical tests over the summer, including having dye intravenously injected into my veins to prepare me for X-rays to evaluate my kidneys, all the results came back normal. Despite that, the flight surgeon at TPS again stressed that it's unlikely NASA would take the medical risk on me. Still, I faxed the reports to NASA and started the waiting game.

Now, on this late August day, I get some good news: I made it through the first and second astronaut-selection cuts. NASA is now contacting my references, so I know that I made it through the medical board and that my application has been classified as "Highly Competitive." About 90 percent of the applicants have been eliminated. In the next cut, in December, NASA will choose who it wants to fly down to Houston for weeklong interviews.

I just found out that NASA has contacted everyone that it's going to call for interviews in this selection, and I'm not on the list. I spent months waiting for the "big phone call." Every time I went to my office and saw the red light on my phone flashing, indicating I had a phone message, my heart started pounding as I wondered if and hoped that "this is it."

Now, I believe that either God's plans for me do not include becoming an astronaut or they do, but just not this time. I love God with all my heart and accept whatever course He wants my life to take. I do feel self-doubt creeping in, however. *Maybe all the miracles that occurred weren't really miracles at all.* I pray that God strengthens my faith and helps me not stumble during this time of confusion.

With my training complete and test pilot school graduation just around the corner, Carmel and I are preparing to head back to the Florida Panhandle. We recently found out that I've been assigned back to Eglin for a tour as a developmental test pilot.

It's been two years since I applied to the NASA astronaut program. Since then, our family and I have really enjoyed our time back in Florida. A few months ago, I decided to give the astronaut program another try, so I resubmitted my application for the latest class. Now, on this August day in 1999, I'm waiting for a bus to take me and nineteen other astronaut interviewees to the Johnson Space Center. Even though I've made it to the interview stage this time, ironically, I feel that I am finally rid of my emotional attachment to the quest to become an astronaut.

The bus arrives at our hotel and each of the handpicked candidates board amidst nervous excitement. Each of these guys and gals is amazing in their own right—a nuclear scientist, an oceanographer, a professor of aerospace engineering, and other incredibly accomplished overachievers. Each is so close to realizing a lifelong dream that they can taste it. I can too. The bus stops at the JSC Headquarters building, where we are greeted by Chief Astronaut Charlie Precourt and the legend John Young, who inspired me so many years ago when he blasted to space on the first shuttle mission. I fight my emerging inner child from asking him for an autograph. I don't think that would go over very well with Captain Young.

Later in the day, I am five hours into a psych test answering questions such as "Fill in the blank: I wish my mother was more_____" and "True or False: I always wanted to be a florist." After a long day, I'm back at the hotel writing an essay of a thousand words or less on why I want to be an astronaut, our homework assignment.

I'm sitting in a makeshift waiting room of a rather old and somewhat dilapidated one-story office building near the back gate of JSC. On the other side of a door, a few feet from me, the astronaut selection board is meeting in a conference room to comb through my application and "Why I Want to Be an Astronaut" essay. The heaviness of this moment weighs on me. What will happen in the next hour or so will set in motion the trajectory of the rest of my life, one way or another.

At the appointed time, Duane Ross emerges from the conference room and says, "Ronnie, we're ready for you. I'm going to take you in and lead you to your seat. Don't shake anyone's hand on the way in." I walk behind him, following his orders. As soon as my posterior hits my appointed chair, John Young jumps right in. "So, Ron, tell us about yourself, starting with high school." I don't get three words out when someone at the other end of the table asks, "How big was your high school?" I get the impression the question was purposely intended to throw me off if I had a prepared speech—I don't.

After I finish sharing my life story, the board peppers me with other questions, most just asking for clarification of things I've already said. Halfway through the process, I realize I'm having a good time. I feel relaxed, probably because everyone seems to be trying to make me feel comfortable. I answer all their questions honestly, as opposed to trying to give the answers I think they're looking for. As the interview ends and they thank me for my time, I feel that it went well. Friendly smiles abound. I hope the smiles are not just because they're happy to be rid of me.

After four days of numerous medical tests, claustrophobia tests, tours and meetings with various astronauts, flight directors, and space program managers, our group of candidates arrives for a NASA interview week tradition, the Thursday Night Social at Pe-Te's BBQ. We enter a somewhat dilapidated joint just outside the front gate of Ellington Field through swinging doors that look like they're straight out of an old Western movie. Ellington

Field is where NASA flies its T-38 aircraft, a supersonic jet that astronauts use for flight training.

I'm feeling really good about the week. Through the grapevine, I heard that I made a good impression on the board. John Young confirms this when he tells me, between bites of brisket, that he really enjoyed my interview and that I did well. Later in the evening, veteran astronaut and member of the selection committee Nancy Currie pulls me aside and says, "Ron, I really enjoyed meeting you at your interview, and I don't know how the selection will turn out, but I want you to know that I would consider it an honor to fly in space with you."

Her remark truly humbles me. I thank her and let it sink in. Her words were incredibly kind. She didn't have to say that. I'm somehow able to keep everything in perspective and not let any of those comments go to my head. The comments, though, really put a nice ending on an incredible week.

It's been about ten months since my NASA interview, and rumor has it that the NASA selection results will be announced in the next few days. When the phone call comes, my life and my family's life will change no matter the outcome. If I'm chosen, then we'll have a few weeks to pick up, move, and get settled in prior to the start of training. If I'm not chosen, I'm going to start a very demanding job as the operations officer of the squadron. To date, twenty-five to thirty candidates are left, from which it is rumored that NASA is expected to pick fifteen to twenty. Four are Air Force pilots, including me, of whom they will probably pick two to three. But, as ever, my chances still remain at either 0 percent or 100 percent, depending on God's plan.

The NASA selection has been rumored to be released within a day or two for the past three weeks. But NASA has not said a word about when it will announce the results. The test wing here at Eglin had planned on holding off on choosing its new operations officer, but since the NASA results are so delayed, they went ahead and assigned me to the position starting this Monday in late June. Normally, I would be excited about diving into a new leadership post, but this incredibly high state of turmoil is just another tremendous source of stress.

The squadron is a few weeks away from a biannual inspection, and it will fall on my shoulders to ensure it is up to speed. Holding my breath all these weeks waiting for the NASA announcement along with everything else has become, at times, extremely hard to bear.

I've been sitting here at my work desk reflecting on the fact that today, July 20, 2000, is the thirty-first anniversary of the first landing on the moon—thirty-one years ago today, the day that I was floating on a sea possibility as a deep desire to follow in the footsteps of the *Apollo 11* astronauts was burned into me.

I feel really restless today, almost jumpy. I decide to burn off some energy by going to the gym. Even at the gym, in the middle of a fairly intense workout, however, I'm still restless. Halfway through a set of sit-ups, I realize that daily Mass is starting soon in the base chapel and I decide to go. I think, *I'll just do one more set of sit-ups and leave.* Just then, intense stomach spasms attack me and I decide to go to Mass right away.

In the small base chapel, the aroma of pine rises above the sweet, pungent smell of incense. Behind the altar stands a simple wooden cross framed by blue curtains on either side, no doubt to hide the cross during non-Christian or secular ceremonies. On the right side of the altar stands an American flag, and on the left side stands an Air Force flag. Only three other people are here as I find a spot in the wooden pews as Mass begins. The Scripture readings comfort me. I receive communion, and an intense joy—the type you experience when you're with people you love and who love you; a feeling of loving unity—surges through me.

After Mass, I go to an even smaller chapel to spend some time in silent prayer. The fact that the NASA call is coming any day now has preoccupied my mind. I pray intensely that I only want what is God's will in my life. "Lord, if becoming an astronaut is the absolute best way for me to serve you and if it's the absolute best path to salvation for myself, the family entrusted to me, and all those that I love, then I pray that I become an astronaut. If this is not the best way nor the best path, then please, I beg you, do not let me become an astronaut." After some time lost in intense prayer, I return to the here and now.

Not long afterward, on my way to the base shoppette to grab a quick lunch, a squadron mate informs me that NASA calls have been going out over the last couple of hours. I drive straight to my office. The whole way there I keep thinking, *Your will, Lord, not mine,* and I again give my life to Jesus and pray for His grace.

Entering my office, I see the flashing red light on my phone. I pick it up, mash the *message* button, and hear, "Hi, Ron, this is Charlie Precourt from the Astronaut Office at JSC. I was wondering if you could give me a call back at your earliest convenience. Thank you." Every nerve cell in my body goes on heightened alert. *Charlie Precourt, the chief of the Astronaut Office. Would the chief astronaut call all the finalists or just the ones they want to hire?*

After taking a few moments to gain some semblance of composure, I dial Charlie's number while standing next to my desk. Charlie—what many people call him at NASA, where things are relatively informal—answers on the second ring.

After some brief small talk, he gets right to the point. "Ron, we were wondering if you'd like to come work for us. If you're still interested, we have an astronaut candidate spot for you in the next class." I fight the urge to hoot and holler. I simply say, "Sir, that is great news, and I am honored to accept your invitation."

Charlie explains to me that the Class of 2000, the seventeenth class of astronauts since the original Mercury Seven, will begin on August 28. This leaves my family a little over four weeks to move and get settled in. He also directs me not to tell anyone but my family. The NASA administrator needs to call members of Congress from the home states of each of the selectees, he says, before NASA will make a formal announcement. I thank him for the confidence that he and the selection committee have placed in me and express how excited I am to begin training. We say goodbye and hang up.

All in all, I think the call couldn't have lasted for more than three minutes. However long it was, it represents an abrupt shift in the direction of my life. Everything that I've worked for over the past exactly thirty-one years has led to this moment, and everything that will come after this moment will be affected by those three minutes.

Immediately, I leave the squadron. I don't want to run into anyone and be forced to keep a poker face if they ask if I got the call. I drive straight back to the chapel realizing that, in all likelihood, the call came in sometime while I was there earlier. In the chapel, I thank God for all the blessings that He has bestowed upon my family and me. I spend some time in complete adoration of and in gratitude to Him.

Sometime later, I start my drive home. I want Carmel to be the first person I tell, and I want to tell her in person. From the very start, we have been in this together, and she has supported me at every turn, through every defeat and victory. At times, this road was grueling for her too, especially since it seemed so crazy, maybe even reckless, to pursue such an impossible dream.

When I arrive home, I hurry through the door and deliver the news. Carmel hugs me with an intensity that I haven't felt since we hugged before I deployed to the Persian Gulf. This hug, like the one in 1990, marks an inflection point. Back then, it was an inflection point leading to violence. Today, it's an inflection point leading to, exactly what, I don't know. But with absolute certainty, we know that we are heading down a path together that is the right one for us.

In my mind, I run through all the amazing things that have happened over the past few years to get to this moment. I feel amazingly blessed. I pray that I am able to continue to serve God on this new and exciting path. Serving Him is truly my only goal in life. This has been a truly amazing, blessed, unbelievable journey. When I look back on all the incredible miracles that have gotten us to this point, I realize that our God is truly an awesome God.

Amen!

# CHAPTER 9

# Road to the Launchpad

✦ A heavy, moist coolness permeates our cramped cylindrical sleeping quarters outfitted with a metal hull, a covering that can't be more than a few inches from my head. A strangely familiar sound emanates from the hull, almost like the crackling and popping of a roaring campfire. I have no idea what's making the noise, but it's helping me settle in and unwind after an incredible day—a long day that started on the surface of Earth and ended in this amazing but hostile environment. From our one "window," the viewport in our tiny sleeping quarters down near my feet, a light shines out into the darkness. *Are any strange creatures lurking outside, just beyond the beam of light?* With that thought, I drift off to yet another boundaryless world.

The next morning, my alarm jolts me awake. The white spotlight that was shining into the darkness beyond our viewport is now replaced by wavering rays of light. I imagine the sun has peeked above towering thunderstorms on the horizon, casting a golden glow on the surface of the ocean some sixty feet above us. Some of that light is penetrating the ocean depths, illuminating our new home in an undersea habitat called *Aquarius*, nestled on this April 2006 day in the beautiful Conch Reef a little more than five miles off the coast of Key Largo, Florida.

I'm lying on the top of three bunks on the right, or the starboard side, of the habitat, across from three identical bunks on the left, the portside. Below me, in the middle bunk, rests

Nicole Stott, a beautiful soul who makes all in her presence feel immediately comfortable. Nicole has a great sense of humor and a beautiful laugh that vibrates on a frequency that penetrates deep into all beings within range. She is a fellow classmate in the astronaut Class of 2000, affectionately called "the Bugs." Nicole is my closest friend in the astronaut corps, warm and caring. Really, she is much more than a friend; she is family. Besides being close friends with Nicole and her husband, Chris, Carmel and I are also godparents to their son, Roman.

Below Nicole, on the bottom bunk, rests habitat technician Jim Buckley, a salt-of-the-earth—make that salt-of-the-sea— kind of guy. Although thin and small of stature, Jim has all the makings of a tough and competent drill sergeant. He appears to be intimately aware of every bolt, fastener, and wire here, and I'm grateful that he has that level of expertise.

Across from me, on the port top bunk, sleeps veteran space flyer Dave Williams, a Canadian astronaut. Dave got the nod to lead this, the ninth NEEMO mission, short for NASA Extreme Environment Mission Operations. Commander Dave, as we affectionately call him, is one of two medical doctors on board. He is a tall, likable guy who tends to wear shorts that are way too tight. But there's no sense telling him that because we're stuck with what we brought to our new undersea home.

Below Commander Dave rests the other MD, University of Cincinnati physician Tim Broderick. Tim is one of the most inquisitive people I've ever met. His natural, almost childlike curiosity, cultured over decades, has given him a wide breadth of expertise in many subjects, from medicine to robotics to computer science.

Below Tim, on the bottom bunk, we have our other hab tech, Ross Hein, a tall, thin guy many years younger than his counterpart, Jim Buckley. Besides being a Mr. Fix-It of sorts, Ross has a wealth of knowledge about marine life, which should prove useful as we get to know our neighbors.

Even through our small viewport, I can see that the coral reef we now call home is teeming with marine life of all sorts. The first glimmer of subsurface light served as a wake-up call to them. This call has now advanced to a full-blown rush hour of activity. I take a cue from these new neighbors and climb out of my bunk to start our first full day on the ocean floor. This mission is set to last nearly three weeks, the longest NEEMO mission to date. In addition to providing us all with some great spaceflight training, it includes a full schedule of scientific experiments. We'll be simulating that we have landed on the lunar surface and will conduct experiments outside during our seawalks, which will serve as simulated moonwalks. We will also conduct many experiments inside, primarily involving telerobotic surgery and other health-related experiments centered on lunar exploration.

I say good morning to everyone as they awaken, and I head to the bathroom. In this case, "bathroom" means the Atlantic Ocean. The habitat is divided into three parts. The main living quarters are called the "main lock" and are located in the bow, or front, of the habitat. I'm walking in the opposite direction, toward the stern, passing through the entry lock on my way to the area known as the wet porch, a portion of the habitat that is open to the ocean. On the deck, in the aftmost, or rear, part of the habitat, metal stairs descend into a pool of water. This water, which for some reason we call the "moon pool," is the open ocean, but because the air pressure inside the habitat is the same as the water pressure outside of it, the water does not rush in and flood the interior. When you submerge an inverted empty glass into water, the trapped air inside the glass prevents the water from filling it; likewise, the ocean water outside of *Aquarius* is maintained right at the interface of our habitat by the air pressure inside.

I trade my sweatpants and sweatshirt for a bathing suit, grab a scuba mask, and descend the stairs into the slightly chilly water, which snaps the last bit of sleepiness out of me. I'm now crouching in the moon pool, submerged to my neck, with my bare feet perched on a grate encrusted with barnacles and algae. The grate is attached to the legs of our habitat, and the ocean floor is about ten feet below me. I don the scuba mask, take a deep breath, hold it, dunk my head into the water, and pull my body into the ocean. I make the very short swim of about six feet to a submerged inverted gazebo filled with air. I pop my head into it, leaving everything from my neck down in the water.

A school of excited fish of various sizes, including some rather large and colorful angel fish, follow me and start circling my lower body, catching me off guard. Then I realize why they're all here. My presence has signaled to them that it's breakfast time and I'm about to provide the meal, which, of course, is what's left of *my* last meals. It's all part of the wonderful circle of life. *Hakuna matata!*

I finish my business, firmly establishing my place in the food chain, then I make another breathless swim back to the foot of the steps leading to the wet porch. Once back inside our artificial habitat, the aquatic silence I just experienced is replaced by the mechanical hum of pumps and fans, and the cold, wet chill of the ocean is replaced by the relatively warm, humid air of our undersea home.

I take a quick shower and head back into the main part of the habitat just as folks are starting to eat their breakfast. It's bound to be a hectic day, so I sit at the sparkling stainless-steel galley table and spend a few moments enjoying some oatmeal and the incredible view through a large viewport.

A tranquil alien landscape mesmerizes me. The azure-tinted water is so clear that it can almost be mistaken for air. The habitat sits on columns anchored to the seafloor, which elevates my vantage point by fifteen or twenty feet. The size and sheer number of fish around the habitat give me the impression that I'm much higher up than I actually am. I feel as if I'm looking out from a mountain ridge toward a valley of light blue snow.

Far in the distance, various human-made objects—storage tanks, guide wires, and platforms—are engulfed in activity. All the morning commuters are heading off toward their destinations as I watch from the picture window of my mountain retreat, cup of hot coffee in hand.

Suddenly, a blizzard of small particles rains down past the viewport, as if a strong gust of wind has sent a large amount of snow airborne from our roof. The snow gust is actually some sea creature spawning directly above us. A large fish, probably a grouper, just released thousands of unfertilized eggs in the hope that they will be fertilized and produce the next generation. I'm content to pretend that it's all just snow.

The fish seem more like they're flying than swimming, flying through a light blue, effervescent atmosphere at different altitudes and speeds. A rather large sea turtle lumbers up to the viewport and stops. He, or she, looks right at me, and I swear I see curiosity on the creature's tiny face. I think back to the aquarium I had as a kid and how I would look in at my fish and wonder whether they could see me. Now, *I'm* in the fishbowl. After a minute or two, the turtle departs to take care of some turtle business.

A short time later, three spotted eagle rays fly by in tight formation. Each animal's wingspan seems to be eight to ten feet across. As the formation starts a seemingly effortless right-hand turn toward the habitat, distinctive white polka dots against the dark background of each of their diamond-shaped upper bodies become apparent. They look like a formation of futuristic stealth aircraft on an attack run, each trailing a shockingly long stinger. As they pass close to the viewport, the white polka dots reveal a dark center—a polka dot within a polka dot.

These creatures disappear, and a large school of small, fast-moving fish takes their place on the undersea performing stage. There must be several hundred of them swimming in unison. I believe these neon-blue fish with prominent, deep, almost-purple scales and dark black eyes are called blue chromis. They hypnotize me. Unlike the spotted eagle ray formation, which seemed to have a leader that the others were following, this school appears to have no leader. It's as if the entire school abruptly and rapidly changes direction simultaneously, so the turn appears to happen at every point in the school all at once. I can't even see the turn. One moment they are all going one way, and the next moment they're going somewhere else, with no visible transition, as if they are acting as a single organism with a single brain. I wish I could sit and ponder how all of this is possible, but my day needs to get going as well.

Hours later, I'm back at the galley table after a long day. The sun has set, and the ocean is now dark. Looking out the main viewport, hundreds of species of fish of all sizes and colors are visible thanks to our habitat's exterior lights. We have had a busy day finishing moving into our new home and workspace, and it's been wonderful, but I'm exhausted.

Apparently, the soothing campfirelike noises I heard last night were actually snapping shrimp feeding on the algae growth on *Aquarius's* hull. Now, I'm looking forward to hearing the crackle of the snapping shrimp again as I drift off on my second night "sleeping with the fishes."

Several days later, I'm assisting Nicole and Tim on their seawalk. They have just donned wet suits and dive helmets and climbed down from our porch to the ocean floor. Each of them trails an umbilical that provides fresh air. I feed out the umbilicals to make sure they don't get tangled as the seawalkers traverse on foot from the habitat.

I tend to the task while standing in the moon pool up to my waist as several dozen schoolmaster fish, about one to two feet long, swim over and align themselves next to me. They are perfectly still, parallel to each other. I move a little to the left, and they all follow me to the left. Wherever I go they follow, seemingly watching my every move. They are beautiful fish with slender silver bodies adorned with bright yellow vertical stripes and matching yellow fins. All of their little black eyes, each inside a bright yellow ring, seem to be aimed directly at me as they make small, graceful, seemingly effortless fin movements to stay in formation. *Why are they here? Are they expecting a meal? Are they just curious? Are they here to evaluate my umbilical-tending performance?*

What a bizarre scene. I start whistling "Whistle While You Work" to see how the fish will respond. Maybe they'll all start helping me tend to the umbilicals. Then it dawns on me: *I can whistle!* Because the environment of our habitat is approximately two and a half times the pressure at the surface, none of us undersea rookies could do that when we first arrived. It's funny when nothing but air comes out when you try to whistle. But somehow, today is the day I've figured out how to do it down here. I wonder what I'm doing differently. Apparently, a part of my brain has been running a whistle fluid mechanics subroutine and it just finished compiling.

After a little over an hour outside, Tim and Nicole return home, and I assist them out of their helmets and gear. The schoolmaster fish stayed right next to me the entire time. I like to think they helped. As we all climb out of the moon pool, I say goodbye to my new friends.

Our next task for today is to prepare for a live video conference with the crew aboard the International Space Station, the ISS. Not long after we set up the video equipment, we see live video from the mission control center at Johnson Space Center and a lower-left corner thumbnail video of our crew, all crammed in front of our video camera. A couple of minutes later, a female voice from NASA says, "*Aquarius*, are you ready for the event?" Commander Dave replies, "The crew of NEEMO Nine is ready!"

Moments later, we get a view from aboard the ISS. Floating in the center of the screen are US astronaut Jeff Williams and Russian cosmonaut Pavel Vinogradov.

Jeff shares with us his experience on *Aquarius* in 2002, when he served as the commander of the NEEMO 3 mission. As he describes the lessons he learned during his six days here, it dawns on me how surreal this conversation is. Here we are, on the bottom of the ocean, talking with folks in space who are traveling at five miles per second—folks in inner space having a nonchalant conversation with folks in outer space as if it's totally normal and routine. The awesomeness of this experience just keeps growing.

+

A day later, facedown, covered in sand, with seventy feet of water above me, I struggle to get back to my feet. Commander Dave and I are on a seawalk, our wet suits and diving helmets simulating lunar space suits. Each of us is also wearing a large aluminum boxlike structure that simulates a life-support back-pack. It contains weights on rails that can be adjusted to deter-mine the effects of changes to our center of gravity on our ability to conduct tasks such as timed walks and runs, picking up rocks, and kneel-and-recover and fall-and-recover drills.

Following the last adjustment, the fall part was easy; the recover part is proving challenging. A combination of weights and floats are attached to me to simulate lunar gravity. Even though I'm experiencing a pull of gravity that is one-sixth of what I would experience on the surface of Earth, I'm still strug-gling to get to my feet.

I rest for a moment, facedown on the bottom of the ocean. My perspective is limited to the sand and small rocks I can see through the faceplate of my helmet. Radio transmissions from *Aquarius* and mission control in Houston periodically drown out

*The NEEMO 9 crew prepares for a night dive. Standing in the "moon pool" of Aquarius's wet porch are Canadian Astronaut Dave Williams (right rear), University of Cincinnati physician Tim Broderick (left rear), Ron Garan (right front), and Nicole Stott (left front).* Credit: NASA

the sound of my breath and the bubbles escaping from my helmet. I roll over on my back, which shifts the weights to a position more advantageous to standing. As I manage to get to my feet, I think, *This center of gravity location needs to be removed from the list that engineers are using to design the next-generation lunar space suit.*

Before we left Houston, I initiated the development of the Lunar Surface Exploration Lessons Learned Database. During this mission, we have been entering the key points that we have learned directly into the database. It's important to capture and document this so that the architects of our nation's Vision for Space Exploration can use the data when developing lunar exploration missions.

After getting to my feet, I start into a timed run between two markers on the seabed. Bounding across the surface, I flash back to memories of watching the *Apollo* astronauts bound across the lunar surface. I approach the finish line and lift my left leg for what will probably be the last step before I complete my "race." As my foot starts to come down, a stingray with a four-foot wingspan glides under it and I see its black eyes looking up at me. I get the impression that the ray is thinking, *Go ahead. Step down and make my day.*

I avoid stepping on it as I hear a crackling transmission in my helmet from mission control in Houston: "Watch out, Ron. We see a stingray below you." They've been watching everything unfold through my helmet camera. *The Apollo astronauts never had to put up with flying moon creatures with penetrating spike weapons*, I think.

✦

The next day, Dave, Nicole, Tim, and I make our final checks on our scuba gear as we stand in the moon pool just before 0600 hours, a little more than an hour before sunrise. An external light dimly illuminates the ocean water. Beyond the radius of the light lies the inky black ocean. From this perspective, it seems that the only things that exist are what our external light illuminates. Beyond that is vast nothingness, a void. I know there is a whole world out there beyond the reach of our lights, but I can't shake the feeling that we're about to step, or swim, into a great unknown. One by one, we submerge our heads under the habitat hull and press out into the darkness.

My plunge into the ocean is accompanied by the soundtrack from *Jaws*, which is playing in my paranoid mind. As we swim south, we all turn on our flashlights. Four pencil beams of light shoot off in different directions into an alien world. I'm looking through a soda straw of light, seeing only what's directly within the narrow beam. Everything outside the beam is covered by an opaque sheet of black. This is how I have traveled through large portions of my life—not seeing much more than what's right in front of me, not realizing the immensity of the world just outside my soda-straw perception.

Dave leads us to a nice sandy spot with towering coral surrounding us on all sides. We all find spots on the ocean floor to settle in, turn off our flashlights, and wait for the big show. Already, the first signs of light are becoming evident. The black ocean is starting to turn dark grey, and I start making out the general shapes of the terrain. Vague outlines of dark coral formations appear, and I can see my hand when I hold it out in front of my scuba mask.

I sit on the ocean floor, facing east, digging the bottom part of my scuba tanks into the sand to support my back. It's as if I'm sitting in an underwater Adirondack chair. Around me, I see that all of us are settled in nicely, four trails of dimly lit bubbles making their swift climb to return our borrowed air back to our planet's atmosphere.

Not long afterward, the first ray of morning light penetrates diagonally through the ocean depths, illuminating the coral reef like a theater spotlight. Then, off in the distance, I see what we've been waiting for: a shimmering, dancing bead of slightly orange-tinted light. Our planet has rotated just enough to bring the star at the center of our solar system into view from our vantage point on the bottom of the ocean. Our coral reef neighbors have taken notice as well. As more wavering light beams pierce the water, the ocean becomes less opaque and the surrounding coral comes alive with far more color than I'm used to seeing in the daylight. It's as if the coral has bloomed during the night, only to wither and retreat again in the full light of day.

We've all been taught as children not to stare at the sun, but from this depth, it's probably OK. I'm transfixed by its constantly changing appearance, happily dancing through the waves to greet us. Soon, the light of day floods the entire ocean bottom. I marvel at the enormous difference in the scene before us and the one of less than twenty minutes ago. A large spotted eagle ray glides by a few feet away. Now, beyond the towering coral that surrounds us, I see numerous additional coral structures in all directions and schools of fish and other marine life. I notice, a few feet to my left, an Atlantic stingray that apparently had buried itself in the sand for the night. The only parts of the ray sticking out above the sand are its eyes and tail. All that was hidden from my view a short time ago has been illuminated.

The whole experience seems even more poignant as I remember that today is Palm Sunday, which recognizes Jesus's triumphant arrival to Jerusalem. Jesus's words, "I am the light of the world. Whoever follows me will never walk in darkness, but will have the light of life" have, I believe, taken on a richer, deeper meaning for me. Jesus preached a gospel of love, and I wonder if somehow love serves to bathe darkness in light. Maybe love is the star in the center of our spiritual solar system.

Dave, using hand signals, asks for the status of our air quantity remaining. Since we're all getting low on air, he raises his left hand over his head with fingers extended and makes a chopping motion, pointing south in the direction of a refill station called Kamper. Dave then swims off to the south, and we all follow.

Kamper Station is an inverted undersea air-filled glass dome, elevated about four feet above the ocean floor on steel legs. After a short swim of about five minutes, we arrive there. Tim and

I swim under it and pop our heads up into the waiting air pocket while Nicole and Dave wait nearby. In the dome, we see two refill hoses, which we attach to our tanks. I open a valve, and a hissing noise signals that the air is flowing. We take off our scuba masks, remove our regulators from our mouths, and are able to speak for the first time since leaving the habitat before dawn.

I push a button on an intercom and hear Ross's voice with a forced, whiny telephone operator accent say, "Hello. *Aquarius* Base. How may I help you?"

I tell Ross that the four of us are refilling at the Kamper Station and that the sunrise was spectacular.

"It always is," Ross replies.

Having left without eating breakfast, I wish that we had brought some food. It's always amazing to have a snack while we wait under ninety feet of water for our tanks to fill.

After our tanks are set, we head back in the direction of the habitat, gliding in formation a few feet above the coral below us. The closer we get to the habitat, the more familiar everything seems. Up ahead, I see a coral formation that I recognize. A moray eel lives in a little nook on the far side of that coral. As we pass over it, sure enough, I can see the eel's beady little eyes and golden-yellow head poking out. *We're back in the neighborhood.*

We come to a stop near the habitat, and an unusually large barracuda swims right up to me and stops inches from my scuba mask. Its menacing mouth full of haphazardly placed and ill-aligned teeth transfixes me. I imagine the damage those pincers could do if this guy wanted to harm me. But now that the creature has stared at me with its small black eyes for what seems like minutes, I sense a curiosity in this prehistoric-looking predator. And then, in a flash, the creature darts off—probably in pursuit of its next meal. He or she—I really don't know—probably sized me up as not worth the effort. Or maybe it was just welcoming me back home.

✦

More than a week has passed in our habitat, and I'm back in my favorite writing spot at the galley table. It's almost noon, and it appears to be a sunny day on the surface. In the days since we first arrived in this undersea world, I have frequently gazed up at the sun through the ocean depths. Whether I'm out in the water on a seawalk or here inside the habitat, staring up through the viewport, I am always mesmerized by the dancing, shimmering light that has traveled from the star at the center of our solar system—ninety-three million miles through the vacuum of space, about fifty miles through our atmosphere, and then through about eighty feet of azure water—to its destination on my retinas. It's been nine days since I've seen the sun in the way I'm accustomed to as a surface dweller—that is, without its light having to pass through that last eighty feet of the journey.

As I wait for my lunch to heat up, my ears pop, almost to a beat. A rhythmic pressure pulses in my head and sinuses. Tight pressure comes, squeezes for a second or two, then retreats, over and over. *Is something wrong with me?* I see that the depth gauge in the galley is bouncing up and down to the same slow beat as the habitat seems to be rocking back and forth, and I remember that we received a forecast for rough seas this week, with eight- to ten-foot swells. The measured depth of our habitat and the respective pressure of our environment are changing with each passing wave.

I stroll down to the wet porch to see if the changing pressure is causing water to flow into the habitat. Entering the porch, I inhale and immediately cough as a breath of warm, almost hot, moist air hits my lungs. I see a fog, but moments later it's gone—and then it's back again. As the pressure changes with each passing wave, the relative humidity in the habitat has changed enough to cause this fog. The whole scene seems eerie. It's as if we are in the belly of a whale and are watching from the inside as it inhales and exhales. Or maybe we're in the heart muscle of a giant beast and are witnessing the flow of blood as the heart slowly beats. Then I realize the truth: This is the rhythmic pulse of our planet. I'm getting a glimpse into the timeless cycle of energy that has given life to every creature in this world from the beginning of time on Earth.

The *ding* of a timer, announcing the readiness of my midday meal, pulls me back to the galley. I sit down to a bowl of rehydrated beef stroganoff as a goliath grouper lumbers past the viewport. *Is this Stella or Lucy?* Shortly after arriving on *Aquarius*, we realized that two huge groupers live under our bunkroom viewport. Nicole named the massive creatures after her two pet German shepherds.

At the moment, I see only one of the beasts. It has to be more than six feet long, and it must weigh 300 pounds. Its brown, blotchy, spotted body, along with its spiky dorsal fins, makes it look like a prehistoric blimp with two yellow and black eyes and a huge frowning mouth. In spite of their frowns, the groupers seem to be curious, docile creatures that routinely lumber over to say hi when we are out on dives. I wonder if Stella, or maybe Lucy, realizes I'm having my lunch.

This afternoon, we all change into T-shirts that commemorate the twenty-fifth anniversary of the first space shuttle flight and gather in front of a laptop for a videoconference. It's been two and a half decades since that launch served as my second calling to embark on a career that would lead me here, living and working on the bottom of the ocean. Besides celebrating the shuttle anniversary, we are celebrating the halfway point of our mission too. We are patched into celebrations taking place with both the Topside Team in Key Largo, which monitors our mission, and mission control in Houston.

Most of our families are at the Houston gathering. It is wonderful to see and hear everyone. Any remarkable experience is always enriched when you can share it with your loved ones and friends.

*The NEEMO 9 crew gather at the galley table inside the Aquarius habitat during celebrations to recognize the halfway point of the mission and the 25th anniversary of the first space shuttle launch. From left to right are Canadian Space Agency astronaut Dave Williams, NASA astronaut Nicole Stott, NASA astronaut Ron Garan, University of Cincinnati physician Tim Broderick, Aquarius hab tech Jim Buckley, and Aquarius hab tech Ross Hein (seated in front).* Credit: NASA

The next day, Dave and I are back on the seafloor wearing our simulated lunar exploration suits. We're using PVC pipes to build a structure that will simulate a lunar communication relay station. Several robotic vehicles accompany us on our seawalk to help us with our tasks. One is a rover called *Skuttle* that a flight controller in Houston is remotely driving along the seafloor. Occasionally, it will drive over with a tool that we need, but it's also providing camera views to mission control. I climb up the jungle-gym-looking structure about seven feet to the top. The climb is easy in the simulated lunar gravity field. As I'm attaching one of the last bolts to it, a familiar voice comes across the speakers in my helmet ear pads. "Ron, you're looking good out there," says Carmel, who, at the moment, is in mission control with our three sons. One by one, each of the boys says hi.

I feel deeply connected to my family right now, even though they are 1,200 miles away and I'm on the bottom of the ocean. The normality of the exchange seems out of place. Later, after I've climbed down from the structure and am back on the seafloor, I hear Nicole shout over the radio from inside *Aquarius*, "Knock it off, knock it off, knock it off!" Right at that moment, *Skuttle* rams into my leg at full speed. Apparently, one of my sons was asked if he would like to remote drive the rover. At the controls, he saw in the rover's camera his dad bounding across the seafloor and decided to drive straight for me. The rover weighs only a few pounds, so it is no big deal. We all have a good laugh about it.

On another day, at dusk, Dave, Tim, Nicole, and I push off the wet porch and immerse ourselves in the undersea world. The normally vibrant colors of our coral reef neighborhood are replaced with a dim, more monochromatic hue, announcing the approaching night. A nurse shark joins our formation for a few moments as we head east, then it peels off for something more important. Above us, five or six large permit fish form up to start their evening hunting party, their large silver foreheads protruding nearly vertically up from their dark eyes—killing machines on a mission.

Leaving the habitat no longer feels like going out on a scuba dive; it simply feels like we're going *outside*. We continue to head east as a blanket of night engulfs us and our undersea world rapidly dims. As we get far enough away from *Aquarius* to escape

*A NEEMO 9 crew member works outside of Aquarius during
the NEEMO 9 mission in 2006.* Credit: NASA

the glow of the habitat lights, Nicole and I proceed down one
sand finger off the reef, and Dave and Tim proceed down another,
about ten yards away. We all settle into our sand patch observation spots eighty feet below the surface, turn off our lights, and
watch in total amazement as the marine world comes to life.

Overhead, the shimmering moon dances. The wavering,
cool blue moonlight subtly illuminates the sand, coral, and
everything around us, like highlights being brushed on an ever-
changing masterpiece by an invisible underwater artist. From
this depth, the moon looks different than the sun. Even through
eighty or ninety feet of water, the sun still looks harsh. The
moon, by contrast, seems inviting, a soft beckoning to adventure. I imagine what the moonlight must look like sparkling on
the rippling surface of the ocean. I imagine what it would feel
like to swim to the surface and poke my head above the water,
inhaling fresh, cool ocean air.

I think about the surface of the water, the interface between an ocean of water and an ocean of air. If I had never been above the surface, if I had lived my entire life underwater—if, say, I were a fish born with human intelligence—would I even know there was an interface to something else? Could I even fathom another world out there? Would I have any clue about the boundaries between our world and the rest of our universe? Would I have the slightest idea that the bright, shimmering light that I see in the day and the dimmer, cooler light that I see almost every night are actually two heavenly bodies an incomprehensible distance away from both my home within an ocean of water and the ocean of air above it? Would I have any clue about the cosmic dance of these heavenly bodies that has taken place for eons?

Maybe I do realize there's an interface to a bigger world out there. I swim as fast as I can toward it. I smash through, only to find that, as soon as I break through the confines of my three-dimensional world, I am in a one-dimensional world that exists between up and down. I'm thrust into a world where I no longer have control of my movement, and an invisible hand reaches out and yanks me down back into the comfortable and familiar. How could I possibly know the true nature of the universe from this undersea vantage point?

To see the bigger picture, I would have to invent a way to escape the confines of the undersea world and immerse myself in the world above. And what would I think if I were able to look back at the world from which I came, if I were able to look back at the surface of the ocean from this newfound vantage point? It's easy for me, born on land, swimming through life in an ocean of air, to look at the world down here from my above-the-surface perspective and realize it's only a partial story. But even we land dwellers see only a piece of the puzzle. Would I have a similar revelation if I went to space and crashed through the interface between our ocean of air and the rest of the universe, if I were able to immerse myself in what exists above?

Suddenly, I'm distracted from my fantasy by an otherworldly scene of thousands upon thousands of bright blue undersea stars. Anything we move through the water creates swirls of bright blue neon light. Each kick of a fin or movement of a hand creates an incredible light show. Individual points of light of countless bioluminescent plankton surround me and Nicole. Behind the clear plastic of our scuba masks, we look at each other with pure amazement. The inconceivable awesomeness of our world envelops me in a strong embrace. We continue to take in the dark undersea world for nearly two hours. I notice many new creatures that I have not seen in the daytime. It seems that life on the reef is more animated once the last photons of sunlight dissolve into ink.

At the predetermined time, Nicole and I head over to Dave and Tim and start back toward the habitat. We know it is somewhere up ahead, but all we see as we swim west is blackness. After about five minutes, I start to see a dim glow. It reminds me of flying a jet at high altitude at night. Areas of the United States are completely devoid of lights. When flying over them, it is always nice to see, up ahead on the horizon, the dim glow of an approaching city. The closer one gets, the brighter the light becomes, and soon the dull, dim glow transforms into a sea of individual points of light. The same scene is playing out now as we approach the habitat. In both the high-altitude and the undersea versions, the lights are beckoning us to the warm comfort of home.

We arrive at *Aquarius* and take a few minutes to explore around the habitat and say hi to our neighbors, seeing what they're doing on this fine evening. Then we stick our faces up against the galley viewport, and Ross takes a photo of us wayward travelers.

After reentering the habitat and getting out of our gear, we sit down around the galley table and share our impressions of the experience over a round of very satisfying hot chocolates. It's a little after 2300 hours. It has been a long but memorable day. I'm looking forward to tomorrow, my first Easter on the bottom of the ocean.

Nicole, Tim, and I plaster our faces to the bunkroom viewport. Outside, Dave proceeds away from the habitat, using a system we call "hookah." Equipped with only a mask and fins, he breathes through a small regulator attached to a long hose that feeds out from the habitat. He sees the perfect spot on the coral reef to deposit his precious cargo, an STS-107 mission pin. We thought Easter morning would be the perfect time to honor the friends we lost on Space Transportation System mission 107, known to most everyone as simply space shuttle *Columbia*.

As Dave prepares to place the pin on the reef to honor the crew of STS-107, I'm hit with a flood of memories from that horrible February morning three years ago. I woke up that day, strolled out to the living room in our home a mile from the south gate of the Johnson Space Center, and turned on NASA TV to watch Rick Husband and his crew land *Columbia* at the end of their fifteen-day mission.

A month or two earlier, I had been with the crew out at the ten-story-high shuttle landing simulator at NASA Ames in California. My job at the controls of the instructor console of the world's tallest flight simulator was to input malfunctions and other challenges as the crew tried to land. They did a great job during the sim, and I was confident that, when it was their turn to bring *Columbia* home, a great landing would be the exclamation point on yet another successful mission.

As I sat in front of the TV on the day of their scheduled return to Earth, I heard NASA TV announce that *Columbia* was overdue for landing. *They aren't going to make it to their landing in Florida,* I thought with dread. *Space shuttles just aren't late.* In the immediate aftermath of the shuttle's demise as it attempted to return to Earth, months of accident investigations ensued, followed by several years of working on the return-to-flight effort. The funerals, memorial services, and tree plantings now replay in my mind. A pang of sweet sadness wells up inside me, the emotion I experienced as I rode in the funeral procession through Amarillo, Texas, as hundreds, or maybe thousands, of people lined the roads, all saluting as Rick's flag-draped coffin passed by.

A cold evening a couple of weeks after the accident, I flew myself in a NASA jet to Washington, DC, to hand-deliver recovered onboard videotapes that were discovered among *Columbia's* wreckage. I watched one of the videos while sitting next to a National Transportation Safety Board video technician in the vacant NTSB headquarters late at night. I felt a kick in the gut and noticed my heart rate climbing sky high when we realized that a specific tape we were watching was a recording of the last moments of the crew's lives. We were the first two people to watch the video, so we did not know how long it would last. We did not know what horrors we would be the first to witness.

I experienced mixed feelings when the burned and mangled tape ended abruptly just before the crew compartment broke up. Seeing the compartment explode would have accelerated our investigation into what happened and increased the chance that we could prevent it from happening again. But I was relieved that the last recorded moments of the crew's lives showed them happy, excited, and acting in a professional manner.

I have lost friends in violent crashes before, in the Air Force, but the shuttle tragedy three years ago was different. I have never been able to put my finger on what was different, but now, as Dave is laying the pin on the reef against the backdrop of the beautiful undersea world, I realize what it is: guilt. Rick Husband, William McCool, David Brown, Kalpana Chawla, Michael Anderson, Laurel Clark, and Ilan Ramon—all of *Columbia's* crew—put their trust in us, and we let them down. In our arrogance, we thought we had the whole picture.

*Columbia* was ripped apart not just because of foam that broke off from the external tank and impacted the leading edge of the shuttle's wing. Our arrogance also caused its destruction. We thought that we had it all figured out, which blinded us to the reality of the situation. Because foam had hit shuttles before without incident, NASA managers decided it wasn't a problem this time. They even turned down an offer to survey *Columbia* with high-powered ground-based telescopes. As the shuttle reentered the atmosphere, the damage caused by the impact of the foam allowed superheated plasma to enter the wing, which eventually ripped the shuttle apart. I don't know if we would have been able to save the crew if we had done anything different, but if we had correctly assessed the situation, at least we could have tried.

*Columbia's* crew members put their trust in NASA, in our country, and in humanity to keep them safe as they furthered our understanding of our place in the universe. Despite the mishap investigation board's findings, a root cause of the astronauts' deaths was arrogance—arrogance that limited perspective and led to the loss of seven wonderful humans.

After the pin-laying ceremony concludes and Dave returns to *Aquarius*, we begin a videoconference with my family in Houston and Monsignor Bob Sable at the Vatican. Years earlier, Pope John Paul II selected "Father Bob," my old chaplain at Shaw Air Force Base, to serve on the Vatican's Supreme Court. Using audiovisual technology made possible by the space program, Father Bob leads my family and our NEEMO 9 crew through an Easter prayer service. He blesses our mission and gives a special blessing for the laying of the STS-107 pin on the reef. It's incredible to share such a special Easter service, led by a dear friend on the other side of the ocean, with my family in Houston while I'm on the bottom of the ocean. This is without a doubt the most unique Easter I have ever experienced. What a tremendous opportunity and blessing.

Happy Easter 2006!

In nearly the third week of April, I depart the wet porch by myself just before nightfall to engage in my last opportunity to spend some quality time with our neighbors. I swim under the habitat, toward its bow, wearing just swim trunks, a scuba mask, fins, and a hookah regulator. After nearly three weeks of wearing heavy gear, it's liberating to explore outside without all that cumbersome stuff weighing me down. Being alone here as the undersea world grows dark also provides me with some rare quiet time alone. This is the first time since arriving on *Aquarius* that I'm able to go outside by myself without the constant crackle of our communications gear and the pinging of our diver tracking systems. It's peaceful.

The fish are so used to us being here that they come right up to us. Some are very curious. Everything seemed so alien when I first arrived here, as if I were leaving one world for another. But this is not another world, and it no longer seems alien. I belong here. This is now part of my home. My world is now bigger. Being out here feels as if I'm out for a stroll in my front yard, one that we share with numerous other creatures. I say goodbye to them one by one.

With the mission drawing to a close, I contend with mixed feelings. On the one hand, I am very much looking forward to reuniting with my family in Houston. On the other hand, I am going to miss being a resident of Conch Reef.

I spend about another half hour simply enjoying the ocean. As darkness falls and the lights of the habitat come on, I head toward the wet porch and then I stop. A sergeant major fish guarding a nest clings to *Aquarius's* hull. I bring my hand toward the small yellow-and-black-striped fish, and it darts toward my hand in attack. The message is clear: *Move along, human.* I let it be and head under the hull, savoring the fact that this is the last time for this mission that I'll be able to fully enjoy our undersea world.

Beeping alarms are going off simultaneously throughout the habitat, each of our watches marking 1600 hours. It's time to start the long process of decompression, which will slowly bring the habitat down to sea-level pressure. About an hour ago, our crew increased to seven with the arrival of James Talacek. James is responsible for monitoring *Aquarius's* life-support systems and watching the crew for signs of sickness and oxygen toxicity during the course of the seventeen-hour decompression.

Before the venting of the habitat atmosphere begins, the heavy steel hatch that separates the wet porch from the entry lock is closed, sealing us all inside a smaller *Aquarius*. As we start the decompression, we six NEEMO 9 crew members climb into our bunks and begin a series of twenty minutes of breathing 100 percent oxygen and then five minutes breathing cabin air, which has basically the same composition as our atmosphere. We continue this series for three cycles to flush nitrogen from our bodies. To pass the time while we're confined in our bunks, we'll watch movies on a portable DVD player that we set up just below the viewport in the bunkroom. First up is *The Life Aquatic with*

*Steve Zissou* and on deck is *Wedding Crashers*. After such a busy mission, it's wonderful to relax during this last part of it.

I reflect on the past eighteen days, and I can't possibly praise enough the outstanding and professional performance by our hab techs, Jim and Ross. The success of the mission is due in large part to their incredible talent and dedication. In addition to all their help, we owe them a great debt of gratitude for the marine biology tutorial they provided.

I think about an experience we had earlier today too. We spoke with *Mercury* astronaut Scott Carpenter, who came to Topside Team headquarters to congratulate us on a successful mission. Besides being one of the original Mercury Seven astronauts, he was also instrumental in the *Sealab* undersea research program and the first person to become both an astronaut and aquanaut. We all really enjoyed discussing the differences and similarities between our time on *Aquarius* and Scott's time on *Sealab* with him.

As night falls, the marine world remains busy, which is evident just above the monitor showing Bill Murray's character leading Team Zissou on undersea adventures. Schools of fish are highlighted in the spotlight off the bow of *Aquarius*. The groupers Stella and Lucy lumber past the viewport continuously, while the sudden disappearance of schools of fish signals the arrival of barracudas. Enjoying a movie while experiencing our last look at the neighborhood sea life is utterly relaxing. We all start to drift off to sleep in our bunks as Jim, Ross, and James prepare to take turns monitoring the decompression throughout the night.

It's 0830 hours, and a loud hissing is making it difficult to hear folks when they speak. A little while ago, when our decompression reached sea-level pressure, James initiated what we call "blowdown." By opening a valve, he allowed the higher-pressure air outside the entry lock to rush into the lower pressure of our present home in the main lock. At this point, most of the nitrogen absorbed by our bodies during this mission has been released and the threat of decompression sickness as we ascend to the surface has theoretically been reduced to a safe level. We took seventeen hours to slowly bring the pressure down to sea-level pressure from two and a half times sea-level pressure. We will take only a few minutes to bring the pressure back up to two and a half atmospheres.

I wiggle my jaw and force a yawn to try to equalize the pressure in my ears. My eustachian tubes are not keeping up with the rapid pressure change, but after many years of flying aircraft, I'm used to this discomfort. Once the pressure inside the hatch is equalized with the pressure outside of it, James opens the hatch that was sealed prior to decompression. Wearing bathing suits and T-shirts, I and the other five members of the NEEMO 9 crew proceed to the wet porch. Safety divers, who will escort us to the surface, greet us. We each don a scuba mask and hold a regulator attached to a small bottle of air.

Starting with Nicole, followed by Tim, me, Dave, Ross, and then Jim, we duck under the habitat hull, grab a line that stretches from the habitat to a boat floating on the surface, and one by one, we slowly ascend the line. As I do, my eyes gravitate back to *Aquarius* in a final goodbye to the incredible place that we have called home for the past eighteen days and to the neighbors with whom we've shared this paradise. I look up to the surface and reflect on how wonderful it will be to arrive back on land and reunite with my family.

I can see the interface between an ocean of water and an ocean of air getting closer. The hulls of other boats nearby, protruding down into the water, come into view. As my head breaks the surface, I close my eyes and immediately remove my regulator and mask. The fresh, cool, moist sea air rushes into my chest as my lungs expand in a deep breath. I can taste it. It's the taste of Earth.

I lay my head back in the water, a liquid pillow embracing me as I take in my first moment returning to the surface of Earth. As I open my eyes, directly overhead beams a bright half-moon set against a beautiful sunny blue sky. Under the iridescent moon, I gently bob up and down in the calm Atlantic. A slight, cool breeze blows across my face, taking clinging seawater with it. What a familiar and welcoming sight. The haunting beauty of the moon has enticed me throughout my life to pursue a career that could possibly send me there one day, a career that so far has led me to this particular slice of the paradise we call Earth.

It's poignant that we just spent the past several weeks simulating that we were on the moon and the first thing I see when I return to the surface is the real thing. I hope that the accomplishments of this mission will, in some small way, help humanity return to the moon—this time to stay.

I swim over to a ladder on the stern of the research vessel *Legacy*. As I climb the ladder, I see another boat, about 100 yards away, carrying some of the family members, friends, and colleagues who have arrived to celebrate the end of the mission. Some are on the boat while others are in the water snorkeling so they could watch us ascend from *Aquarius*. It's great seeing so many smiling faces, including my godson, Roman Stott. We enjoy a wonderful ride back into port. I use the time heading to shore to reflect on what I've experienced undersea. It will probably take a long time before I will be able to mentally process it all.

Two days later, I look down at the glittering Gulf of Mexico six miles below my window seat on a commercial flight. Offshore oil rigs and the wake from tankers cover the deep blue canvas, and whitecap waves dot the surface. From this altitude, they appear as ripples radiating out in different directions and then crashing into one another. I think about the seeming chaos on the surface of the ocean, but I know there's more to the canvas— there's depth hidden beneath the churning top layer. My mind penetrates the two-dimensional surface and into the three-dimensional deep. An entire world below, out of view, teems with interdependent beauty, energy, and life. A vibrant ecosystem exists just beyond that surface veil, hidden from my present vantage point. *What other layers of understanding are presently veiled from my awareness? Where else requires a deeper exploration, inquiry, and immersion?*

For at least the past hour, I've had my face pressed to the window, attempting to process the past few weeks while my heart is pulling me toward home, toward my family. I think back to the highlights of the mission and to all that I learned and experienced. I think back to yesterday, arriving back on shore and being greeted by our extended team, and to the splash-up party at the oceanfront home of one of *Aquarius's* supporters. I think back to sitting underneath a blanket of stars, chatting with Scott Carpenter about renewable energy, as one incredibly bright star streaked overhead. The "star" was actually reflected sunlight bouncing off the aluminum hull of the International Space Station as it flew over the Florida Keys, still bathed in sunlight. From the ISS's orbital perspective, the sun had not yet set.

Probably the biggest impression I will take from these past several incredible weeks is the sheer awesomeness of the undersea part of our planet. My childhood trepidation about the ocean, partially thanks to Steven Spielberg, has been replaced by a deep appreciation for the gift of our oceans and a strong desire to go back and once again live among marine creatures.

I gaze out upon this vast gulf, astounded by the incredible level of interdependence that exists below that sparkling blue surface. I spent a lot of time on the mission mesmerized by the linked and seemingly altruistic behavior of schools of fish.

Their behavior, I believe, reflects a complex network of inter-acting components. The collective actions of the individual fish within the school appear to be linked by a dense web of intricate connectivity.

No one fish could do what the entire school can. It seemed almost as if the school itself had some form of networked consciousness capable of forming complex patterns, as if there was some sort of evolutionary non-zero-sum algorithm that was playing out in their collective action, as if each individual fish sensed somehow that it was part of something larger and more important, a community with a common purpose: to survive.

Up ahead, I can make out the coast and Gulfport, Mississippi. If I squint and use my imagination, I can almost make out the Houston skyline. Every fiber of my being is pulling me back to Carmel and our three wonderful sons. I can't wait to be home.

# CHAPTER 10

# Kibo, Hope for Tomorrow

✦ On this late May day in 2008, we level out at 39,000 feet above mean sea level as we cross the Texas coast and head out over the Gulf of Mexico. All four aircraft in our formation begin producing contrails, announcing to the world that we are starting our journey. The four twin-engine supersonic T-38 jets, each with a prominent NASA logo painted on its tail, look beautiful. These are sleek white jets with a blue stripe running their length from the black pointed noses to the exhaust nozzles, all racing to a magical place steeped in history.

Our formation is vertically sandwiched between two interfaces to two separate perspectives of reality. I guess we are about halfway between two important interfaces—the interface between our planet's atmosphere and ocean and the interface between our planet's atmosphere and space. Up ahead awaits the Kennedy Space Center, a historic jump-off point to extraplanetary destinations.

I'm in the front seat of the number three aircraft wearing an oxygen mask, a blue helmet with a NASA logo on the front, and a blue NASA flight suit with an American flag on my left sleeve, and, on my right, a gold and black diamond-shaped STS-124 mission patch that gives a nod to our objective to install the Japanese Laboratory on the ISS. In the back seat sits my spacewalk partner, Mike Fossum, wearing an identical flight suit and a maroon helmet brandishing a logo from his beloved alma mater, Texas A&M University. Strapped to the ejection seat, I can hear and feel the hum and vibration of the aircraft engines. At this altitude, the sky is darker than it appears from the ground, a beckoning to what's to come.

The flight lead for this trip to the Kennedy Space Center is STS-124 commander Mark Kelly, an experienced astronaut and a great leader. In Mark's back seat sits Greg "Taz" Chamitoff. We will deliver Taz to the International Space Station to begin his six-month tour of duty. Also flying in the formation are the other members of the STS-124 crew, *Discovery's* pilot, Ken Ham, whom we call "Hock," Karen Nyberg, a classmate of mine from the astronaut Class of 2000, and astronaut Aki Hoshide of Japan. I couldn't ask for a more capable and fun group to go to space with.

About a hundred miles out in front of us, my thirteen-year-old son, Jake, looks out the window of the NASA-leased private jet that is carrying him, his brothers, and Carmel to the same destination. The atmosphere inside the jet is relaxed, but there's palpable excitement too. Jake feels out of place. He understands that flying on a private jet to watch his dad launch into space this week is a unique event that very few people will experience. He realizes that this is not a normal trip. This is a trip with a timer counting down to a major event that will change his life and the lives of everyone in the family, one way or another.

I think back to the goodbye I shared with my family and I'm reminded of another time when I said goodbye before heading out on a journey not knowing exactly what I was heading toward. I think back eighteen years ago, saying goodbye to Carmel before flying over the ocean toward the Persian Gulf. I think about our last embrace then and my somber realization that I might not ever see her or hold her again. Back then, there was no guarantee that we would enjoy life together and raise a family together. Thankfully, we have been able to do all that and more.

We have been able to travel down a path that has led us to this surreal moment.

Heading out to the Persian Gulf all those years ago was the first time in my life I had to say goodbye not knowing where I was going or when or if I would return. All I knew was that I was heading toward danger, toward a situation where the stakes were incredibly high and the gravity of the situation was pressing in on me. This is similar yet different.

As I peer out at the dark sky and think about what's beyond, I, yet again, feel as if there's something much larger at work here, something just beyond the veil of reality. I feel as if I'm standing before a boundary between a comfortable yet incomplete day-to-day reality and a greater and richer understanding of the miraculous creation that surrounds us constantly. I feel like I'm on the verge of escaping a small and limited subset of reality and shedding the false self-confidence that I use as a crutch to function in the "real world."

I look down at the Gulf of Mexico and think back on my time living two years ago in that beautiful and wonderful coral reef on the bottom of the ocean. For several weeks, I was immersed in an incredible environment of awe and wonder. A new world and a new existence opened up before me. A certain sense of structure, a distinct pattern of pulsating life existed within that beautiful coral reef. I emerged from the ocean with a newfound appreciation for the incomprehensible miracle that is life on Earth, an appreciation that was born from gratitude—gratitude for the opportunity to experience the ocean from that perspective and gratitude for the beautiful gift of our planet's oceans, a beauty that is currently hidden from my visual perspective by the surface of the ocean, which veils its depth, true beauty, and meaning.

Up ahead, I see the West Coast of Florida and think about the comfortable and familiar—the coconut oil smell of beaches, air-conditioned strip malls, ubiquitous and multivaried restaurants, sturdy and well-designed highways, the endless cycle of daily commutes to and from seemingly all-important jobs and careers. I think about post offices, taxes, tailgate parties, late-night television, and everything else that marks humanity's presence on this planet. At the moment, it all seems irrelevant, eclipsed by the monumental journey we are heading toward.

Way off in the distance, hidden behind the curvature of Earth, stand the Kennedy Space Center and Patrick Air Force Base. It was at Patrick that I took my entry physical prior to joining the Air Force nearly three decades ago. I remember a beautiful morning in 1983 driving east on Florida State Road 404, the Pineda Causeway, toward the base. As I drove on the causeway over the Indian River, a spectacular sun rose directly in front of me. It seemed to light the sky on fire as it peeked out behind towering pink-orange cumulonimbus clouds announcing the start of a glorious new day. I distinctly remember the transcendental beauty of the scene compelling me to wonder where this journey would ultimately take me. I'm still wondering about that.

My gaze transitions from the horizon in front of us back to the sky above. Intellectually, I know that just beyond that sky exists an interface to an expanded perspective of reality that acknowledges and incorporates that we live in a universe that's billions of light-years across and contains an incomprehensible number of solar systems. I'm looking forward to crashing through that interface in a few days. Right now, I'm again hurtling toward a microscopically small point on a microscopically small planet. Despite the utter insignificance from the cosmic scale of what we're heading toward, this is the most exciting thing I have ever had to face.

I feel like I'm slicing through the atmosphere toward a sharp edge, an inflection point that will forever change the trajectory of our lives. As I head toward it, many people that I've met along the journey of my life—extended family, friends from high

*The crew of STS-124 leaves crew quarters at the Kennedy Space Center and heads to the "Astrovan" to start the journey to the launchpad, May 31, 2008. First row: Ken Ham (left), Mark Kelly (right). Second row: Ron Garan (left), Karen Nyberg (right). Third row: Japan Aerospace Exploration Agency astronaut Aki Hoshide. Fourth row: Greg Chamitoff (left), Mike Fossum (right).* Credit: NASA school and college, Air Force buddies, and many others—are all converging toward this same microscopically small point on a microscopically small planet to watch me and six of my friends leave Earth.

Passing Orlando, still heading east, our four-ship descends toward the Kennedy Space Center. Up ahead, I see the massive vehicle assembly building, what we call "the VAB," and can just make out a tiny American flag painted on the side of it. At least it's tiny from this perspective. In reality, it's the size of a football field. We drop down to about a thousand feet above the ground as we pass by the VAB, aiming for the historic launchpad 39A. As we approach it, Mark begins a left turn.

Tucked in tight on Mark's right wing, I can see below us, on the inside of the turn, the launchpad with space shuttle *Discovery* cocooned within the servicing structure. A wave of nostalgia rolls over me as I remember that all the manned *Apollo* missions started their journey to the moon from this spot and the first space shuttle mission started from this pad too. Two of the most significant impacts on the direction of my career began on this very spot. I have come full circle.

Each of us takes our turn landing on the runway, where if all goes well, we will land again in a couple of weeks when we bring space shuttle *Discovery* back to Earth.

A few days later, on May 31, I step out of the Astrovan, the van NASA transports astronauts in, and onto launchpad 39A. A soft breeze caresses my face. I inhale, filling my lungs with warm air laced with moisture extracted from the Atlantic Ocean. It's a beautiful day. The sun is shining brightly, but it's not too hot, even with us all wearing our bulky space suits. All seven of us tilt our heads back to fully take in an incredible sight. *Discovery* is no longer cocooned behind the steel of the rotating service structure. She is exposed, perched on her external tank. She looks like a sprinter cocked in her stance, ready to spring into high-speed action.

It's eerily quiet on the launchpad. I can hear the hum of distant waves crashing against the beach and the cry of seagulls. All the bustling activity of the past few days has concluded. The only people within three miles of the pad are the seven of us and a handful of technicians to help us strap in. Then they'll close the hatch and depart to a safe distance. I've experienced countless beautiful sunny days like this, days that remind me to be grateful to be alive. On the surface, this is a day like any other—just a normal day. It's normal except for the fact that very shortly, the seven of us will be way up there inside that spaceship strapped to four and a half million pounds of explosives. And in a few hours, someone is going to light the fuse. *This is it! We're really here! It's really going to happen!*

We all make our way to the launchpad elevator and ride it nearly 200 feet up. Once we arrive, we take turns starting the journey from the pad to our spacecraft. When it's my turn, I walk across the narrow gantry on the orbiter access arm that connects the pad to the space shuttle. Something feels different. I've walked across this gantry many times, but this time I won't be walking back across it in the opposite direction. I look down at its grated floor. Below my feet is a 195-foot drop to the concrete launchpad. The gantry floor is painted yellow with black arrows pointing in the opposite direction as if they're saying, "You're going the wrong way!"

A twinge of pain shoots through my lower back as I squirm in my seat to get comfortable. A few hours ago, the rest of the STS-124 crew and I climbed through *Discovery's* hatch. One by one, we made our way to our respective launch positions. In my case,

*Ron Garan makes final preparations before climbing through*
*the hatch and into space shuttle Discovery for the launch of*
*the STS-124 mission on May 31, 2008. Credit: NASA*

I am on the flight deck sitting behind and directly between Mark Kelly and Ken Ham. To my right sits Karen Nyberg. Directly in front of me, on *Discovery's* control panel, a digital clock reads "00:09:00." It shouldn't be long before we exit from the nine-minute hold and things will get real busy.

"Time to head to the roof!" exclaims astronaut Mike Foreman as he and some of our astronaut colleagues escort Carmel, our boys, and the family members of my crewmates from an office on the fourth floor of the Launch Control Center, which we call the "LCC," down a hallway to a small flight of stairs leading to a door to the roof. A few hours ago, the families were bused here from their hotel in Cocoa Beach. The blaring sirens and flashing lights of their police escort added to the surrealism of the day. Once on the roof, they each take turns climbing a small ladder for the last few feet of their ascent to their launch-viewing positions.

The last few days have been a whirlwind for our families. NASA has done everything in its power to keep them comfortable and busy. The busyness is by design, to get everyone's mind off the impending danger. For the most part, this has worked well. What NASA can't control are the numerous friends and family members who continually ask the crew's children and spouses if they're nervous or worried that something terrible might happen. The very thing that all the activity is designed to take their minds off is undone by careless comments that bring the awareness of the danger back into the forefront of their thoughts.

But nothing can shield them from the reality of the situation as they walk to the edge of the roof with a perfect view of *Discovery* on the launchpad a few miles away. For my seventeen-year-old son Ronnie, the abstract idea of me flying in space one day instantly transforms into something with great weight and potential reper-cussions. It becomes real. He and his brothers have seen me training for spaceflight for years and always knew what the training would lead to. But seeing the shuttle poised on the launchpad with me inside it makes the reality of the moment sink in.

As Ronnie and the rest of the family make their way to the edge of the roof, he thinks about the times that other shuttle missions have gone wrong. There's a low chance it will happen again on this flight, but he understands that a low chance is not a zero chance. He also realizes that this is an exciting and momentous event. He tries as best he can to put the danger out of his mind so he can enjoy the experience.

In my headset, an unrecognized voice from the Launch Control Center transmits, "Countdown clock will resume on my mark. Three, two, one, mark." I watch as the last digit of *Discovery's* timer clicks from zero to nine seconds and continues its free fall. Another voice from the LCC proclaims, "T-minus nine minutes and counting."

My heart rises in my chest and lodges in my throat. There's no turning back now. I think about Carmel, Ronnie, Joseph, and Jake. I think about my mom and dad and stepdad and all the family and friends who are watching and waiting for the big show. I am so thankful for them all. This moment would not be possible if it were not for their love and support. I say a silent prayer for them and our mission. I feel determination, confidence, and peace rising in me as my heart descends from my throat back to where it belongs. It's time to get to work!

Leaning against a bleacher railing at another launch viewing area, Bill "Kanga" Rew, now a major general, nervously watches the descent of the countdown timer. The viewing area is about four miles due west of our current location on launchpad 39A. Separating it and the pad are bayous and marshes that are fed from the Indian River farther to the west. The flat terrain provides an unobstructed view of the spectacle that's about to unfold on this beautiful day.

Kanga notices a man next to him dressed in the black cassock of a Roman Catholic monsignor. Father Bob, who has made the trip here all the way from the Vatican, turns to Kanga, says hello, and asks, "Who do you know on the flight?" After they figure out that they are both my guests, they exchange stories of how they met Carmel and me. Kanga shares with Father Bob the significance of the obstacles I overcame to get accepted to test pilot school and into the astronaut program. Although Father Bob knows some of the story, Kanga puts it in terms of his perspective as a military pilot. Kanga remarks that my persistence got me to the footsteps of my dream to launch into space.

Father Bob politely reminds Kanga of God's role in the journey. Kanga agrees and quotes his favorite Bible verse, Philippians 4:13: "I can do all things through Christ who strengthens me," he says, then he adds his own motto, "Your attitude determines your altitude." Father Bob then shares my favorite verse of Scripture with Kanga, Romans 8:28: "And we know that all things work together for good to them that love God, to them who are the called according to His purpose."

*Discovery's* countdown timer clicks below T-minus six minutes. The seven of us inside the spacecraft limit our conversations to what it takes to get the job done. We have practiced the choreography of our part in getting this rocket off the ground so many times we could do it in our sleep. The countdown timer seems to be accelerating in its free fall to zero.

Carmel and the boys have settled into their spot near the edge of the roof of the Launch Control Center. Everyone is laser-focused on what's about to happen. My seventeen-year-old son Joseph feels the intensity building. He notes that the clock is ticking to a huge situation that no one in our family has any control over. As the countdown clock clicks below T-minus four minutes, he trusts that every one of the hundreds of engineers and technicians who worked on *Discovery* all got it right.

As the countdown timer clicks below two minutes remaining to launch, a female voice from the LCC transmits, "*Discovery*, close and lock your visors and initiate oh-two flow." Just as we've done hundreds of times in the simulator, we close our helmet visors, cutting ourselves off from the cabin atmosphere. With the flip of a switch on each of our space suits, cool oxygen flows into our helmets. Once we all are flowing oxygen to our suits, the next call we hear is, "GLS is go for auto sequence start," which means the computers on board *Discovery* are controlling the spacecraft and everything looks good.

Moments after the countdown timer descends below ten seconds to go, I feel vibrations developing into a rumble that seem to be rapidly approaching us from below. The digital engine display on all three main engines rises to 100 percent. Our pilot, Hock, says calmly, "Three at a hundred. Hang on." I raise my left arm and point my wrist mirror toward *Discovery's* overhead windows. In the reflection, I see towering white steam from the main engine's exhaust billowing behind us against the backdrop of the Florida coast.

Although I can't see them from my vantage point, bricks are blowing out from the launchpad at supersonic speeds. Some are ripping through the launch perimeter fence, some are being lodged into various surrounding structures, and others are flying off into the Florida swamplands never to be seen again. Structural fatigue from the many previous launches from this pad has finally reached its limit.

Carmel, our boys, and all the other family members on the roof of the LCC watch as the white steam slowly billows out from below our spacecraft. Friends from my Air Force years, including Gilly and Tav, and many other friends and family from other viewing areas are also transfixed on this one small historic jump-off point. Even my high school football coach Tony DeMatteo is on hand to take in the spectacle. From the vantage point of the distant observers, the shuttle lumbers slowly off the pad as the countdown timer clicks to zero. Over loudspeakers, the official NASA launch announcer proclaims, "Booster ignition and liftoff of shuttle *Discovery*. *Ganbatte kudasai*—best of luck to the International Space Station's newest laboratory!"

*Carmel Garan and sons watch the launch of space shuttle Discovery
from the roof of the Launch Control Center at the Kennedy Space
Center in Florida on May 31, 2008. Left to right: Joseph Garan,
Jake Garan, Carmel Garan, Ronnie Garan.* Credit: NASA

From our perspective, we spring from the launchpad as if the entire shuttle has just been released from a giant slingshot. We are going somewhere, and we are going there fast. The launchpad disappears quickly below us as we leap into the sky. Light streams into the cockpit as *Discovery* rolls to put us on the correct trajectory to rendezvous with the ISS. Mark transmits, "Houston, *Discovery*, roll program." I can hear the vibration of the engines in his voice. At this moment, the space station is passing the northern end of the eastern seaboard about 210 miles southeast of Halifax, Nova Scotia, traveling northeast at five miles a second. We will spend the next two days catching up to the ISS.

On the roof of the LCC, Carmel takes her hands off the shoulders of our sons, raises her fists in the air, and lets out a spontaneous, "Woo-hoo!"

*Discovery's* digital clock is now counting up. As it passes thirty seconds, we are heading straight up at 600 miles per hour and accelerating rapidly. I watch as all three engine displays decrease, indicating that they are temporarily reducing thrust to slow our acceleration to ensure that we do not rip the orbiter apart by exceeding the dynamic pressure limits as our velocity approaches the speed of sound.

From his viewing location on the NASA causeway, JP Reilly, one of several of my Air Force friends, watches the rising column of white "smoke" as it continues accelerating upward. He can't help but think back to his time in Saudi Arabia during Desert Storm watching US Patriot missiles launching to intercept incoming Scud missiles, hoping and praying that they found their prey. This time he's not watching machines of war dueling in hypersonic jousts. He's watching seven humans ascend beyond the limits of our world for the benefit of all.

Approaching two minutes into the flight, we are already twenty-two miles high. The solid rocket boosters have completed their job of getting us out of the thickest part of the atmosphere. Right on cue, I see a bright flash through both the starboard and port windows as the rocket boosters separate. Without the boosters, it feels as though we transitioned from traveling on a bumpy gravel road, which shook us and bounced us around the cockpit, to a smooth road that permits us to really punch the accelerator now!

Somewhere in my brain, a subroutine starts running based on the acceleration I'm feeling. As our acceleration continues, we are all being pushed down into our seats more and more. Our displays indicate that at the moment, we are traveling at 13,000 miles per hour, and the velocity is increasing rapidly. But my brain is extrapolating relative speed, not in numbers but in something else, maybe in relation to flying a jet at the speed of sound, or twice the speed of sound, or the speed of a bullet. There's nothing with which to compare the acceleration I'm feeling. I instinctively know that we are traveling at an incomprehensible speed—ludicrous speed.

But I'm also aware that *speed is life*. The faster we fly, the more options we will have if something goes wrong. I continually update our plan if we are to lose an engine, or two, or three. At the moment, if we lose an engine, we can make it across the ocean and land in Zaragoza, Spain. The mood on the flight deck is determined focus. All four of us are concentrating, monitoring, and planning. If something goes wrong, it will go wrong fast and we will only have moments to react.

As we pass an altitude of fifty miles, Mike Fossum breaks the tension when he calls over the intercom from the middeck, "You have three people on the flight deck that need to do a big high five." Fifty miles is the altitude at which first-time fliers become certified astronauts. The first-time fliers on the middeck, Aki and Taz, have already exchanged their high fives. On the flight deck, Karen, Hock, and I, now officially "flown" astronauts, also happily comply. I turn to Karen as we high-five with our gloved hands. Best I can do with Hock is give him a strong pat on his shoulder—strong enough that he can feel it through his space suit but not so hard that it causes him to hit a switch or the controls.

The acceleration continues to the point where we are all being pushed into our seats at a force of three times our weight. Again, I watch as the engines throttle back, this time to keep us from exceeding three g's. We are approaching the moment when all three engines will shut down. It is critically important that they all cut off at the exact moment needed to ensure the proper trajectory for our rendezvous with the ISS.

Eight and a half minutes after the launch, the engines abruptly shut down, precisely according to plan. We all instantaneously transition from three g's to weightlessness. It's as if the elephant that was sitting on my chest suddenly decided to get off me. I suppress the bubbling awareness that my lifelong dream of flying in space has just come true! There's still too much to do.

When we are safely in orbit and on a good path toward the ISS, I unstrap and float out of my seat. I lightly grab the back of Hock's seat to stabilize my ascent as I twist to face backward. In what seems like slow motion, I gently glide through the artificial atmosphere of the flight deck toward the aft control panel, which contains the controls for the doors to the payload bay, where we store large equipment. Right now, the doors are cocooning our primary cargo, the Japanese Laboratory. It is now Karen's and my job to open up that payload bay. *I'm in space! I made it! I'm really in space*, I think as I grab on to the control panel to stop my motion.

I float up to the overhead windows above the flight deck to get a quick peek. There she is—Earth. I have a view of the planet looking almost straight down at the surface. The view is a little disappointing. Years of hearing how wonderful the planet looks from space have burdened me with some lofty expectations. I just feel like I'm looking out of the window of a jet flying at a very high altitude. *Was this whole, long, difficult journey just for this?*

Karen joins me at the control panel, and after moving a few switches and entering some commands to the onboard computers, the massive payload bay doors start to open. As they do, soft blue light floods the bay. Shortly, everything in that bay, including the Japanese Laboratory, is bathed in earthshine, light reflected from the planet. The earthshine fills me with anticipation for what may be next. The farther the payload bay doors open, the wider the view of the planet becomes. As the doors near the full-open position, the horizon comes into view. An iridescent, incredibly thin blue line separates the ocean from pitch-black space. At this moment, my perspective pivots abruptly. I no longer feel that I'm looking down from a jet flying at high altitude. I'm looking at a planet, a planet that I, Karen, and the rest of the crew are no longer on. A planet in space.

✦

After many hours, everyone is settling in nicely. But we're all exhausted from a long day that started on the surface of Earth and ended in this amazing but hostile environment. This is a strange new existence. We all had an extremely abrupt entry into this new weightless world. It was an attack on the senses. Everything feels new and exciting. In this new existence, we can throw out all those silly rules we have on Earth—like you can't sleep on the wall.

As it's time to get to sleep, each of us scopes out a spot to attach our sleeping bags to. On the forward wall of *Discovery's* middeck stand rows of lockers. This looks like as good a spot as any. I affix my sleeping bag to one of the lockers and climb inside. After what seems like about thirty minutes since I started the journey toward sleep, I notice that the rough inside of my bag is rubbing against my arms and legs as I move up and down like a sea buoy. To my right, Taz seems sound asleep. To my left, Karen fidgets out the last remnants of an incredible day. I feel a battle going on within me between the restless pent-up energy of the most uniquely exhilarating day of my life and the sedative side effects of a shot of the antinausea medicine Phenergan that Aki injected into my right butt cheek an hour ago. Looks like the Phenergan will win out as the interior lights on *Discovery's* middeck dim while I drift off to yet another boundaryless world.

Today, June 2, has lived up to its hype as being the busiest day of our mission so far. Since we arrived in space two days ago, we have conducted maneuvers to get on the correct path to catch up with the ISS. Mike and I have also prepared our space suits and tools for our first spacewalk, which is planned for tomorrow.

Hock calls out, "There she is!"

I float over to a window and see what looks like a bright star—a bright star that will be our home for the next eight days.

As we close in on the ISS, the enormous structure takes shape. It reminds me of an X-wing fighter from the movie *Star Wars*. At this distance, the massive solar arrays serve as the wings of the starfighter. The closer we get, the more impressive this magnificent home in the heavens appears.

We arrive 600 feet beneath the ISS and execute a 360-degree flip under it so that its crew can take detailed technical photos of the thermal protection tiles on *Discovery's* belly. After completing the maneuver, Mark manually flies *Discovery* up in front of the space station and slowly backs in.

Just entering into orbital sunrise, 210 miles above the South Pacific, Karen calls out, "Eight inches," followed quickly by Hock adding, "Point oh-nine." *Discovery's* docking port is presently eight inches away from the ISS docking port, and we are closing in at .09 feet per second. About a second after Karen calls out, "Two inches," we all hear and feel a "thump, thump, thump," indicating that the two vehicles have captured each other. Aki calls out, "Capture light," indicating that *Discovery's* onboard computers agree that we are captured. Hock transmits over the radio, "Houston and Station, capture confirmed."

All of us on the crew sigh in relief. After traveling almost a million miles to catch up with the ISS, our tolerance for docking was only plus or minus three inches. We also each give Mark a high five for a job well done as ISS crew member Garrett Reisman rings the ship's bell on board the station while announcing over the radio, "*Discovery* arriving." Although we're captured, we're not quite docked, and we still have a great deal of work to do before we can equalize the air pressure between the two vehicles and open the hatches.

Once everything is set and we open the hatch to the space station, Mark calls over to the ISS crew through the hatch, "Hey, you guys looking for a plumber?"

We're carrying spare parts for the space station's broken toilet. We each take turns floating through the hatch from the small, cramped space of *Discovery's* middeck to the relatively spacious accommodations of the ISS. Each of us is greeted with a hug from Garrett and Russian cosmonauts Sergey Volkov and Oleg Kononenko, all of whom I've met before. There's a constant stream of greetings in both English and Russian. It is really wonderful to see these guys again. I think they're happy to see us too since it means their broken toilet is one step closer to being fixed. As soon as our orbital reunion is over, Mike and I begin transferring all of our gear and space suits into the station's airlock in preparation for tomorrow's spacewalk. When the time comes, we will seal off the airlock from the rest of the ISS and exit through its hatch into space for those "walks."

Once everything has been loaded into the airlock and as we approach the end of our long day, we start a routine called "campout" that we will continue on each of the three space-walks we will conduct on this mission. Campout entails me and Mike locking ourselves in the airlock the night before a spacewalk. Sealed in there, we will then lower the air pressure to reduce the chance of getting the bends during the next day's walk.

Spending an extended amount of time before the spacewalk at reduced air pressure helps purge some of the nitrogen from our bodies. This happens while we prepare our space suits and tools and while we sleep. The purging of nitrogen is not unlike what we did during the NEEMO 9 mission prior to returning to the surface of the ocean, but this time, instead of returning to sea-level pressure, we are going to a much lower pressure.

In accordance with our planned routine, as we are winding down for the day and setting up our "campsite" for the night, we play Pink Floyd's *The Dark Side of the Moon* on our iPod-driven speakers. When we wake up tomorrow, we will switch the mood and play Led Zeppelin as loud as we can stand as we prepare to go out the door into the vacuum of space. For some reason, Led Zeppelin has become our out-the-door theme music of choice. It doesn't matter what Led Zeppelin songs we will listen to as long as we hear "Kashmir" before we head out into the great unknown.

✦

"Hey, Ron, comm check," transmits Mark Kelly the next day over the ISS intercom system, which my space suit is presently tied into.

"Loud and clear," I respond as I wonder how long I've been asleep.

Hours ago, after listening to the obligatory "Kashmir," we suited up with the intent to head out the door. Shortly after we were all "buttoned up" in our respective space suits, Mike experienced a problem that prevented him from communicating with mission control. This means a delay while mission control tries to figure out what's going on. This also means some downtime for me, which apparently led to a micronap.

I took this nap right before potentially undertaking the most incredible thing I can ever imagine—stepping out into the vacuum of space for the first time! *How is that possible? Where was this ease to fall asleep the last two nights when I really needed it?* Except for the first night, I have not really been able to sleep in this weightless environment. I am so tired right now that I'm not sure I will be able to accomplish my tasks outside. I hope my fatigue doesn't lead me to do something stupid.

With Mike's communication problem fixed, Mark, Garrett, and Taz detach me from the wall and stuff me into a part of the airlock called the "crew lock." Mike is already in there, shoved in headfirst. I go in feetfirst, then the guys wedge in all of the equipment we're taking out with us. When everything is in, there's no room left to move. Mark closes the hatch, sealing us off from the rest of the space station. All that's left to do before we can open it and head outside is reduce the crew lock air pressure to vacuum.

Initially, the air inside the crew lock is pumped back into the station, but below a certain pressure, the rest of the air is vented out into space. When the air pressure inside the crew lock is reduced to zero, Mike receives "the go" to open the hatch. With a turn of a crank and a yank, the hatch opens inward. Cool blue earthshine floods the crew lock, bringing with it space itself. At least, that's what it feels like. Technically, we are already on our spacewalk even though we're both still inside the space station.

After we make some final checks, I hear Hock transmit over the radio, "OK, boys, you ready to rock and roll?" Mike responds, "We're ready to rock and roll," and with that, he heads out through the hatch. I watch as his feet retreat away from me, out of my field of view. With Mike outside, I now have the room to flip over and point my head toward the hatch. I can now make my way to the source of the earthshine. I slide over the open hatch, which is filled with the glowing blue Earth. I start handing our equipment out to Mike, who is hanging on to the bottom of the ISS.

When everything but me is outside, it's my turn. The fatigue I felt earlier evaporates as thoughts and emotions bombard me. I need to block out everything but the task at hand. I'm about to leave our artificial home and immerse myself in space. Mike, being the "old head," having gone on three previous spacewalks, feels the need to give me some words of advice: "Ronnie, don't look down."

I don't have a choice but to look down. Down is the way out. *Just do it like we've done hundreds of times before in training,* I think. But this time there's no bottom of a pool six feet below. Earth is 240 miles below me, sliding by silently at five miles a second. Everything feels so unreal, as if I'm watching it all unfold in a movie.

Now comes the moment of truth. I reach through the hatch with my left hand and find an exterior handrail exactly where I expected it. I pull my head and shoulders through the hatch.

The rest of my body slides through the circular opening, which is the doorway to our orbital construction site. As I move farther out, I transition my grip to another handrail farther from the hatch opening. My feet slide through the hatch, and I apply a slight rotational force to the handrail, which rotates my feet down toward Earth. The horizon spins left, placing more sky below my feet than over my head.

I experience a surreal sensation of imbalance. Sights, sounds, and emotions that seem otherworldly bombard me. The foundation of my concept of reality is being challenged by a life-and-death here and now. Everything seems out of place. I'm leaving the familiar behind and pressing into a dangerous unknown. I'm now face-to-face with Mike, both of us hanging from handrails on the bottom of the ISS. I can't actually see Mike's face since both of our gold reflective visors are down, protecting our eyes from the harsh daylight side of the orbit.

After we both check each other over to make sure that nothing dislodged as we exited through the airlock hatch, Mike and I separate to perform tasks on different parts of the space station. My first task is to climb to the top of the truss, the station's backbone. It's a 365-foot-long rectangular structure, jam-packed with all kinds of equipment, that stretches out on either end of the station. Attached to the truss are the station's massive solar arrays that sweep out like giant wings. Once I climb my way to the top, I have to unbolt a large boom and hand it off to the ISS's robotic arm that Aki and Karen are operating. We will use it after undocking to inspect *Discovery's* thermal protection system, and later, we will take the boom back to Earth.

Hand over hand, I make my way to the top of the ISS. I've practiced taking this path dozens of times before in a giant pool known as the Neutral Buoyancy Lab, where we practice spacewalking. But in the pool, there's an up and a down. The gravity vector, which always points toward the bottom of the pool, keeps us oriented. Here, there is no up or down. A critical piece of my

*Ron Garan on a spacewalk during the STS-124 mission.* Credit: NASA/Fossum

internal navigation system is missing. Making matters worse, there's that 240-mile drop to the bottom of this "pool." I'm not concerned about falling to Earth. Intellectually, I know that I am already falling toward it.

Mike and I, the entire ISS, and everyone in it are falling toward Earth. But because we are also traveling across Earth at an incredible speed, we're not getting any closer to Earth in our free fall. Earth is curving away from us at the same rate that we are falling toward it.

I arrive at the top of the truss with the exhilaration of a mountain climber reaching the summit. In every direction, I see the magnificent International Space Station. Everything is framed in the beautiful glowing Earth. The busyness of this spacewalk so far and the sheer number of tasks that are in front of us have done a good job of keeping my mind occupied; but every now and then I have a moment to attempt to take it all in and process it.

I can see all the way down the length of the 365-foot-long truss. The far end of it is as crystal clear as the part that's right in front of me. None of the light from the far side of the truss was attenuated during its journey through the vacuum of space to my eyes. It traveled through nothingness. My present visual perspective of reality is not being filtered. It's as if scales have fallen from my eyes and I'm seeing things clearly for the first time.

It reminds me of the time I had to pick out targets through the thick smoke of Iraqi oil fires or when I was observing schools of fish through the azure water of Conch Reef or just everyday life on Earth. Until now, I have been observing the physical world through one filter or another. Adding to this new perspective is the fact that in relation to Earth, my point of view is changing at five miles per second. When we see a situation from two points of view, we can see it in stereoscopic vision. Multiple points of view allow us to then begin to see depth. I'm seeing Earth from an ever-changing point of view. I'm seeing it from another dimension. It's as if my perception of reality is being dolly zoomed.

The cinematographic technique where the camera is dollied, or rolled, back while it is zoomed in, or vice versa, comes to mind—the technique that Steven Spielberg used in *Jaws* to get the viewers' attention and broaden their perception of reality. The term can also be used as an analogy. If we dolly zoom a situation, we zoom out to the widest perspective possible while we also focus on the worm's-eye details on the ground. An additional consideration of a dolly zoom is looking at a situation over the longest time span possible without losing the importance of each individual moment. In other words, we're not overly focusing on the short term and ignoring the long term or vice versa.

Now I am seeing the world in the widest perspective possible for me at this moment. Even from here, I can actually see a familiar big bend in the Euphrates River below. From this altitude, the bend looks tiny. But even so, I can identify that river bend as our roll-in point on the first daylight raid of Baghdad seventeen years ago. Zoom in, and everything in that conflict is all important—the violence, destruction, the mission, self-sacrifice, and camaraderie. Zoom out, and all that blurs into insignificance. Dolly zoom, and both perspectives are appropriate and integrated. Depth is added to the situation. It is no longer two-dimensional—no longer simply us versus them, good versus evil.

With the boom unbolted, Aki, using the ISS's robotic arm, backs it away from the truss. Other than cleaning up my worksite and packing up, my first task is complete. It's now on to *Discovery*'s payload bay to help prepare the Japanese module for extraction and installation. Retracing my "steps" back down to the underside of the space station, I slowly make my way toward *Discovery*, which is docked to the forwardmost part of the ISS.

The sun has set, and I'm almost at the shuttle. I climb "down" the docking port and have one hand on the ISS and one hand on the shuttle. The entire payload bay is filled with the massive Japanese Laboratory, referred to as the JEM, short for "Japanese Experiment Module." It's also nicknamed "Kibo," which means "hope" in Japanese. When we install it later today, it will be the largest part of the station. Kibo is almost thirty-seven feet long and weighs more than 35,000 pounds. Attached to its silver metallic frame is its own robotic arm. Future crews will use the laboratory to conduct scientific experiments inside and outside of the ISS to help us better learn how to live and work in space and to improve life on Earth.

Yesterday's spacewalk went great, and we successfully added the JEM to this orbiting outpost. Earlier today, we opened the hatch to the JEM and all of us explored it. I now have a couple of minutes of free time before we need to start campout in preparation for tomorrow's spacewalk. I look out the big windows of the newly installed laboratory and do some earth gazing.

I have no idea what part of Earth we're over, so I look at a flight path program on an ISS laptop to determine our location. We have just crossed the West Coast of Africa, and our path will take us over Rwanda. In the distance, I can see the lush green of the Land of a Thousand Hills.

Moments later, Lake Kivu floats by. I see the rolling hills surrounding the lake through smoky haze and smoke from crop fires rising up, seemingly to the limits of the atmosphere. I try to pinpoint an orphanage I visited on the lakeshore, but I can't make it out through the smoke. A couple of years ago, I was there as part of a combined Engineers Without Borders and Manna Energy Foundation development trip that ultimately provided clean drinking water for the orphanage and electricity for a nearby hospital. I think of the kids I met in the orphanage and my time in Rwanda.

I stayed in the capital city of Kigali my first night before heading out into the countryside. I distinctly remember checking into the Hôtel des Mille Collines, the establishment featured in the movie *Hotel Rwanda*. I felt a barely perceptible undertone of the collective horror, shame, pain, trauma, and guilt from the genocide that occurred in the country in 1994. It seemed to hang over it like a sorrowful mist. Going into the lush and fertile countryside, the next day I was struck by the incredible contradiction between the beauty of the country and the beauty of the people and their horrible past. How could the genocide have possibly happened?

Looking out at beautiful Earth from the vantage point of orbit, I again feel an incredible, and I'll add sobering, contradiction that fills me with an intense sense of injustice. From here, I see beauty, but I also see the smoke-filled effects of humanity. If I dolly zoom, I see a different contradiction—people in destitute poverty working day and night barely eking out an existence. But I also see these same people filled with happiness and generosity.

I remember seeing lush and fertile hills teeming with all kinds of fruit, flowers, and animals, but I also remember seeing a memorial I visited near a hospital where the skulls of countless genocide victims were lined up row after row. I remember seeing the small chapel where I gave a presentation about space exploration to a group of schoolchildren. That chapel was the site of a massacre during the genocide. Bullet holes and bloodstains were still visible on its concrete walls.

These are not isolated scenes. These are just a few of the many examples of the incredible injustice that exists on the planet below. Over 5,000 children die every day from waterborne disease on that planet—children that we have the power to save and the responsibility to protect. Facts like these make us look ridiculous from space. *Why are we OK with the status quo? Why are we not all filled with outrage? Why do we not have the courage to rise above the walls we've built that don't protect us but only isolate us?* The injustice and suffering that we allow on our planet infuriates me and fills me with deep sorrow. *Why do so-called evolved modern humans allow that? Why is it so easy to turn a blind eye?*

Later in the week, in our last campout of the mission in preparation for our third and final spacewalk, I think about the past few days. Each morning before heading out into the great void, the music of Led Zeppelin has flashed me back to my days playing football when we would scream Led Zeppelin loud enough for our ears to bleed before heading out of the locker room onto the gridiron of conflict. It was a ritual designed to prepare us for an entirely new perspective—a perspective shift from the routine here and now to one where heightened awareness and heightened physical performance were required for success. This is true in our spacewalk preparation as well.

With Pink Floyd's *The Dark Side of the Moon* gently leading us toward pre-sleep relaxation now, I begin taking a multivitamin. It is truly a process, just as using the toilet is a process, but I'll leave that unpleasant description out. As for the vitamin, I first use a straw to sip some water from a bag. Then I open my lips to insert the pill, but as I do, water starts to float out of my mouth. Unlike on Earth, where I sip some water then insert the pill, here, I find out the hard way, I must put the pill in first to avoid sending liquid floating off in multiple directions. Gravity doesn't pool the water in my mouth below my lower lip like it does on Earth. This is just one of the many things to get used to here.

After I successfully take the vitamin, Mike and I climb into our respective sleeping bags. It feels surreal trying to fall asleep while floating in a bag that's traveling around Earth every ninety minutes. Adding to the surrealism is the awareness that when we wake up in the morning, we will slap on our space suits and yet again head out into space. I still have not yet figured out how to sleep in weightlessness.

My problem is that my head settles into an uncomfortable position that I can't avoid. For my entire life, gravity has gently pressed my head into a comfortable pillow. Now, gravity has abandoned me. Up here, there's no use for pillows. As we both try desperately to fall asleep, I continue a habit that began shortly after we arrived in this new existence, thinking to myself if I fall asleep right now I will get "X" hours of sleep before we have to get up. Right now, that "X" is about six hours.

A few minutes after I close my eyes, I notice a streak of light that seems to be moving rapidly. It seems as though it traveled from one side of my head to the other, a short distance from my eyes, which are still closed. The light was bright enough to catch my attention but not bright enough to hurt when looking at it. I think it had a slight yellow tint to it, although it's hard to say since it came and went so quickly. The light seems to streak by every minute or so. Then I see a point of the same light not traveling in a line but blossoming in one spot in the form of a bright fuzzy circle of light exploding into my perception. But it dissolves as fast as it arrives. Since I've noticed these lights, I've been wondering, *How am I seeing this with my eyes closed? What's going on?*

Then I remember hearing other astronauts describe experiencing similar phenomena on their space missions. There's a plausible theory that the light is caused by cosmic rays zipping through the eye and hitting the retina, giving off energy in the form of photons. Likely these rays, high-energy subatomic particles that mostly originate from outside our solar system, emanate from supernova explosions of distant stars. On Earth, to some extent, our atmosphere protects us. But not up here. *How far did these particles travel before finding my eyes? How many more high-energy particles are penetrating my skull right now, and what damage could they be doing to my core processor?* In reality, this has been happening continuously since we've been up here, but we only notice it when other more pressing things aren't distracting us and when we are in a dark place.

The luminary dance of fast-moving light seems to last for hours. I've been checking my watch periodically throughout the night to see how many hours remain before we have to get up. Then, as I feel the coming day accelerating toward me, the strange lights fade out, not because there's a reduction in the amount of supernova radiation hitting my retinas but because the flashes of light are fading out of my attention as I drift off to sleep. On some level, I am finally, fortunately, getting some kind of rest. I somehow become a silent watcher of my own sleeping mind as a dream rises up into my consciousness.

I'm standing on a mountain summit, and cold wind blows across my face. I inhale deeply, filling my lungs with cold, crisp air. I hold the thin mountaintop air in my lungs, savoring it like a fine wine. Out in the distance roll mountains beyond mountains. They appear blue, with each more distant mountain a lighter shade of blue than the one in front of it. This gradual lightening continues ridgeline after ridgeline far out into the distance until the distant mountains dissolve into the same pale blue as the sky. I stare out into that blue abyss where rock and sky are one.

I slowly exhale and feel myself climbing up through the atmosphere as the mountains retreat below me. I ascend past the clouds and into orbit. I see beautiful Earth slowly turning below and the curved horizon with a glowing thin veil of blue atmosphere off in the distance. I continue to climb away from Earth, accelerating rapidly. I pass the moon, then what looks like a planet, and another, and another. It's all a blur of color and motion, and it's all beautiful. As I continue to exhale, I fly past countless stars until I see the entire Milky Way Galaxy as it too retreats away from me. Many more galaxies come into view as I continue my exponential acceleration away from everything.

The rapid pace of my motion makes all the galaxies appear to merge into one fuzzy shrinking blob of light, similar in appearance to the light flashes I experienced before I drifted off to sleep. The fuzzy blob continues to rapidly shrink to a single point. Then, as I approach the apparent space between an exhale and an inhale, the single point disappears. All that is left is silent, still, peaceful darkness. There is a familiarity to this "place." It almost feels like I've been here before. *Am I still moving? What does the word "moving" even mean in this matterless void without form and without name? What does it mean to move in a realm of no thing?*

I inhale and notice that I am rapidly moving toward a bright dot that blossoms into a fuzzy blob. As I dive into the blob, galaxies again go whizzing by me but this time in the opposite direction. I'm hurtling back toward the Milky Way and dive right into it as individual stars streak by. I'm decelerating as I head toward one specific star as a familiar blue planet comes into view.

I pass through the atmosphere and am standing on the mountaintop as I approach myself still at high speed but rapidly decelerating. The disembodied part of me, the silent watcher of my dreaming mind, shrinks as I continue my inhalation and descent. The trajectory is taking me directly toward my head. My shrinking is accelerating at the same but opposite rate that speed is decelerating. I enter into the molecules of my skull and brain and continue shrinking and moving. Past the atoms. Past the ones and zeros of subatomic particles. Past what lies beyond until my inhale is complete and I am back in a silent, still, peaceful darkness. Back in a matterless void without form and without name, to a realm of no thing.

I am in the same place I was before. I have traveled in a circle. Both directions took me to the same peace, the same truth, the same unity. But I can't stay here.

I exhale for the second time, and I become aware of another dimension, a dimension of depth and height to time itself. I'm contemplating time and wondering how long does *now* last?

*What if I had only one day to live?* I wonder. If *now* is defined as one day, then I would have one *now* left in my life. If *now* is defined as one hour, I would have twenty-four *nows* left, one minute, then 1,440 *nows* remain. If the present *now* lasts for one second, then I'd have 86,400 *nows* left. If a new *now* arrives every millisecond, then I would have 86,400,000 *nows* left.

In my hypothetical twenty-four-hour remaining life span, as I get closer to the end of my life, if I continually reduce the duration of *now*, then I would never reach the moment of death. I would be immortal. Obviously, the human mind is not normally capable of functioning on excessively small time scales, but nonetheless, time can be cut into an infinite number of slices; and on a scale that's beyond the physical dimension, each moment has an infinite vertical dimension. Time, as I experience it when I'm awake, flows in a line between past and future. But it also flows in a line perpendicular to the line between past and future. The intersection of these two lines is *now*. *Could the now be a perpendicular doorway between the finite linear timeline that we "know" so well and the infinite exponential existence that is usually just beyond our perception? Could it be that there is only one indivisible now that has ever existed or ever will exist? Could it be that linear time is what the eternal now looks like when it's filtered through our finite minds? Is it yet another filter partially masking reality like the azure water of Conch Reef?*

As I head back out to the vast cosmic scale of galaxy clusters, the *now* gets longer and longer. A new *now* arrives every millisecond, then second. But the farther out my exhale takes me on the physical scale, the *now* slows further and further. Each *now* is passing by a day at a time, a week, a month, a year at a time. If the duration of each *now* continues to increase, I will never reach the point where an exhale becomes an inhale. I will remain in an eternal exhale. I enter back into the void beyond the physical universe, and each *now* passes so slowly that it has no conceptual meaning. Time has disappeared into the void as well. I am no longer exhaling or inhaling. I am back in the dimension "between." How long have I been here? What does that question even mean?

I inhale time back into existence as I, again, head back toward a point of light that I *now* know contains the physical universe. As I return to the mountaintop, each *now* passes at a dizzying speed. The farther I dive into the microworld of subatomic particles, the faster time itself passes. Each *now* is cut into smaller and smaller pieces. If *now* continues to be cut into ever smaller pieces, I will be caught in an eternal inhale. But I do arrive back at the point where the unimaginably large meets the unimaginably small and the unimaginably fast merges with the unimaginably slow. It's a singularity where all dimensions fold into one. A singularity where the energy of inhalation and exhalation form one perfect continuous circle. Where existence is a gently curving line leading us back to our one true home. Where there is no up or down, forward or backward, slow or fast. All that remains is pure existence, pure freedom, pure love.

I feel as if I have entered into eternity. I don't mean a place where time goes on forever but a placeless existence of no time, where past, present, and future are one. An existence where the words "birth" and "death" have no meaning. A state where I just *am*. A state of pure, still, peaceful existence. Timeless contentment where everything merges into nothing and nothing merges into everything.

In this dark stillness I wonder, *Am I alone? Is my awareness all that exists? Are there others like me out here somewhere?* There appears to be no one but me here, but I know that I am not alone. Others inhabit this nonspace. I feel wrapped in warmth and well-being, protected and cared about. I feel a constant sustaining and protective energy flowing to me. Although I acknowledge that I cannot see others, they exist here, whatever "here" means. There is an unbreakable force that ties us together. In this boundaryless existence, I understand how everything is intimately tied together and dependent on each other without losing the realization of my own distinct existence. *What would happen if I exhale again?*

All that is me that now drifts in an existence beyond the senses, beyond seeing, and beyond hearing knows, on some level, that I'm still rooted in the material here and now. I'm sleeping in an airlock on a space station orbiting the planet we call Earth. I ponder what the vacuum of space really means. At present, the ISS and shuttle are engulfed in nothingness. Even though we are still close to Earth, we have entered into the predominant state of the universe, a state of nothingness. There's vastly more empty space in the universe than there is matter. It's a wonder that the same can be said for our own bodies. Our atoms and the space between them mimic the marvelous structure of the universe. I rest in silence in this realization in the space between an inhale and exhale.

Nevertheless, rising up through the stillness, I hear a dull tone like a single note. Slowly, it becomes louder, as if it's approaching me. I'm hearing music. I recognize the tune from somewhere, but I can't place it. I hear childlike voices singing individual letters. It's a happy melody, but there's a silliness to it. Then it dawns on me. It's *The Mickey Mouse Club* theme song. My eyes open as a blurry airlock slowly comes into focus. Across from me, I see an unhappy Mike Fossum as we hear over the radio the voice of capsule communicator Shannon Lucid, the "capcom." "Good morning, *Discovery*, and a special good morning to you, Mike."

At this moment, gathered in mission control in Houston, are representatives of the Texas A&M Corps of Cadets with their impeccably pressed uniforms and spit-polished shoes. Even Reveille, the Texas A&M rough collie mascot, is there. They are all there because today is the day that Mike's wake-up music was scheduled to be played. But instead of the Texas A&M "Aggie War Hymn," what all the Aggies gathered in mission control were there to partake in, someone on the crew who will remain nameless—Mark Kelly—decided at the last minute to substitute the fight song for the Mickey Mouse theme song.

Looking at Mike Fossum, I don't think he appreciates the joke yet. I feel for him, but deep inside I get a chuckle out of it. I'm sure Mark swapped in the Mickey Mouse song to lighten the stress on his crew during this tense and challenging mission. He did it knowing that Mike has a great sense of humor, even if he's not showing it at the moment. Meanwhile, in spite of the abrupt and unexpected start to the day, Mike and I both dive straight into our spacewalk preparations.

I climb out of my sleeping bag, and with a gentle push of my finger, I fly across the airlock and grab a handrail that my iPod is tethered to. I gently hit "play" on the iPod and let it go. It floats off until it hits the limit of its tether then bounces back in the opposite direction as Led Zeppelin's "Dazed and Confused" initiates our pre-spacewalk morning routine. I think back to the vivid dream I just had and marvel at the idea that in a couple of hours, Mike and I will again depart our artificial somethingness and enter a void of complete nothingness. Like a couple of mountain climbers breaking camp for a big climb, Mike and I will make our final preparations with our tools and gear.

Many hours have passed since we've started our day. My tasks so far during this spacewalk have primarily involved unbolting a large, failed 500-pound nitrogen pump that is contained inside a box made of white fabric and installed inside the ISS truss. Now that the pump is ready to be removed, I have to strap my feet to the end of the station's robotic arm and drag the module out of the truss. I position myself to slide my toes under a bar at the front of the foot restraint. After a struggle that causes me to sweat, I position my feet under the toe restraints.

I rotate my left heel outward until my left boot heel locks into position with a felt but not heard click. I do the same with the right boot. Now, with the task of attaching myself to the arm complete, I pause for a second and attempt to take a deep breath. But before I can inhale fully, the expansion of my chest is stopped by the hard upper torso section of my space suit. *Taking a full breath is highly overrated,* I think, as I radio to Aki and Karen that I'm ready to go.

Aki and Karen's job is to use the ISS's robotic arm to back me away from the truss and fly me over to a storage location on the far portside of it. Far from me on the other side of the truss, I can see a barely visible, tiny white figure. At this moment, Mike is preparing the storage location for this broken pump and the new pump for its journey back here.

My feet jerk backward as Aki and Karen move the arm, with me attached to it, away from the truss. I fight the momentum that wants to pitch me forward. Extreme tension fills my back, thighs, and feet as I act as a mechanical latching device by holding on to handrails on the huge box as it's slowly retracted from an orbital home that doesn't want to let it go. After we back away from the truss a sufficient distance, the arm's motion is paused as Aki and Karen put a series of commands into the computer that will take the arm on a preplanned trajectory to the pump's new home. A few seconds later, the arm starts to propel me and the big white box I'm holding up above the ISS.

As the last remnants of light from the orbital sunset dissolve into black, and as the arm continues to propel me above the space station, I become conscious of the danger of the situation. It's not that the level of danger has suddenly increased, it's just that at the moment, my only job is to hold on to this box. Up until this point, accomplishing my tasks has taken extreme focused concentration, during which time I've had to block out of my awareness all but the task at hand. Now, with a long ride on the arm in front of me, I have almost nothing to do but think.

As the lights of the ISS retreat below me as I'm propelled into the dark, empty, cold universe above, I feel surrounded by danger on all sides. There are literally dozens of things that could kill me in a split second. I start running through a few of these scenarios in my mind.

For instance, if something as small as a speck of paint, traveling at hypersonic speed, happens to hit my space suit, it would, no doubt, rip through the suit and ignite the 100 percent oxygen environment inside it, ending my life in a fiery explosion. If I somehow survive the explosion and I'm not ripped into a million pieces, I would die within seconds after being exposed to the vacuum of space. Seeing the countless small craters in the ISS, caused by the impact of minute orbital debris, makes this scenario a little too probable for me to ignore. If this were to happen, it would happen without warning. Eventually, I remind myself that there's no use worrying about something I have no control over and decide to make better use of this break in the hyperfocused action.

Approaching the top of the arc across the space station, a complete blanket of darkness envelops me. The lights of the station are far below, out of my field of view. My helmet lights are illuminating only what's right in front of me, a 500-pound box and my gloved hands that are holding it. Everything else in my field of view is just black.

While still imperceptibly moving toward my destination on the far side of the truss, I let go of the pump unit with my left hand, reach up, and turn off my helmet lights. *This was probably a bad idea*, I think, as the last remnants of my hold on the material universe, that is, my view of the box and my hands, disappears and I am completely and utterly engulfed in cold, crushing darkness. I realize that I still have a foothold on the real world when the sound of my own breath and the low hum of my space suit's fans rise into my awareness. I cling to that sound as it anchors me in a deep ocean of all that I have ever known. I feel the tops of my feet rubbing up against the inside of my boots as I float up in my suit slightly. I can feel the bars from the foot restraint digging into the top of my feet, holding me in place.

In this pitch-blackness, I have no sensation of movement other than the slight relative movement between my body, the space suit I'm wearing, and the bars of the foot restraint. Intellectually, I know that in relation to the ISS, I am traveling from one point on the truss to another in a long arc being drawn out by the motion of the station's robotic arm. Presently, I am near the apex of this arc about a hundred feet above the space station, which I trust is still there, but I would have no way of knowing if it wasn't.

In relation to Earth, my body, the robotic arm, and the entire ISS are traveling in formation together above Earth at 17,500 miles per hour. I try to wrap my mind around the concept of that speed. I think back to growing up in Yonkers and the seemingly never-ending walk from my home to my high school, which was probably about three miles. At the speed I'm presently traveling, that journey would take less than a second.

A pinpoint of light traveling very fast from left to right catches my attention and pulls me out of my sensory deprivation daydream. It is far above my head, which I guess means it's far above the ISS and far above Earth. It must be a satellite traveling at a higher orbit than the space station. Because of its higher orbit, it must still be bathed in the light of the sun, making it appear as a fast-moving star. As I keep the path of the object in my sights, many more pinpoints of light blossom into view. Then they dissolve into the true picture as the Milky Way, in all its glory, shines in stunning radiance.

It's almost as if a dimmer switch was controlling all the lights of the Milky Way—a dimmer switch that has been slowly turning brighter ever since my pupils began dilating when I turned off my helmet lights. What only moments ago was suffocating black darkness that crushed in on me from all sides, making me feel as if I were shrinking into nothing, is now replaced with the certainty of the incomprehensible vastness and grandeur of the universe. I feel myself expanding out into the beauty that is unfolding before me. For a moment, the pump and my gloves come into view, illuminated by the cool blue-tinted light of the Milky Way. Then a brighter, harsher, less beautiful light seeps in from below. I recognize it as the lights of the ISS. We are starting to approach back down to the truss.

I twist myself to look toward the direction of travel. Below, I see Mike working on the truss, a bright white humanoid form gracefully moving back and forth in fluid motion bathed in a cone of floodlights like theater spotlights highlighting a play's focal plot point. It looks like Mike has the new replacement pump ready for me to take back. My respite from deep concentration is over. It's time to get back to work.

Aki and Karen stop the arm a few feet above Mike, who positioned himself to help guide the old pump into its new home on the truss. Together, Mike and I secure the old pump to the truss and I grab the new one as Mike releases it. Now, it's time to retrace my path back to where I started, following the same arc across the ISS. As I again rise away from the station into the darkness, I see out ahead an almost imperceptible paper-thin curved grey line dissecting the darkness above and below it. We are heading toward orbital sunrise.

The higher I rise into the arc, the more perceptible the grey line becomes. It now includes bands of blue in addition to grey. But the bands are not continuous or homogenous. They are made up of many individual layers. My attention is drawn to the darkness of space directly in front of me. My gaze is drawn out into the distance. I try to focus, but there's nothing to focus on. My eyes move down and away from this infinite cave of crushing darkness revealing a faint dark grey band without shape or form as if it were blended or smudged from the infinite darkness above.

As my eyes continue down toward the horizon, I see grey band after grey band, each successively lighter and softer than the band above it, until my eyes reach a band of luminescent pale blue pinned up against a band of dark blue. These grey and blue bands are sandwiched between the pitch-black darkness of space above and another area of pitch-black darkness below. The darkness below is Earth. We must be over the ocean because I don't see any artificial light.

Now, between the dark blue band and the dark Earth, another band has formed. It's a brilliantly thin layer with a yellow-orange hue signaling the impending arrival of light from our star that will cast out the darkness from the surface of Earth. I can now make out a fiery band of bright red closest to the planet. Scattered within the red band are areas of black, the silhouettes of tiny thunderstorms penetrating up into the awakening atmosphere. All of the bands seem to be expanding in width and increasing in warmth. Sprinkled throughout this marvelous scene are subtle highlights of pure white light, a hint at what's about to happen.

In a flash, a yellow-orange laser beam pierces my visor and impacts the back of my retinas. It is blinding, and I can feel the intensity of the light rapidly increasing. I have to look away. As I do, I see the band of blue exploding with bright colors—red, purple, orange, green, and turquoise—each in turn becoming dominant.

Then, as my body continues to travel eastward at five miles a second, propelling me out from behind the shadow of Earth into the light of our star, brilliant, pure white light streams out from behind Earth. I am engulfed in colorless radiant light that seems to be emanating out of cold emptiness and traveling through cold nothingness. The light streams over and around me, and a hint of peaceful serenity awakens inside me. The star at the center of our solar system is now fully out from behind Earth's horizon, continuing its ascension to its rightful place above, bathing the highly reflective metallic ISS below me in radiant white light and Earth below in light that stretches from a palette of yellow to red. The pure white light is bouncing off the station and out into every direction.

Beyond my view of the sparkling ISS, a rocky coastline on an unrecognized continent drifts into view—sunlight bathing newly awakened snowcapped mountains into the glory of a new day. Framing the snowcapped mountains are glowing red-orange clouds stretching out as dotted lines hugging the coast. The clouds are almost pink or maybe the color of smoked salmon. I imagine there are people down there somewhere just starting their day who are also witnesses to this exquisite beauty from a different but no less compelling perspective. I wish we could share notes.

The complex immensity of the ISS against the backdrop of our indescribably beautiful Earth 240 miles below thrusts me into a singularity. The entire universe peels away; the blanket of danger, the thoughts of upcoming tasks, the feelings of fatigue, the excitement of being in space are all displaced by a singular vision of beauty. Thoughts of any kind are rendered speechless as an inner stillness takes hold of me. From deep within this stillness, a subtle joy starts to bubble up within me that explodes in a sensation of peaceful love and appreciation.

Certainty floods me, a certainty that seems not to be derived from thoughts but from something deeper, truer, more primordial. Deep within me, I experience, in an intense wave of love and gratitude, the unity of our planet and every living thing on it. For a few moments, all that exists is the beauty that is before me. I bask in it but soon feel myself being reluctantly pulled away by the noise of my own thoughts.

An inner voice like an alarm clock sounds off, reminding me of all I need to accomplish when my joyride on the arm ends. But as my mind recovers from the shock of a few moments immersed in complete awe and wonder, I'm also filled with gratitude for the International Space Station itself—not necessarily for the technical accomplishment it represents, which places it among the greatest technological accomplishments in human history, but for something much more important. The ISS, in a very real way, represents what we as humans can accomplish when we acknowledge and embrace the true nature of our unity.

The fifteen nations that make up the partnership that constructed the ISS have not always been the best of friends. Some were on opposite sides of the Cold War, opposite sides of the Space Race. Some fought wars against one another and purposely targeted civilians in an attempt to break one another's will. I think back to all those years I spent training to fight the Russians and the times I sat nuclear alert, waiting for the balloon to go up. I think back on my visit to East Berlin and the face of that young mother who couldn't follow me back through Checkpoint Charlie into freedom. I think back on my time in combat. The dark ugliness of a landscape of violence and burning oil fires, in contrast to what is presently before my eyes, fills me with sadness for how off course we are from reaching our true destiny.

I believe all the nations of the ISS partnership agreed to set aside their differences and accomplish this amazing achievement in space because they got a taste of the awe I'm experiencing now and they wanted more. They glimpsed the wonder and beauty of our home planet. They glimpsed this physical manifestation of our underlying unity—a unity that once experienced makes all the things we quarrel over seem trivial and tragically unnecessary. The truth that is blatantly apparent from this vantage point is that every living thing on the planet and the planet itself are inexplicably interconnected and interdependent. Humans have evolved to be the stewards of this sacred contract, and we've been sleeping on the job. What's obvious from this vantage point of physical detachment from Earth is that we are not *from* Earth, we are *of* Earth—all of us, every living creature.

✦

*The STS-124 and Expedition-17 crew members pose for a photo in the Destiny laboratory of the International Space Station. From the left (front row) are Karen Nyberg, Japan Aerospace Exploration Agency astronaut Akihiko Hoshide, Ron Garan, Mike Fossum, and Ken Ham. From the left (back row) are Russian Federal Space Agency cosmonaut Oleg Kononenko, Greg Chamitoff, Garrett Reisman, Mark Kelly, and Russian Federal Space Agency cosmonaut Sergey Volkov.* Credit: NASA

It's been a couple of hours since our spacewalk ended, and I'm alone on *Discovery's* middeck. I am out of my space suit, have cleaned myself up, changed into pants and a crew polo shirt, and want to get something to eat. My stomach is letting me know it's been a long day without any food. As I place my crew notebook on a Velcro patch on a locker in *Discovery's* middeck, the book flips open in weightlessness, exposing the inside back cover. On that page is a copy of a pencil sketch of Earth from the perspective of the surface of the moon. A fourteen-year-old boy named Petr Ginz drew it in 1942 while he was a prisoner in the Theresienstadt concentration camp in German-occupied Czechoslovakia.

*This photo that was taken aboard space shuttle Discovery during the*
*STS-124 mission shows the inside back cover of Ron Garan's crew notebook.*
*On that page is a copy of Moon Landscape, a pencil sketch of Earth from*
*the perspective of the surface of the moon drawn in 1942 by fourteen-year-old*
*Petr Ginz while he was a prisoner in the Theresienstadt concentration*
*camp in German-occupied Czechoslovakia.* Credit: NASA/Ron Garan

Theresienstadt served as a way station to the extermination camps. The sketch, called *Moon Landscape*, depicts sharp, craggy mountains reaching up from a barren lunar surface partially obscuring Earth, which hangs in the blackness of space. Africa, Europe, and the Middle East are clearly visible. I was inspired to bring this sketch with me to space when I heard that Ilan Ramon carried a copy of the drawing with him on STS-107. When the shuttle broke apart on February 1, 2003, the copy of the drawing was destroyed on what would have been Petr Ginz's seventieth birthday.

When I heard about the drawing and learned about Petr's short life, I was moved. Petr was an insatiably curious boy filled with hope for the future. He represents the best that we offer as a species. He epitomizes the innocent search for meaning and understanding that I believe is imbued in every human. We then choose what we do with that spark. Petr chose to share it with us. He continued to search and share for the rest of his life, a life that ended in Auschwitz at age sixteen.

Petr's story is also a story of what could have been. A story of loss. A life cut short because of the insanity of the human ego. On some level, I identify with Petr. Petr was born into a mixed family, as was I. According to the insane laws of the Nazis, children from mixed marriages were sent to a concentration camp at the age of fourteen. If I was born in the same town at the same time as Petr, I would have met a similar fate. I think back to the time I was attacked for my Jewish heritage. The capacity of human hatred has not changed much over the years.

But these things are not why I brought the drawing with me to space. The drawing and Petr's story struck me as a symbol of hope and the resilience of the human spirit even during the darkest times. Petr Ginz is proof that man-made walls cannot conquer the human spirit. He is proof that there exists a force infinitely stronger than the empty and false worldview that leads humans to degrade and commit violence against each other. Petr was a bright light shining in the darkness of Nazi hatred, and I wanted to bring his spirit with me to space. It serves as a source of inspiration on a very challenging mission.

With this our third and final spacewalk complete, the hardest and most demanding part of the mission is over for me. In preparation for this, my first space flight, I didn't know how I would perform. As a rookie, I worried that I would make some irreversible, catastrophic mistake—a mistake so bad it would make me wish I had never pursued becoming an astronaut. Now that the part of the mission I was most concerned about is over and everything went great, I feel deep relief and gratitude.

I am so grateful for everyone who supported me and is praying for me. It's almost as if I can feel their prayers. I think of the communities of cloistered Carmelite nuns that I have come to know over the past few years—one in New Caney, Texas, which I met through our church in Houston, where we now live, and one in Rome, Italy, which Father Bob introduced me to. Folks who devote their lives to the service of others have always fascinated me. I believe this mindset is epitomized in those nuns who remove themselves from the world to devote themselves in prayer for others. I felt their prayers during the most challenging parts of the spacewalks. I have also felt the prayers of my family and friends. Most of all, I have felt the prayers and love from Carmel, who has always been my strength, my rock that I cling to in life's storms.

My feeling of gratitude is so sublime and intense that I start to sob. Alone on the middeck of a space shuttle docked to an orbiting outpost, this combat-hardened fighter pilot and steely-eyed test pilot is crying—crying tears of gratitude. I have to abruptly pull myself together as Hock floats down from the flight deck to use the head. I'm standing between him and *Discovery's* only toilet.

"You guys ready for a little theme music?" asks Garrett Reisman moments after Hock undocked *Discovery* from the ISS.

"Yeah!" replies Hock.

Garrett, who we are bringing back to Earth now that his ISS mission is complete, hits play on his iPod, which is connected to external speakers that he set up on *Discovery's* flight deck. *Discovery* slowly backs away from the space station, accompanied by the melodic "The Blue Danube," which was the choice of another soundtrack.

With the theme from *2001: A Space Odyssey* playing in the background, Hock will fly a complete 360-degree loop over the space station. The enormous outpost is framed by a succession of breathtaking backdrops—the West Coast of South America and the Amazon jungle—and, as we approach orbital night, the station's massive solar arrays glisten with a golden glow. We all take pride in seeing the Japanese Experiment Module in its new home. The station has gotten a lot bigger and more capable because of our visit.

All of us crammed together in the flight deck bask in the glorious view and the success of our time docked to the ISS. I think back on our experience. In many ways, traveling to space was moving from one world to another. When we crashed through the interface between Earth's ocean of air and the rest of the universe, we entered into a new existence. I remember that when I left Shawbu Dhabi after Desert Storm, I was looking forward to returning to the "real world." I was yearning to break free of our self-imposed prison. I noted that our "prison" was a cordoning off of a small part of reality separating out the full richness of life. Being here has given me a broader view of the full richness of life and the reality of the world we live in.

"The Blue Danube" really is the perfect backdrop for this moment. A spaceship is an especially sterile and artificial environment. Normally, all we hear are the sounds of pumps and fans. Music is a tie back to the natural. It's a tie back to normality, back to home. I remember hearing about efforts to use music to do the same for patients in hospitals. The unnatural whirring and buzzing of machinery is the same in both alien environments.

With Johann Strauss's beautiful waltz still serenading us, the ISS is framed against Shanghai at night. The city is aglow, like a glistening jewel. Each of us has our face pressed against one of *Discovery's* windows. The whole scene below looks somehow biological. The city has glowing tentacles reaching out in all directions to other radiant cities. The scene looks like a micro-scopic photograph of nerve cells. In effect, they are. Every city is like a giant nerve cell in the brain of a superorganism called humanity. But as my gaze shifts from Earth to the infinity that lies beyond and the Milky Way comes into focus, I realize that the brain analogy does not end at the orbital perspective. It pervades the universe.

I once read that the total number of neurons in the human brain fall in roughly the same ballpark as the number of galaxies in the observable universe. On the cosmic scale, matter and dark matter are structured into stringlike filaments. Clusters of galaxies form at the intersections of these filaments. Every-thing in between is basically empty. From the cosmic perspec-tive, the structure of the universe bears a great resemblance to the structure of a human brain. It is obvious from this vantage point that everything is interdependent and as such nothing can be taken in isolation. For example, when we consider how the human brain functions, we cannot consider it as an individual organ operating in isolation inside a single cranium. We live in a complex hyperinterconnected society. Our technology has linked billions of individual brains together. Information flows from brain to brain in countless directions at the speed of light.

With our loop around the ISS complete, Hock maneuvers *Discovery* to head out into the darkness and away from the incredible outpost that served as our home for eight days, seven-teen hours, and thirty-nine minutes (but who's counting?). As the ISS shrinks to a point of light and again starts to resemble a bright star, my gaze shifts back to Earth, where we'll be in a few days, and I'm filled with the certainty that humanity is a superorganism whether we realize it or not.

✦

With my eyes closed, I lay my head back in the salty Atlantic, a liquid pillow embracing me as I just let go and float. Maybe *float* is the wrong word now that I know what it feels like to really float—to float weightless. Maybe *suspend* is more accurate. Maybe I'm suspended on a surface between an ocean of water and an ocean of air. Suspended on a surface between here and beyond, between now and then. Even though my ears are submerged, I can still hear the countless bathers and beachgoers. Their combined voices sound like a continuous buzz, suggesting that I am also suspended on a surface between me and everyone and everything else. *Is there even such a surface?*

It's mid-June, and as I float in the Atlantic Ocean fifty feet off the coast of Cocoa Beach, the sun's warmth on my face feels so good. I'm so grateful for that giant nuclear reaction at the center of our solar system. I'm so thankful that our planet is at the perfect distance for that energy to spark and sustain life. I'm so grateful that the sun is the perfect distance away for me to bask in its warmth. I feel its heat on my face, energy that has traveled ninety-three million miles through cold and empty space before arriving here on my cheeks.

My weight pushes me down into the water, and the water pushes back, keeping me floating on the surface. In a very real way, I now realize that the feeling of weight is actually the gravitational attraction of the entire planet pulling me toward the center of Earth. I can also feel the weight of the atmosphere pressing against the front of my body, as if I'm wrapped in an enormous lightweight blanket. Probably anyone could experience the sensation of the weight of the atmosphere, but it's particularly acute for me because I just spent two weeks in space without the weight of the atmosphere above me and I remember the difference.

I open my eyes and see, off to the east, a rising crescent moon set against a beautiful sunny blue sky. The faint moon unsuccessfully tries to blend in and hide in that blue. The moon looks so different now—different from this surface perspective. It's the same, yet somehow it isn't.

How will I ever fully explain what I just experienced? How can I possibly explain the constantly changing colors of Earth or the simultaneous feeling of detachment and connection while in orbit? How will I ever be able to fully describe the beauty of dancing neon curtains of green and red auroras that seemed so close I could almost reach out and touch them? How can I possibly share my memories of the glowing, iridescent emerald waters of the Caribbean or the bright tan and crimson of the Libyan coast against the deep blue of the Mediterranean? How will I be able to completely explain the majestic splendor of the snowcapped mountain ranges of the Himalayan Plateau that seemed to jut out through the limits of the atmosphere or the incomprehensible vastness of the African continent?

Will time help me process my experience? If/when time works its magic, will I be able to explain why the moon feels different now? Since returning to Earth less than twenty-four hours ago, I've already been asked countless times, "What was it like to be in space?" So far, the only response I've come up with is, "It was wonderful!"

One thing I know for sure, I appreciate life down here a lot more than I did before. Here, I am floating in an incredible ocean on an incredible planet on Father's Day after spending a couple of weeks in space with some incredible people. I am so grateful for all that we have here. I am particularly grateful for my family. It is wonderful to be here in Florida with Carmel and the boys. As a Father's Day present, our youngest son, Jake, even gave me a video he made of the launch and landing experience from his perspective. I can't imagine life being any better than it is at this moment.

My gaze fixates on the sky, a light blue canvas that mere hours ago, I and six of my friends were propelling through, riding on a high-tech fireball at hypersonic speed. From below, I'm sure we looked brighter than the brightest shooting star I counted on my way over to Operation Desert Storm. From here, at this moment, the sky looks so big, but I know that it's not. I know in a very real way that the beautiful blue does not extend very far from me, and beyond that is the cold vacuum of space. With the sound of a human beehive buzzing in my ears, I propel my mind back through that thin band of blue and back into space, back to that boundaryless world without form, and I realize that part of me never left. Floating in one of our planet's oceans, I know that I will forever remain with one foot on Earth and one foot in space—immensely grateful for both perspectives.

# CHAPTER 11

# Three Ships Pass in the Night

✦ The alarm on my NASA-issued Omega Speedmaster watch goes off at 0830 Alma-Ata Time—ALMT—on April 4, 2011. I am in bed in my assigned room at the cosmonaut crew quarters building in the Kazakh town of Baikonur. As I awake into full consciousness, the weight of this important day sinks in. This is my last day on Earth. Well, hopefully not my last, but if all goes as planned, it will be my last day on the planet for the next six months, the last time I will feel the breeze on my face or hear the birds sing during that time.

Today will be divided into two parts, delineated by 1900 ALMT. Everything up to 1900 should be leisurely and relaxed. But 1900 is *showtime*. It will be the opening bell with all actions from that point on having the expressed objective to get us off the planet.

Before lunch, I spend some time with Carmel and Jake on the grounds of the cosmonaut crew quarters facility. Together, we stroll through the renowned cosmonaut grove. Beautiful trees line either side of a stately promenade steeped in history. Each tree was planted by a cosmonaut before their flight, a Russian tradition that started with Yuri Gagarin, whose tree is the oldest in the grove. Not far from Yuri's tree stands a sapling that I planted a few days ago, adding my name to the long list of space travelers who started their journey to space from this same historic spot. As my family and I walk together, I feel deep

*Ron Garan (center) participates in the ceremonial tree-planting ceremonies
at the Cosmonaut Grove in Baikonur, Kazakhstan, on March 29, 2011.
Ron is assisted by Russian cosmonauts Aleksandr Samokutyayev (left)
and Andrei Borisenko (right).* Credit: NASA/Victor Zelentsov

gratitude for the love we share. Everything seems a little more precious. Each touch, caress, and hug carries a special sweetness. I also long to have my other two sons, Ronnie and Joseph, here, but because they're in college, they couldn't break away from their studies for such a long trip.

As Carmel, Jake, and I arrive back at the entrance to the crew quarters building, we share a private moment. In our own special way, we acknowledge the last physical contact we will have for the next half year. After we say our goodbyes and I enter the building, the countdown clock ticks closer and closer to the fateful moment, and I continue to note all the "last on Earths" I'm currently experiencing—all those things that I will not do again until I return. My last full meal on Earth is lunch with my crewmates, our backup crew, our flight doctors, and a few management personnel here in the crew quarters building. It's the typical Russian fare that falls squarely into the category of comfort food. Eating this meal has me reflecting on the fact that the most bizarre thing about preparing to launch into space is how normal everything feels. The thing that gets everyone through this intense experience is treating it as if it's routine, like any other trip. But, of course, it's not like any other trip.

After lunch, we are afforded a few hours of rest and final preparations before the real fun will begin at the Baikonur Cosmodrome launch facility, about a forty-minute drive due north. I start reflecting on the almost three-year journey to this historic launchpad. We are a few hours away from journeying in a Russian Soyuz spacecraft from the same pad where Yuri Gagarin became the first person in history to launch into space almost fifty years ago to the day. In mere hours, I, along with my Russian crewmates, will commemorate the anniversary of the day in 1961 that humanity became a species no longer confined to Earth. This fact fills me with a sense of poetry. I am the same age as Yuri's tree in the cosmonaut grove.

My personal mission began the same year when I was born on a natural spaceship called Earth, a spaceship that has been traveling through the universe for the past four and a half billion years. Now, I will again leave the cradle of humanity and step out beyond our world. I will participate in what I believe is the continuation of the story of human migration. Missions like the one I'm about to embark on are the baby steps in a journey that began 200,000 years ago in Africa, and that, starting in 1961, included the possibility for humans to migrate to the stars.

In these hours before our 1900 opening bell, as I rest in my assigned room in the crew quarters facility, I reflect on the irony of being here to launch into space from the Baikonur Cosmodrome. Baikonur is a former top-secret Soviet military installation. Despite my extensive time training with Russians, the novelty of being embedded in the Russian space program has not yet worn off. I doubt it ever will. I spent the first fifteen years of my adult life as a Cold War fighter pilot preparing to fight the Russians, my country's most menacing enemy at the time. The emotion of being a fully integrated member of a Soyuz spacecraft crew is warm and palatable. This is a glimpse into the possibilities of the human spirit when we agree to set aside our differences and work together toward something big and meaningful.

During my time working with the Russian cosmonauts, I have become filled with hope and optimism as stereotype after stereotype that I had been conditioned to apply to the Russians has fallen by the wayside, exposing that underneath, we are all simply human. I feel a deeper, larger sense of belonging, which extends to a radius of 4,000 miles, the radius of Earth. In a few hours, we will extend that radius just a little farther. I'm most looking forward to seeing Earth again from space and watching as Sasha and Andrei experience that incredible vantage point for the first time.

*April 1, 2011, three days before launch. Soyuz TMA-21 crewmates and their*
*backups ask, "What kind of world do you want?" in Russian and English.*
*Left to right: NASA astronauts Dan Burbank and Ron Garan*
*and Russian cosmonauts Andrei Borisenko, Anton Shkaplerov,*
*Aleksandr Samokutyayev, and Anatoli Ivanishin.* Credit: NASA

My Soyuz commander, Russian Air Force pilot Aleksandr Mikhailovich Samokutyayev, is a fun-loving, likable guy who goes by "Sasha." He is tall, capable, and seems to enjoy life moment by moment. Although he always appears to be looking for an angle or is concocting some scheme to get the better of a situation, I've learned to trust him. Sasha's polar opposite is our other crewmate and future ISS Expedition-28 commander, Andrei Ivanovich Borisenko. Andrei, who also was a member of the Russian military, having worked for the Russian Navy, is smaller in stature and softer in voice than Sasha. Andrei has a gentle demeanor but seems devoted to getting the job done right. I'm looking forward to leaving Earth with these guys.

My alarm wakes me from a short nap. It's 1900. Our "real" day starts now. After a snack that we're calling dinner, we meet with some of the Russian Space Agency managers before we begin the launch ceremonies. First up is the traditional signing of the doors of our crew quarters rooms. With cameras of all sorts rolling and snapping, I add my signature with a Sharpie to the dozens of previous space travelers who spent their last few days on Earth in the same room. Next, a Russian Orthodox priest smashes Sasha, Andrei, and me in the face with a holy-water-drenched brush as we receive his official blessing on behalf of the Russian Orthodox Church. This signals the start of our journey. We head down a flight of stairs and out into the Kazakh night.

As soon as we step out of the cosmonaut crew quarters building, we are met by a barrage of camera flashes of the many friends, family, and coworkers who line the path to the buses. I recognize many faces in the crowd. A constant stream of people wishes us well in two languages. Once I board the bus, I spot Carmel and Jake, who stand directly in front of my window seat. I blow them both a kiss and try to memorize their faces.

The bus pulls out of the parking lot to take us to the launch facility, and everything gets oddly quiet. The silence catches me off guard. I guess this is the traditional time for self-reflection. Outside of my window stretches pitch-blackness as we travel across the Kazakh Steppe.

As we arrive at the Baikonur launch facility, we're ushered into a room where we watch a wonderful sendoff video with messages from the friends and family of each of us on the crew. I really appreciate that. It is taking some of the sting out of the awareness of impending long-duration separation.

Not long afterward, we change into our space suits and have our last few words with the managers who represent the many people who worked to get everything ready for launch. Then we board a bus that takes us to the pad. There, a beautiful sight greets us: Our rocket is completely covered in a layer of white ice. I hear something that reminds me of whales exhaling through their blowholes. It's the rocket venting oxygen. White oxygen vapor bathed in the light of floodlights billows up from it. The rocket appears to be alive.

On our walk to the foot of the launchpad, senior managers, two by two, grab hold of each of us by the arms on both sides. This is yet another Russian space program tradition. I'm thankful for the help because it's hard to walk in these space suits! But I also think the tradition is meant to represent the many thousands of people who helped bring us to this launch.

Then, in an interesting tradition I was not aware of, each of us receives a kick in the butt from one of the senior Russian space program managers as we step toward the ladder to the launchpad, as if to provide one last measure of encouragement. This reminds me of when Gumby Carr swatted Carmel on the butt as we walked up the aisle after exchanging wedding vows. Maybe this is kind of the same idea, or maybe not.

At the base of the rocket, I see painted on the top of it an American flag and Russian flag side by side. That image is being burned into my mind as a strong unidentified emotion wells up inside of me. As the emotion reaches full force, I identify it—it's pride. Not self-pride or national pride. I feel proud to be human. If Steven Spielberg were directing this scene, he would have dolly zoomed that image and then dolly zoomed my look of pride as I stand in my space suit at the foot of the launchpad, all accompanied by an inspirational soundtrack. Never in all my years as a Cold War fighter pilot would I have thought this possible. If you had told me then that I would one day serve as a fully integrated member of a Russian spacecraft crew and would launch into space with a couple of Russian military officers from a former top-secret Soviet military installation, I would have thought you were insane. It was not one of the scenarios I thought possible to play out. But here we are.

I sense that I am not alone in these feelings of unity. Everyone here is looking at the three of us as one single unified crew. By extension, all of the people working on this mission, regardless of what nation they come from, are also on one unified crew with a unified mission. The three of us standing here are not only representing

*Aleksandr Samokutyayev (bottom), Ron Garan (middle), and Andrei*
*Borisenko (top) wave from the base of the rocket before they board the*
*Russian Soyuz TMA-21 spacecraft, named after the first human in space,*
*Yuri Gagarin. Baikonur Cosmodrome, April 4, 2011.* Credit: NASA/Cioffi

our nations, we are representing our species. I'm sure that everyone
else here feels that as well. I feel like I am floating on a sea of possibility. I would love to continue to soak in this rare glimpse of the
unity that our species is called to, but it's time to go.

Sasha, Andrei, and I wave goodbye to everyone at the
launchpad, then, along with a launch technician, we climb the
remaining steps and enter a small rickety elevator that will take

us to the pointy end of the rocket. On the elevator's ascent, we pass through clouds of venting oxygen. When we reach the top and are let out, each of us signs the entry hatch before climbing inside the spacecraft and taking our assigned spots while some other launch technicians already near the entry hatch look on.

✦

We've been lying on our backs, knees in our chests, for a couple of hours now. Each of us has been cinched down to our custom-molded seats by Russian launch techs who were determined to ensure that nothing would dislodge their human cargo. At the moment, I have nothing to do but wait and think. Music that sounds like a Russian military marching tune flows through our headsets from the launch control room.

As I lie here strapped in the rocket, I think back a few weeks to when I was getting ready to leave Houston, which in many ways was the first step on this journey to space. At that time, not only did I start to think of the wonderful things I would miss during my half year away from Earth, I also thought about the darker side of life here. Two days before my departure for Russia, Carmel and I visited our friend and my former STS-124 commander Mark Kelly's wife, Congresswoman Gabby Giffords, at The Institute for Rehabilitation and Research in Houston. A few weeks before that visit, Gabby was the victim of a violent attack. During a community event in Tucson, Arizona, a lone gunman shot her in the head. Eighteen other people were shot, six of them killed. When we entered her room at the institute, she recognized us, but she had obviously been through hell.

That senseless tragedy highlights how far we've strayed from the unity that we as a species are called to. But I do not believe that violence is an indispensable part of our human character.

Our numerous transgressions do not diminish the pride I feel for being human. What I experienced a few hours ago on the launchpad is our true calling. That unity is our destiny. But until we reach that destiny, we will unfortunately continue to have our hearts broken.

Underneath my space suit right now, on my left wrist, I wear a bracelet with Gabby's name on it. In my small way, I want to carry into space her indomitable courage and spirit and the hopes and prayers of all those affected by the tragedy. I also want to carry the strength and unity of the Tucson community with me as its members exemplify the beauty of life on our planet—beauty, even in the face of a senseless tragedy.

The bracelet is also a reminder that one of the most difficult parts of being in space is being separated from everyone we love. Hanging over us all is the possibility that something horrible could befall a loved one while we are helplessly stranded in zero-g. I think back to when Mark's twin brother, Scott Kelly, was the commander of the ISS. I was Scott's backup for that mission. I had trained to take his place should an event arise that could prevent him from going to space. But that event, the shooting of his sister-in-law and others in Tucson, happened only *after* Scott was on board the ISS.

During an in-orbit news conference shortly after Scott received the call we all fear—the call that someone we love has been seriously injured or killed—he reflected on the fact that even an emergency on the ground doesn't excuse us from our duties and responsibilities in space. We are expected to play the cards we're dealt. He also reflected on how even such a horrible event can bring us together. A news anchor conducting the interview from Earth agreed and noted that Republican and Democratic members of Congress had decided to sit with each other as a sign of support for Gabby during the State of the Union Address that was scheduled for later that same evening. This was yet another glimpse into the unity that is our destiny.

Now, lying here on my back with my knees in my chest, U2's song "One" begins to play in all three of our headsets. A few days ago, each of us picked a couple of songs that the Russian launch personnel could pipe into the spacecraft to help us pass the time during periods of relative boredom. I chose "One." At a very deep level, I knew that my Russian crewmates and I were about to embark on a mission of unity for all of humanity and I felt that "One" was the perfect theme song for what we were about to do.

As I think about the words straining forth from the melodic substrate, I experience a certainty of beauty.

> One love
> One blood
> One life
> You got to do what you should

I understand why the words are beautiful. They represent unity, a beautiful concept. But I don't understand why the underlying melody is also beautiful. I try to dissect what is physically happening. Each individual note is nothing more than a mathematical equation, a sine wave with a specific frequency that traveled on a radio carrier wave from the launch control center to our spacecraft to the small speakers in our headsets. The speakers converted the electrical frequency to vibrational energy that traveled the short distance to my eardrums. Although my brain cannot make out each of these individual notes, when they are all taken together, my brain perceives the vibration they cause on my eardrums to be something beautiful.

> One life
> With each other
> Sisters
> Brothers

Each of the notes lasts for only a short time, but all the notes together make up the song. Some of these notes, when taken by themselves, may not communicate beauty to me, but nonetheless, the overall beauty of the song would not be possible without these specific notes.

This being the second time I've strapped myself to tons of high explosives with the intention to light them, I'm yet again pondering my own mortality. Each of us, like the individual notes of a song, only exists for a brief time. *Am I and all of us like the individual notes of the song of the universe?* Our unique note lasts for the duration of our physical life, but the contribution of that note to the overall song lasts forever. Only you can be the specific note represented by your potential. No one can play your note but you.

*One life*
*But we're not the same*

To think of our lives in this way makes it apparent that not only am I a distinct individual, I am also the universe. The orbital perspective represents two sides of the same coin, and so in keeping with that idea, when we dolly zoom out to the big-picture perspective from space while focusing on the worm's-eye details on the ground, each of us is dolly zooming out to the scale of the entire universe. We do that without losing our individuality. When we choose to be kind to someone or help someone or some creature, it's not that we're necessarily being altruistic anymore than we are being altruistic to our hand when we pull it back from a hot stove.

*We get to*
*Carry each other*
*Carry each other*

There's a distinction here that is becoming unmistakably clear as the countdown timer marches closer to the moment of truth.

I think back to a thought I had during our third and final spacewalk of the STS-124 mission. I noted that what was clear to me from the perspective of the spacewalk is that we are not from Earth, we are *of* Earth. In that same vein, we are not in the universe, we are *of* the universe. Every moment of every life from conception to death and beyond mimics the all-encompassing life of the universe. And when we exhale for the last time and the link between us and from where we came is severed, it is in death that we escape the gravitational pull of the mass of the universe and weightlessly step outside of our physical limitations, travel full circle, and return home. The universe is infinite and as such, every point in it must also be infinite. I am two dolly zoomed sides of the same coin. I am both a distinct finite individual and the infinite universe. It's not that I'm a universe and you are a universe. It's that we are the same universe. We are one, all of us—every living thing.

*One . . . life*
*One*

*E pluribus unum*

It's been a little while since our music selections have ended. They did their job of passing the time and helping us relax. So far, I've found this time remarkably peaceful despite the fact that I've felt vibrations and valves opening and closing and heard fans and motors turning on and off. The vehicle feels alive and primed, ready to go. Lying here strapped inside the rocket, I think about all those people who are close to me who I know are watching here in Baikonur, on TV, or online.

As the countdown timer passes ten seconds remaining, I feel barely perceptible vibrations and hear a loud hissing. Slowly and steadily, the vibration and sound increase in strength to a long crescendo. When the clock hits zero, we're propelled upward. In recognition of the fiftieth anniversary of the launch of the first human to space, Sasha keys the mic and calmly says in Russian, "In the words of Yuri Gagarin, *Поехали*—We're off!" I, on the other hand, let loose with a "Woo-hoo!"

This first stage of the launch has a lot less vibration than I remember from my shuttle launch. A small stuffed animal dangling from our control panel proves that. Sasha's daughter, Anastasia, picked out the toy, a dog with brown floppy ears, to serve as our zero-g indicator. He's not for us but for the folks watching our internal camera view on live TV. When he starts floating, that will indicate to all the viewers that we've made it to space. Right now, he's being pulled down toward us at a force of two g's and increasing and rotating in a circle in response to the maneuvering of our engines. Right on cue, the tension in the string holding him momentarily goes slack as the four strap-on boosters of the first stage separate, leaving only the core engines firing.

Still pinned to my seat by the acceleration of our second-stage core engines, I feel and hear a small explosion. Pyrotechnic charges have fired, which have jettisoned our rocket fairing, sheets of protective metal bearing the name and likeness of Yuri Gagarin. Since we are no longer cocooned inside the fairing, the windows of our capsule are now exposed. We are heading toward the blue glow of orbital sunrise. How many sunrises will I see in the next six months?

As opposed to my launch experience in the shuttle, where I was inside a relatively massive vehicle, this launch almost feels as if we're *wearing* the rocket. We are so cramped inside our little spacecraft that we feel everything—every pump, fan, and explosive bolt. The g-force from the rocket's acceleration is pushing me deeper into my seat. Then, as the second stage starts to burn out, all three of us abruptly and involuntarily thrust forward out of our seats by the deceleration of the rocket. The toy dog slams into the control panel and bounces off. My

*Aleksandr Samokutyayev, Ron Garan, and Andrei Borisenko launch
from the Baikonur Cosmodrome in Kazakhstan on April 4, 2011
aboard the Soyuz TMA-21 dubbed "Gagarin." The launch took place
from the same launchpad where Yuri Gagarin became the first person
to launch to space on April 12, 1961. Credit: NASA/Cioffi*

face moves inches from the panel. Then all three of us slam back
into our seats with a thud as the third stage engine kicks in and
the second stage is jettisoned. I start laughing and let out my
second "Woo-hoo!" The abrupt and powerful third-stage acceleration amazes me. The toy dog is again being pulled toward us.
We are really on our way now!

At the precise moment, the last engine shuts down. Our zero-g indicator does its job, and the dog starts floating gracefully to the limits of its leash. It feels great to be back in space after almost three years of preparation. To think—just eight and a half minutes ago, we were on Earth. The launch was significantly more fun than I had anticipated. I feel like Fred Randall from the movie *RocketMan*. I want to yell, "Can we do that again?!" but I restrain myself. There is still a lot to do before we can unstrap and get out of our seats. Probably the most important tasks at hand are the course corrections we must perform to get on the right path toward the ISS.

We must have two critical pieces of information before we can make a course correction to change our spacecraft's trajectory. We need to know where we are and where we want to go—our current state vector and target. Once we have that information, we can apply the proper force to steer our trajectory to hit our target. We have many different sensors and methods to determine our location and destination, and it's critical that we incorporate all the information properly and precisely. If we can't figure out to a high degree of accuracy where we are and where we want to go, we will miss our goal.

After a few hours of procedures and maneuvers to put our spacecraft on the proper course to "catch up" with the ISS, we unstrap and get out of our space suits. It's time now to start making ourselves at home. It is so wonderful to be back in space, back in the freedom of a weightless existence, and back to this incredible perspective. Unlike the shuttle that maintains a stable attitude as it orbits Earth, the Soyuz slowly rotates about all three axes—pitch, yaw, and roll. Looking out the window, I see Earth, then the moon, then deep space in continuous but varying succession. I feel like we're riding on a slowly tumbling leaf being silently blown around the world by the cosmic wind.

✦

We've completed our tasks for the day, and Sasha and I hang our sleeping bags from the top of the Soyuz habitation module. The bags are positioned so that our heads will point down toward the hatch to the descent module, where we sat on our ride to space. We will sleep like bats. Andrei establishes his bat cave in the descent module. As I climb into my sleeping bag after a very long and exciting day, I think back on the launch. Overall, I found this experience much different than my experience on the space shuttle, not just because it's a smaller vehicle, but mainly because we have only brief periods of time, every few hours, when we have radio contact with the ground.

During the quiet times between contact, it's basically just the three of us—Sasha, Andrei, and me—separated from everyone else in the world. The Soyuz spacecraft is a great and reliable ship, and although it is very small, it is so far surprisingly comfortable to live in, assuming you like the people you're with, which I do!

As I feel myself drifting off to sleep, I think about how amazed and impressed I am with my crewmates. Though this is the first flight into space for Sasha and Andrei, they have both adapted to weightlessness immediately and have acted like they are seasoned, veteran cosmonauts. I know of no way to predict how people will respond after arriving in space for the first time, so I feel incredibly fortunate to be a part of such a capable crew.

Between now and joining up with the ISS, I'm sure we will continue to adapt to our new environment while we prepare our spacecraft for docking. Above my head, down in the descent module, I see rays of blue light in the weightless dust of our Soyuz—light reflected from our beautiful Earth. I'm pulled back in thought to all of the people we just said goodbye to. I think about all those who helped make this experience wonderful, the people who made it to the launch, those who couldn't be here but supported us from home, and all the people who supported us in Baikonur.

I am filled with gratitude to our family escorts, flight docs, managers, instructors, and the Baikonur support staff. The gratitude continues as I transition to my evening prayers and drift off to effortless, weightless sleep. As I let go and rest in the peace of not having to do anything at all, I allow myself to be carried along—carried along on a tumbling leaf being blown around Earth.

"Range, fifty-seven meters. Range rate, decimal two-eight," reports Sasha in Russian to mission control in Moscow. We are closing in on the ISS at a rate of nearly three-tenths of a meter per second. The station has maneuvered to an attitude for the docking that I've never seen before. It's sort of standing on end in relation to Earth and is tilted to the right. It looks like a lopsided letter "I." The entire left side of the station—left from our point of view—is bathed in sunlight as we approach orbital night.

All three of us are back in our space suits and strapped into our respective seats in the descent module. The atmosphere inside the capsule is all business. There's nervous excitement in our artificial air. This is an especially tense phase of our mission, and none of us, of course, has ever docked a Soyuz to the ISS. After over two days tumbling around Earth in our tiny spacecraft, we're ready to board the station and begin our mission. I can't wait to be back inside that amazing and magical place. I'm particularly looking forward to seeing the cupola, the windowed observatory that was installed after my first visit.

Right in front of me, on the control panel of our spacecraft, I see a video image of our assigned docking port on the ISS. After we dock onto the station, our spacecraft will become the highest point on it. On the screen, below our port, I can also see the docking target, a cross within a small circle. The display crosshairs are right in the middle of the target as it slowly grows in the display's field of view.

"We are ready. Standing by for contact. Range rate, decimal one-five," reports Sasha as we pass over the snowcapped Andes Mountains in Chile. Just a few meters from contact with the space station, all three of us are surprised when the docking target quickly moves down and away from the crosshairs. I don't remember seeing that in the sim.

Sasha reports, "Target moved down!"

Mission control responds, "This is nominal," indicating that the movement is expected.

Seconds later, we feel the front of our spacecraft contact the ISS. We rise out of our seats and into our restraints as the massive space station decelerates our relative velocity to zero. Indicators on our control panel illuminate, announcing that we've made contact and our vehicle has been captured by the station. Those watching on NASA TV hear commentator Rob Navias announce, "Docking confirmed at 3:09 a.m. Moscow Time, 6:09 p.m. Central Time. The *Gagarin* spacecraft slips into port at the International Space Station honoring the golden anniversary of the dawn of human spaceflight."

Just like when we docked to the ISS on the shuttle, there's a lot we'll have to do before we can open the hatches and enter our new home. As we're reconfiguring everything that's needed to equalize pressure between the two vehicles, we also take turns getting out of our space suits and changing into our Russian flight suits. Each of our light blue suits bears our Expedition-27 mission patch, Soyuz patch, our respective national flags, and patches of our space agencies. Our Soyuz patch depicts a Soyuz orbiting Earth. Spread across the surface of Earth is an image of the face of Yuri Gagarin. The number 50 is also prominent, recognizing the anniversary of the first spaceflight.

When everything is ready, Sasha opens the hatch between our Soyuz and the ISS. On the other side of it floats Russian cosmonaut and ISS commander Dima Kondratyev, who welcomes us aboard. Sasha is first through the hatch, followed by Andrei and then me. Each of us is greeted with a hug from our Expedition-27 crewmates, ISS commander Dima, US astronaut Cady Coleman, and Italian astronaut Paolo Nespoli, who is celebrating his birthday today. After exchanging brief hellos, we float through the station to the Japanese Laboratory for a post-docking video downlink with our families gathered in the Russian mission control center.

In the bright and spacious Japanese Lab—our JEM—I get nostalgic as I'm transported back three years to the STS-124 mission. I'm filled with warm memories of that wonderful time that, in a lot of ways, served as an awakening for me. As I reminisce, all six of us fly to the far end of the module and align in two stacked rows—Dima, Paolo, and Cady in the back row and us three newcomers in the front. We are all looking into a lifeless video camera. We will not be able to see our families, only hear them. Our families will be able to see and hear us.

Russian Space Agency managers deliver some congratulatory remarks, then the microphone is turned over to our family members who traveled to Moscow from Baikonur after the launch. They take turns offering congratulations, each in their own native tongue. First up is Andrei's wife, Zoya, who proclaims that thousands of people on Earth are proud of us. After Zoya professes her love for Andrei, Sasha's wife, Oksana, says with high-energy excitement, "Boys, congratulations on the successful docking! I love you! I'm proud of you!" Oksana giggles as she sends greetings from all their family members spread throughout Russia.

Next, Carmel congratulates each of us and shares that our sons Ronnie and Joseph spoke to her via satellite phone and were thrilled with the success of the launch. After Carmel tells me she loves me, she addresses my Soyuz crewmates and says that the wives will all "keep the home fires burning warm and welcome you home with open arms at the end of a very successful mission." She adds, "And by the way, Ron, I have your credit card!" We all laugh. I'm sure translation wasn't required in mission control either.

One by one, additional family members send their greetings and congratulations, including Jake, and I'm struck by how much we as humans have in common. This little get-together of people on Earth and in space, people from three countries celebrating their shared humanity, is extremely powerful. I am witnessing the possibility of an emergent civilization where the whole is greater than the sum of its parts. There is incredible strength in this unity and shared humanity.

As the messages of love and congratulations continue to flow through the JEM speakers, I think about how humanity evolved from small tribal communities, to city-states, to nation-states. I see before me the possibility that we can take the next step and become a civilization based on a planetary identity. It's not lost on me that we are here celebrating the docking of this mission that is designated to commemorate humanity's first step into space. It took humanity to leave the cradle of Earth to spark the first emergence of a planetary civilization. It is within our power to go from an identity that thinks, *This is my tribe, kingdom, nation, religion,* to a planetary consciousness.

I'm looking forward to getting settled into our new home. Cady and Paolo lead Sasha and me to our crew quarters on the US part of the station as Andrei follows Dima to his new home in the Russian part. We fly out of the JEM and turn right into the ISS's Node-2 module, which we call "Harmony." In the aft part of the module are four crew quarters—one on the starboard wall, one on the port wall, one on the ceiling, and one on the floor, also called the deck. Cady lives in the port quarters and Paolo on the starboard. My new home is on the deck, and Sasha's is opposite me on the ceiling.

I open a door on the floor of Harmony and slide into my new home thinking, *This feels an awful lot like what it must be like to climb into a coffin.* Basically, all four of our crew quarters are about the size of a small coat closet. Inside, there's a sleeping bag and a laptop computer. Over time, I will deck out my "room" with photos I brought and anything else I can think of to make it feel more like home. Tonight will be my first night in space where I will be sleeping in my own assigned place. All nights on my last mission, I would set up camp somewhere and then break camp at "dawn." For the first time, I'm not a nomadic visitor to space. I'm a resident.

After a couple of hours getting reacquainted with the ISS and our newly enlarged crew, I call it a night. I change out of my Russian flight suit into shorts and a T-shirt. I hit play on my iPod and settle inside my sleeping bag while Peter Frampton's "Float" plays gently in my earbuds. Before sleep overwhelms me, I think back to our video downlink with the families, back to the unifying force of our shared humanity. I think back to the possibility of an emerging planetary identity.

Although Yuri Gagarin's flight was that first step toward a planetary civilization, the inflection point came on Christmas Eve 1968 during the mission of *Apollo 8*. The inflection point occurred when the crew emerged from behind the far side of the moon on their fourth orbit and witnessed something never seen before by human eyes. Commander Frank Borman was the first to witness the amazing sight and called in excitement to the others, taking a black-and-white photo in the process. In the ensuing scramble, Bill Anders took a more famous color photo.

As the crew experienced Earth emerging from behind the lunar horizon, I wonder if they realized the significance of that moment. They had just become the first humans to see Earth as a whole planet hanging in the blackness of space and the first to

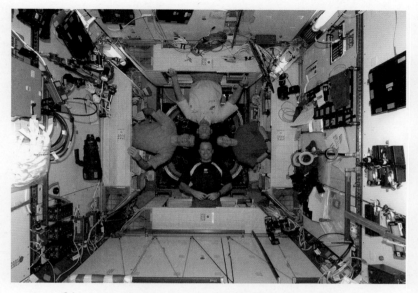

*Four of the six Expedition-27 crew members in their respective crew quarters in Node-2 of the ISS. Clockwise from top: Russian cosmonaut Aleksandr Samokutyayev, NASA astronauts Cady Coleman and Ron Garan, and European Space Agency astronaut Paolo Nespoli. Credit: NASA/Borisenko*

capture that for the rest of us. The famous photograph Anders took, known as *Earthrise*, is probably the most influential photograph ever shot.

With its simple message, that photo revolutionized how we see the world and how we see ourselves: that we are one people traveling on one planet toward one shared future. Back in 1968, for a brief moment, the world was one. People all around Earth, including the Soviet Union, a nation that was locked in a Cold War with the West and the Space Race with the US, declared this a monumental achievement for all of humanity. For a brief moment in 1968, the world rallied around the image of *Earthrise*.

This moment marked an inflection point between two human epochs. It was the spark of an evolutionary phase shift where humanity was given the opportunity to transcend its humble beginnings and ascend to incomprehensible heights, literally and figuratively. But unfortunately, the significance and meaning of the image of *Earthrise* has, for the most part, been forgotten—at least we seem to act as if it has. The video downlink with the families provided a glimpse into how we would treat each other if the truth that we are one people traveling on one planet toward one shared future was brought front and center. With the memory of a glimpse into a possible visionary future still fresh in my mind, I fall asleep in my new home.

My eyes slowly open in darkness. *Where am I?* I blindly feel around trying to determine my surroundings. I feel a hand-rail, a vent, and then a computer. I'm in my crew quarters, but somehow, in my sleep, I've flipped upside down in relation to my stuff. As I turn on the light switch and my crew quarters slowly comes into focus, I experience a sensation I have never felt before in space. I feel truly rested. *How long have I been asleep?* I turn on my computer and start doing the math. *Can it be? Have I really slept for twenty hours?* I float out of my quarters and see Cady working not far from me in the US Lab.

Cady is a retired US Air Force colonel and former polymer chemist. She is friendly, good-natured, and caring. She is someone who sees the bigger picture, and I enjoy her company.

"Cady, I think I just slept through nearly a full day," I say to her in disbelief.

She replies, "Yes, since you had the day off, we decided to let you sleep."

"Wow! I guess I needed that." I thank her and get ready to start my day. I'm looking forward to getting into a routine with our new crewmates.

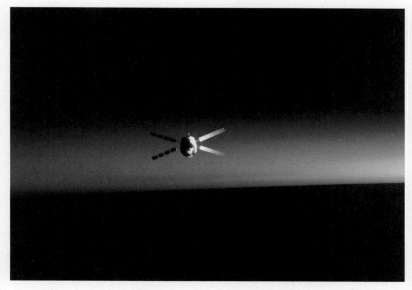

*Ron Garan snapped this photo of the Johannes Kepler ATV (Automated*
*Transfer Vehicle 002) as it flew in close proximity to the Interna-*
*tional Space Station. The unmanned cargo spacecraft was launched by*
*the European Space Agency. Hearing the story of seventeenth century*
*astronomer Johannes Kepler on a radio show years earlier inspired*
*Ron to stay the course toward NASA.* Credit: NASA/Garan

It's the start of another day, and I begin my daily commute.
I fly aft through the ISS, past the US Lab and into "Unity," the
designated name for Node-1. As I pass into Unity, I make a
right turn into Node-3, otherwise known as "Tranquility." Tranquility contains our bathroom, exercise equipment, and my
favorite part of the ISS, the cupola, the windowed observatory
that allows us to look directly into space on the normally Earth-
facing side of the ISS. Of course, at NASA, we have an acronym
for everything. We can't just call things by their normal names.
The NASA term for the bathroom, for instance, is WCS, which
stands for "waste collection system." I set up to shave and brush
my teeth in front of a mirror on the outside wall of the WCS a
few feet from the cupola.

As I shave, I notice that Paolo is in the cupola participating in a family video conference. He's a tall former Italian Special Forces soldier, a great guy with a wonderful sense of humor and some amazing life stories to share. Even though he is speaking to his family in Italian, I sense concern in his voice, so I finish up shaving and brushing my teeth quickly to give him some privacy. I fly to the US Lab to begin my work.

It's a new month, May, and my five Expedition-27 crewmates and I solemnly gather in the cupola, where the six of us squeeze in shoulder to shoulder. Outside the cupola's seven large windows, arranged like flower petals, Earth glides by in beautiful silence. Directly below us, I see the deep blue of the Mediterranean Sea framed by the windswept auburn sands of North Africa as we head northeast toward the West Coast of Italy.

At the predetermined time, Dima grabs the mic and transmits in English, "Houston, Huntsville, Munich, Tsukuba, Moscow, from the station we are halting operations and observing one minute of silence in memory of Paolo's mother." Dima then hands the mic to Paolo, and he transmits, "We are remembering her by looking from the cupola at our beautiful planet. We are sure she has the same wonderful view from where she is now." Paolo then moves a video camera to film and downlink the view of Earth as flight controllers around the world all stand at their consoles and bow their heads in reverent silence.

After Gabby Giffords was shot, Scott Kelly received the call we all fear. Two days ago, Paolo also received a heartbreaking call—word that his mom, Maria Motta, had passed away. He was understandably devastated. Shortly after he got the news, Dima approached him to ask if a certain procedure was completed. Paolo couldn't reply and started crying. Dima was confused and seemed not to know what to do or what was going on. Paolo said, "I'm sorry. My mother just died." Paolo then simply floated away, cleaned up, and started working again. He had no choice but to accept the reality of the situation—no choice but to accept the cards he had been dealt.

The concern I heard in Paolo's voice during the family conference several days ago was because he had learned that his seventy-eight-year-old mother was gravely ill. He had perceived some changes in his mom, but he'd had no idea of the seriousness of her illness. As that family conference approached the end of their planned time, Paolo's mom had said to him, "I'm sorry. I don't think I can hold on to see you when you come back." Paolo shared his mom's condition with us, and we tried to support him as best we could. I can only imagine the helplessness and sorrow he must have felt knowing there was nothing he could do, and in all likelihood, he would never see his mother again.

After his mom passed away and the date and time for her funeral was set, Paolo asked us if he could take a minute off during the funeral to honor her. He thought this might provide him some small sense of closure. We all agreed that we would all go to the cupola and celebrate Paolo's mom at that moment along with Paolo. We sent our request to mission control and in response, we learned that mission control centers all around the world would participate. Members of the entire International Space Station program would all come together in unity and recognize a moment of silence to honor Paolo's mom. All of us, in this small symbolic gesture, would acknowledge and share in Paolo's suffering.

As the end of the minute of silence approaches, we fly over the Italian town of Verano Brianza, near Milan, the location of Maria Motta's funeral. The eyes of all six of us have become a weightless pool of tears. We're crying not only because we can feel and share in Paolo's pain, but because we can feel humanity coming together too. In this moment, the words *one human family* are not just a concept. It's our reality, and it's beautiful.

As the minute ends, we all wipe our eyes and Dima transmits, "Houston, Huntsville, Munich, Tsukuba, Moscow, from the station we are resuming normal operations." We all hug Paolo and then fly off to pick up our work where we left off.

✦

Weeks later, the combined Expedition-27 and STS-134 crews all gather in the JEM for a special event. It's been great seeing Mark Kelly since he and his crew arrived a few days ago on the last flight of space shuttle *Endeavour*. Mark had to make the gut-wrenching decision whether he would continue to train and ultimately fly as commander after Gabby had been so seriously injured in the shooting a little more than four months ago. In the end, two things cemented his decision: his commitment to his crew and Gabby's insistence that he still lead the mission.

With all twelve of us crammed in the JEM in some semblance of order, Paolo keys the mic and transmits, "Houston, Station, on space to ground two, we are ready for the event." On the other end of this historic call is Pope Benedict the Sixteenth.

After some opening remarks, Dima introduces the Expedition-27 crew and Mark introduces the STS-134 crew.

The Pope—dressed in his traditional white papal cassock, sitting behind an ornate desk in an ornate chair with gold trim and speaking in English with a German accent—says, "Dear astronauts, I am very happy to have this extraordinary opportunity to converse with you during your mission. Humanity is experiencing a period of extremely rapid progress in the field of scientific knowledge and technical applications. In a sense, you are our representatives spearheading humanity's exploration of new spaces and possibilities for our future—overcoming the limitations of our everyday existence. I admire your courage as well as your discipline and commitment with which you prepared yourselves for this mission. We are convinced that you are inspired by noble ideals and that you intend to present the results of your research for all humanity and for the common good."

The Pope then addresses his first question to Mark. "From the space perspective, you have a very different view of Earth. You fly over different continents and nations several times a day. I think it must be obvious to you how we all live together on one Earth and how absurd it is that we fight and kill each other. I know that your wife was the victim of a serious attack, and I hope her health continues to improve. When you're contemplating Earth from up there, do you ever wonder about the way nations and people live together down here or how science can contribute to the cause of peace?"

Mark replies, "Thank you for the kind words, Your Holiness, and thank you for mentioning my wife, Gabby. It's a very good question. We fly over most of the world, and we don't see borders. At the same time, we realize that people fight each other and there's a lot of violence in this world, and it's really an unfortunate thing." Mark goes on to say that often people fight over resources, particularly energy. He discusses the solar panels on the ISS, which give us unlimited energy, and he adds, "And if those technologies could be used more on Earth, we could possibly reduce some of that violence."

Then it's my turn as the Pope says, "My second question concerns the responsibility we all have toward the future of our planet. I recall the serious risks facing the environment and the survival of future generations. Scientists tell us we have to be careful, and from an ethical point of view, we must develop our conscience as well. From your extraordinary observation point, how do you see the situation on Earth? Do you see signs or phenomena to which we need to be more attentive?"

I reply, "Your Holiness, it's a great honor to speak with you and you're right, it really is an extraordinary vantage point we have up here. On the one hand, we can see how indescribably beautiful the planet that we have been given is, but on the other hand, we can clearly see how fragile it is. For instance, the atmosphere when viewed from space is paper-thin, and to think that this paper-thin layer is all that separates every living thing from the vacuum of space and that it's all that protects us is a sobering thought. It seems to us that it's just incredible to view Earth hanging in the blackness of space and to think that we are all together, riding on this beautiful fragile oasis through the universe."

I continue, "And it fills us all with hope to think that all of us on board this incredible orbital space station that was built by the many nations of our international partnership accomplished this amazing feat in orbit. Likewise, by working together and by cooperating on Earth, we can overcome many of the problems facing our planet."

After a few more questions, the Pope says, in Italian, "My last question is for Paolo. Dear Paolo, I know that a few days ago, your mom left you. And in a few days, you will come home and you will not find her waiting for you. We are all close to you. I have also prayed for her. How have you been living through this time of pain on the International Space Station? Do you feel isolated and alone, or do you feel united amongst everyone in a community that follows you with affection and attention?"

Paolo responds, "Holy Father, I felt your prayers and everyone's prayers arriving up here where we orbit outside Earth and have a vantage point to look at Earth and feel everything around us. My colleagues on board the station—Dima, Cady, Ron, Aleksandr, and Andrei—were very close to me during this difficult time for me, this very intense moment. As well as my brothers and sisters, my uncles, my aunts, my relatives

*The International Space Station crew, in blue shirts, and the Endeavour*
*astronauts, in black shirts, chat with Pope Benedict XVI. First row,*
*Left to right: European Space Agency astronaut Paolo Nespoli, Russian*
*Space Agency cosmonaut Dima Kondratyev, Mark Kelly, European Space*
*Agency astronaut Roberto Vittori. Back row, left to right: Cady Coleman,*
*Russian Space Agency cosmonaut Andrei Borisenko, Russian Space*
*Agency cosmonaut Aleksandr Samokutyayev, Ron Garan, Mike Fincke,*
*Drew Feustel, Greg Chamitoff, Greg Johnson.* Credit: NASA TV

were close to my mom in her last moments. I am very grateful
for this. I felt very far but also very close, and the thought of
feeling all of you near me at this time has been a great relief.
I also want to thank the Italian and American space agencies
for giving me the opportunity to be able to speak with her in
her last moments."

The Pope then closes with this: "Dear astronauts, I thank
you warmly for this wonderful opportunity to meet and
dialogue with you. You have helped me and many other
people to reflect together on important issues in regards
to the future of humanity. I wish you the very best for
your work and for the success of your great mission in the

service of science, international cooperation, authentic progress, and for peace in the world. I will continue to follow you in my thoughts and prayers, and I impart to you my apostolic blessing."

Dima responds, "We would all like to thank you, Your Holiness, for your kind words."

With that, we all wave to the camera. As we do so, Mike Fincke, one of the *Endeavour* crew members, starts to float up out of view, but I grab his feet and pull him back down.

In space, we always find a way to act a little silly, even in front of the Pope.

# CHAPTER 12

# Home in the Heavens

✦ A very long day is over, and I've sought refuge in our Soyuz spacecraft, docked to the top of the ISS, to watch *Endeavour* as it flies a loop around us. Early today, the *Endeavour* crew members undocked to start their journey back to Earth. Before departing the neighborhood, they are conducting a maneuver to test out new docking systems that future American spacecraft will use.

We are on the dark side of the orbit. Through a window in the Soyuz's descent module, I see what appears to be a bright spotlight against the backdrop of the rotating Milky Way. As we orbit Earth, the Milky Way slowly rotates. Everything in my field of view is turning except one point of light, which is coming from *Endeavour*.

As my eyes adjust to the darkness, I start to make out the silhouette of the space shuttle illuminated by the combination of its own lights, reflected light from cities below, and a crescent moon above. The shuttle is using its reaction control system jets to follow a precise trajectory. Each time one of these jets fires, I see a glowing sphere of ionized gas rapidly spreading out in all directions, including right toward me. Spherical hypersonic shock waves of seemingly luminescent vapor are spreading out in all directions. Waves of glowing high-speed reaction control system exhaust impact various parts of the station with no visible consequence. It's beautiful.

It's been a long couple of weeks with little sleep. About a week ago, Dima, Cady, and Paolo headed home in their Soyuz, leaving

Andrei, Sasha, and me to mind the ISS and host the rest of the STS-134 mission. It's a little sad to look out and see *Endeavour* and realize this is the last time she will ever fly. Her mission has been busy, the highlight of which has been her crew members delivering a device called the Alpha Magnetic Spectrometer—the AMS—which they installed on the top of the station. We hope the AMS will help scientists better understand the origin of the universe by searching for antimatter, dark matter, and measuring cosmic rays.

With Alicia Keys's "Empire State of Mind" playing in the background on this early June day, I put the finishing touches on the crew quarters Cady and Paolo vacated. I want to make sure everything is spotless and ready for the arrival of our new crewmates. Two days ago, a Soyuz launched from Kazakhstan, aiming for a rendezvous with our home in the heavens. Aboard the spacecraft are three friends. I'm looking forward to a reunion with my STS-124 spacewalk partner, Mike Fossum, and with Russian cosmonaut Sergey Volkov, the commander of the ISS back in 2008 when we were here on the STS-124 mission. I'll also be seeing my astronaut colleague Satoshi Furukawa of Japan.

In our communications prior to their launch, Mike and I joked that "we're getting the band back together." Our reunion is especially exciting because in a few weeks, when space shuttle *Atlantis* arrives and docks to the station for the last time, Mike and I will again head out the door to conduct our fourth spacewalk together.

As for Sergey Volkov, I remember him fondly from the 2008 mission as a solid guy with a great sense of humor. He is also an incredible cosmonaut. If I were going to Mars and could take only three astronauts or cosmonauts with me, he'd be one of them—he's that good. Satoshi, who was a surgeon before being accepted into the Japanese astronaut corps, is on his first mission. He's also a great guy. He's very conscientious and has a good but dry sense of humor.

✦

A month later, NASA TV commentator Rob Navias reports, "Garan at the very end of the robotic arm, the Canadarm2, that is being operated by Doug Hurley with the assistance of Sandy Magnus at the cupola workstation. Garan, in the process of installing a portable foot restraint to the end of the Canadarm2 that he will ride like a telephone repairman on the end of a cherry picker to retrieve a failed pump that has been stowed on the ISS after having gone down on July 31st of last year, taking down half of the station's cooling system."

After installing the foot restraint and climbing aboard for the ride, my classmate in both my astronaut class and Naval Test Pilot School, Doug Hurley, who arrived here on *Atlantis* a few days ago, flies me over to the failed pump. There, Mike and I ready the pump for extraction.

"OK, Ronnie, you ready to lift up the pump module?" transmits Mike.

"Let's go," I respond.

"That's fourteen hundred pounds, buddy," Mike adds.

"Well, there's two of us," I say, feigning confidence.

After the pump is safely clear of its support structure, Doug flies me and the module underneath the ISS toward *Atlantis's* payload bay. Once I get there, Mike and I will install the pump on a truss support structure at the very back of the bay for return to Earth so engineers can try to figure out why it failed.

At the moment, I can't see Earth and I'm starting to lose my view of the ISS. My only reference of motion is what's left of my view of the space station. As I lose my last glimpse of it, I also lose my sensation of motion. All I can see is this giant box in my hands. I've been here before. It's been a few years, but it feels eerily familiar.

Suddenly, I feel a strong "clunk" at my feet as my whole body pitches forward and the box tries to pull itself away from me and out of my hands. I manage to keep my grip on the box and my feet in the foot restraints. *What happened?* The most logical explanation is that Doug decided to stop the motion of the arm. When he did that, this massive box wanted to keep going in the same direction. Only my hands and my body connected to the foot restraint stopped it. *But what was the clunk?*

A sobering thought pops into my head. *What if it was the foot restraint breaking free from the robotic arm?* This would mean that I would be heading off into space with no way to get back. I try to twist to get a view of something that can give me a reference point to judge my trajectory, but there's nothing in sight. If I am flying off into space, there would be no way for me to know it. I dismiss these thoughts by realizing that if I just became Earth's newest orbiting satellite, surely someone would say something. Of course, we could have lost communications too. *Oh well, there's no use worrying about something I have no control over. The clunk was probably nothing important.*

After what seems like an eternity, I see *Atlantis's* payload bay coming into view and I'm slowly heading right for it. As I begin to see the entire shuttle, I transmit, "Nice-looking spaceship you got there."

"Why thank you!" replies STS-135 crew member Rex Walheim, who is choreographing our spacewalk from *Atlantis's* flight deck.

"Sweet ride!" I add.

A little over two hours into the spacewalk, I arrive with the pump to *Atlantis's* payload bay. Mike is already here and has prepared the module's new home. Doug is slowly lowering me headfirst the last few feet to the support structure. After the box is firmly seated into the support equipment, I reach down with my left hand and unholster my pistol grip tool, which is basically

*July 12, 2011: Ron Garan is being "flown" toward space shuttle
Atlantis, holding a failed pump module, with his feet clamped
to the end of the robotic Canadarm2. Mike Fossum and Ron
installed the module into Atlantis's payload bay for return to
Earth during the final space shuttle mission.* Credit: NASA

a space power drill. After inputting the required settings into the
tool, I drive a bolt that latches the box into the payload bay for its
trip back to Earth.

With the box delivery complete, I pop out of the foot restraint
and Mike takes my place. Now, I am to translate out of the
payload bay hand over hand while Mike takes the more direct
joyride on the arm. I've made my way down the port edge of
the bay and have climbed up the docking adapter between the
shuttle and the ISS. I grab a handrail on the space station with
my left hand while my right hand still has a hold on a handrail
on the shuttle. As I'm about to leave the shuttle, straddling the
space between these two magnificent spacecraft, it dawns on me
that no one will ever do this again. When I release my hold on
the shuttle's handrail, that will mark the last time a human was
in the payload bay of a shuttle in space because the Space Shuttle

Program is coming to an end. I stop for a moment and let that thought sink in. This moment is too monumental to let it go unacknowledged.

I take a few moments to send some words down to mission control, recognizing the closing of this chapter of US space exploration and thanking the thousands upon thousands of dedicated people who have worked on the space shuttle over the life of the program. With that, I get back to work and start to scale up the ISS to my next high-altitude worksite.

About four hours into the spacewalk, I've made my way to the far side of the starboard truss of the ISS. I am a long way from the airlock. My task is to install an experiment out here that will evaluate the performance of certain materials in the space environment. In front of me stands the Alpha Magnetic Spectrometer. The AMS weighs more than 16,000 pounds. It resembles a giant hot tub wrapped in white material and is perched on the top of the space station.

Beyond the AMS, I see the entire station. *Atlantis* is clearly visible, perched on the front of the ISS like a hood ornament. On the back of the space station, our Soyuz spacecraft extends upward toward deep space. Looking at the AMS, I wonder what mysteries it will unlock. How will that fabulous example of human ingenuity expand our perception of reality? Will it explain the flashes of light I see when I try to fall asleep up here? Will it give us a better understanding of our place in the universe? More importantly, will it give us a glimpse into the potential of our future amongst the stars?

Mike and I have been outside for over six hours. We have completed all of our tasks. I have just put the last of our tools and supplies in the airlock, which I am now inside. All that's left is for Mike to ingress into the airlock, close the hatch, and we can mark this one "done."

"Ronnie, why don't you come back out for a moment?" radios Mike.

*Ron Garan snapped this picture of the ISS and space shuttle Atlantis during the final mission of the shuttle program. Taken during the only spacewalk of the STS-135 mission, July 12, 2011.* Credit: NASA/Garan

"What's up, Mike?" I ask.

"Come on out, and you'll see."

I'm exhausted, and to tell the truth, I was happy to be back inside even if we are still in a vacuum. As I exit the airlock, I see Mike's smiling face through his clear visor. Behind him is a thin, glowing blue line. We are approaching orbital sunrise. Without saying a word, I know exactly what Mike is thinking. Now, I'm thinking the same thing. This is probably the last time either of us will be out on a spacewalk. We've accomplished everything we set out to do today, and now we're going to savor these last few moments.

We watch in awestruck silence as our orbiting home flies out from behind the shadow of Earth. Mike and I hang from the airlock with the newly awakened Earth below our feet. As the indescribable beauty of this particular one of the sixteen new days we will experience today blossoms into radiant glory,

*One of sixteen daily sunrises from the orbital perspective. This one
was over Brazil, August 22, 2011.* Credit: NASA/Garan

I thank God for all He has created. I thank Him for bringing me
to this moment, and I thank all of those fellow crewmates on
"Spaceship Earth" that make it possible. Last, with just a glance,
I thank Mike for dragging me back out here. I pat him on the
shoulder of his space suit and head back into the airlock. He
follows me in and closes the hatch, ending the last spacewalk of
the space shuttle era.

✦

On another day, in front of the hatch leading to *Atlantis*, the STS-135 and ISS Expedition-28 crews are gathered for a ceremony recognizing the last undocking of the Space Shuttle Program.

Chris "Fergy" Ferguson, the STS-135 commander, keys the mic and transmits, "The crew of STS-135, the final space shuttle mission, has brought up with us a special American flag. This flag is significant not only because we brought it up on this flight but also because it flew on STS-1. This flag is not only a symbol of our national pride and honor, but it is also a goal. This flag will be flown prominently here at the forward hatch of Node-2, to be returned to Earth once again by an astronaut that launches on a US vehicle, hopefully in just a few years. Ron, I'd like to turn this flag over to you for you to display on the Node-2 forward hatch."

I receive the flag from Fergy and say, "When we were thinking about where to place this flag that flew on STS-1 and STS-135, we thought the Harmony module would be the perfect place. On our right we have the Japanese Laboratory, and on our left is the European Laboratory. In front of us is the US Laboratory, the Russian Segment, and the rest of the ISS, and above us and below us are hatches where visiting vehicles can bring cargo. But behind us right now is the hatch that leads to *Atlantis*. Thirty-five space shuttles have docked to the mating adapter that is just beyond that hatch.

"During the course of the International Space Station construction," I continue, "all those space shuttles that docked there left behind the legacy of this incredible orbiting research facility that not only is a stepping stone toward the exploration of the rest of the solar system, but it's also improving life on our planet. As we put the flag on this hatch that leads to *Atlantis* and close the hatch after these guys pass through it, we are closing a chapter in the history of our nation. But in the future, when another spacecraft with crew members on board docks to that hatch and when we open that hatch, we are going to be opening a new chapter and raising the flag on a new era of space exploration beyond low Earth orbit. So, it's a great honor to do that."

As Mike and I Velcro the flag to the Harmony hatch, Fergy adds, "When this flag returns again, someday to Earth by astronauts that came up on an American spacecraft, its journey will not end there. Its journey will continue, and it will leave low Earth orbit, perhaps to a lunar destination. Perhaps to Mars."

After Mike and I securely affix the flag to the hatch, Fergy thanks Andrei not only for the wonderful ISS hospitality but also for wonderful Russian hospitality. I then have the opportunity to thank the STS-135 crew for helping set the station up for continued utilization for the rest of the decade and beyond. With that, Fergy and I shake hands, hug, and after everyone exchanges hugs all around, the STS-135 crew flies through the hatch and on to *Atlantis* as we close the hatch behind them.

A little more than a week later, from mission control in the Johnson Space Center, the voice of the capcom, whose job is to communicate with us from Earth, booms over the speakers in the US Lab: "Station, Houston on the big loop. The probabilities are still in the red threshold, and we are planning to have you shelter in place. You have a 'go' to start Message 27-0190. Time until the red conjunction is approximately one hour, thirty-six minutes." *Well, this is not how I thought today would go.*

A "red conjunction" is NASA code indicating that a piece of space junk is projected to pass dangerously close to the space station. In this case, dangerously close means the object will pass into an imaginary "pizza box" shaped region around the station, measuring 2,460 feet above and below it and 15.6 miles on each side. Currently, many millions of objects big enough to cause catastrophic damage to the station upon impact are orbiting Earth, but the same big sky theory we relied on in Desert Storm normally keeps us clear of all that junk here in space.

The fallacy of the big sky theory may just catch up with us though. The sky is not as big as we think. Normally, when we determine that debris will enter our "pizza box," we have enough warning to nudge the orbit of the station to avoid the threat. For some reason, we didn't find out about this object's trajectory with enough time to take evasive action. Now, all we can do is close every hatch on the station and seek refuge in our space-craft. The plan is for Sasha, Andrei, and me to take shelter in our Soyuz and Sergey, Mike, and Satoshi to take shelter in theirs. This could potentially allow us all to immediately undock from the ISS and return to Earth.

The six of us work feverishly to button up all the hatches to isolate the individual modules of the station. This way if the debris hits a module, the closed hatches might prevent the depressurization of the entire space station.

After more than an hour of work, we're all ready to take cover in our spacecraft and split into two crews of three. Mike calls over to us as we float off in separate directions, "Good luck, and we'll see you soon—hopefully for lunch. Either that, or we'll all be together on the ground and back with our families earlier than planned!"

Andrei and I float into the habitation module of our Soyuz with Sasha in trail. Sasha removes mechanical clamps that span the interface between the Soyuz and the station. Sasha then floats into the habitation module and closes the hatch behind him. At the moment, to undock from the station, all we'd have to do is push one button.

We settle into our Soyuz docked to the top of the space station with just under fifteen minutes to spare before our date with the space junk. As we do, I'm picturing the object that is hurtling toward us. We have no definitive description of it, other than that it may be a large spent upper stage of a rocket. Imagine that spent upper stage traveling through space like a bullet. Now increase the size of the bullet so it's as big as a grain silo. Now increase the speed of the bullet about fifteen times. If it hits, it will obliterate us, and our molecules will orbit Earth for decades. All we can do is wait. We have done everything we can to mitigate the risk.

Despite everything, I feel calm. I am at peace with the fact that our situation is now completely out of our hands. Our chance of survival? Either 0 percent or 100 percent. Though I accept that whatever will be *will be*, concern for my family wells up. *Have Carmel and the boys been told what's going on?* It would have been about 4 a.m. in Houston when we started battening down the hatches. *Did a NASA rep wake them up? Did the rep tell them that we are one step away from undocking?* In addition to worrying about my family, I ponder the fact that I'm yet again facing a situation that is elevating the reality of my mortality above the noise level of my awareness. It's not that I suddenly fear death more than in the past, it's that I'm concerned that I have not yet contributed to the world what will become my legacy. I don't want to die until I've completed my life's mission.

In what could possibly be the last minutes of my life, I begin looking back over the lifelong road that has led me here. I've heard it said that the most important thing in life is to leave a legacy. But in light of this current situation, I realize that when we dolly zoom to the orbital perspective and look at things over a long time frame, leaving a legacy loses its importance. Every president, king and queen, sports hero, Nobel Prize winner, business leader, pop star, and politician will eventually be forgotten. When time works its equalizing magic, the best legacy we can ever hope for is to be a historical footnote. Even the physical things we create, every great cathedral and pyramid, will eventually be reduced to dust.

But deep down, I know there is a legacy that we can leave that will *not* fade with time and will grow exponentially. In every given moment of our lives, every decision and action we take gently—or at times not so gently—nudges the trajectory of not only our individual lives but the entire world. These actions are like small course corrections. I think of this in terms of a planet-destroying asteroid that is heading toward Earth. If we knew about this asteroid far enough out, we could send a small spacecraft out to meet it and with a force equivalent to the weight of a feather, give it a nudge. This nudge over the course of the complete journey toward Earth could result in a miss distance of thousands of miles, saving every living thing on the planet.

I ponder life in evolutionary terms. Three billion years ago, Earth was barely inhabitable. The planet's atmosphere had a great deal of carbon dioxide and almost no oxygen. Life was confined to only single-celled organisms, one of which was called cyanobacteria. One day, a cyanobacterium developed the unique and never-seen-before ability to take energy from the sun and transform carbon dioxide into oxygen. In and of itself, that was not a particularly impressive adaptation. For hundreds of millions of years that followed, photosynthesis made little impact on the planet. But after a very long time, the oxygen level of the atmosphere rose as the descendants of these bacteria spread across the planet.

As the oxygen composition reached a critical level about six hundred million years ago, the ozone layer formed. Scientists believe that the formation of complex life was not possible before that. Once the ozone layer was here, which was made possible by a single-celled organism that adapted to perform photosynthesis, an explosion of complex multicellular life occurred that eventually led to the arrival of humans. That tiny single-celled organism that probably lived for only a couple of weeks is directly responsible for the development of all multicellular life on this planet and for a life-form that can contemplate infinity and the meaning of life.

This was the start of a sacred contract where every exhale by a human or animal is matched by an inhale of a plant or tree.

This was the establishment of the "lungs" of our planet, and it was caused by an infinitesimally small accomplishment of a seemingly insignificant life-form. If that creature could think, it would have probably thought, as it faced death, that its life had no meaning. It would not have realized, even if it was capable of rational thought, that with every one of its "exhalations" came the possibility that countless lives and life-forms would come into existence and completely change the face of the planet.

Legacy from the orbital perspective is the projection of the effects, both good and bad, of our daily decisions, words, and actions far into the future. Legacy from this perspective does not require that we get credit for our actions. In reality, credit for the impact we make is irrelevant and will not survive the passage of time. But a hundred thousand years from now, the difference between where our world and civilization are and where they would have been if we had not lived will be vast. We are more powerful than we can imagine!

So even though I feel that my life's mission is not yet complete, I take comfort in the possibility that if my life ends in the next few minutes, I would have already made enough positive nudges throughout my life to make a difference. With that comforting awareness, I close my eyes. If we're not blown to smithereens shortly, we'll have a ton of work to perform to undo this shelter-in-place drill.

Fortunately, when the time arrives, our date with destiny is a no-show. The capcom informs us that we are in the clear. The unknown object has passed us by. A little later, we learn that it passed approximately a thousand feet away from the station. In near-miss terms, this is like a bullet parting your hair. The object was traveling at almost 30,000 miles per hour. That would have left a mark!

✦

In August, six Expedition-28 crewmates, all with full bellies, are gathered in Unity. We just finished a wonderful dinner and are now simply enjoying each other's company. Cans of various Russian delicacies float amongst us. Small metal spoons protrude from each of the opened cans as they float off in super-slow motion in different directions as Tom Petty's "Free Fallin'" plays over the speakers, as we are actually free-falling. I look over at Sergey, who is stretched out with his back arched, imitating a free-falling skydiver.

Times like this, when we are not completely preoccupied with the busyness of the day or facing a rare life-threatening situation, allow us to really enjoy the awe of being in space. Space travel and, in particular, seeing Earth from space, is so awe-inspiring because it is so rare. This same thought struck me after my first mission, when I was jogging through Buffalo Bayou in Houston. As I noticed the trees, flowers, and wildlife during my run, the awe and natural beauty of the scene astounded me, so much so that everything else fell away. No longer did I hear the bustling noise of the city or the buzz of countless conversations from fellow bayou visitors. Awe-induced silence overcame me.

The awe I experienced that day resembled, to an extent, the awe I felt in space my first time here. That day in Buffalo Bayou, I knew that I was experiencing a greater appreciation for the world around me because I was no longer taking it for granted. My time in space had given me this gift. I got the sense that beauty that induces awe and wonder is a manifestation of life's enthusiasm, an outward sign that life itself is grateful and delighted to be alive.

As I reflect on this, I recognize that I feel a deep obligation to share the awe I experience in space with others. I think of it in these terms: Imagine if only a few hundred people in the history of humanity were able to see the miracle of a flower. Shouldn't they feel a responsibility to share that beauty somehow with the rest of humanity? Would there somehow be some level of awe induced simply because of the uniqueness and rareness of the experience? But just because an experience is rare doesn't make it intrinsically more special or more beautiful than a beautiful everyday experience. Miraculous awe surrounds us constantly. We have learned to take for granted the countless miracles that surround us every day.

To me, a miracle is a highly improbable event that brings about beauty and joy, an event that is so improbable that it requires some intervention from beyond the natural world. I think of that intervention as divine intervention and a miracle as having two parts: the event and the receiver. Without both, you don't have a miracle. A highly improbable event can be a miracle only if it brings about recognized beauty and joy. To have a miracle, you have to participate in it.

It strikes me that the first step to participate in a miracle is to recognize the miracle of your own life. If we stacked all the probabilities that you would be you, we would arrive at the mathematical certainty that you are a miracle of incomprehensible statistical proportion. We are all miracles. Every person we encounter every day is a miracle. But we perceive others as miracles only when we see the beauty and joy they bring into the world. We need to embrace the certainty that everyone we encounter is a miracle, even the person who flips us off in traffic, the telephone scammer, the troll who spews nonsense on the internet, and the enemies we face in combat. I now understand that the Iraqi soldiers inside the tanks I attacked in Desert Storm were miracles too. Underneath all our human imperfections is a perfect miracle.

As six space travelers from three nations float in relaxing camaraderie, I experience a profound feeling of belonging with these miraculous others. The awareness that the six of us belong to something special and meaningful is palpable. We are all fulfilling a human need to belong to something bigger than ourselves, and at least in me it is producing a powerful emotion.

But it's a mixed emotion. Mixed in with the sense of belonging, I feel a disconnect for how far we've strayed from our miraculous potential, a potential that could define what it truly means to belong.

The world is complicated. Our planet contains suffering, injustice, crime, terrorism, natural disasters, war, and a long list of other woes. But we also have love, charity, forgiveness, and interconnectedness. Throughout my life, I had found that the complexity of the world, the enormity of its problems, and the sheer terror that world events inspired were so great that to cope, I constructed a simpler framework or worldview in an attempt to incorporate all those factors into something more understandable and palatable.

When I simplified life like this, I had a strong tendency, almost by requirement, to lump situations, people, groups, and nations into categories and place them in the cubbyholes of my self-constructed framework. It was much easier to label an entire group of people than to deal with the myriad complex factors that could lead them to do things that I didn't understand. By placing them into cubbyholes, I built walls and boundaries that separated me from them, from the value that they could bring to a situation, and from potential sources of solutions to the problems that I faced.

I realize that I—that we as a species—have at times become the labels that others put on us, or worse yet, that we label ourselves and put ourselves into groups. As I ponder this, I realize that there's nothing wrong with identifying with a particular group as long as we don't let that define who we are, who we will speak with and work with. But often, labels box us in and erect barriers to collaboration and cooperation. Often, they make us ask the wrong questions: *Is he a liberal or a conservative? Is she religious? What religion is he? What denomination? Is she like me? Are we in the same group? Can I trust his words because we're cut from the same cloth?*

*The Expedition-28 crew enjoying each other's company during a break in the action. First row (left to right): Japan Aerospace Exploration Agency astronaut Satoshi Furukawa, Mike Fossum. Back row (left to right): Ron Garan, Russian Space Agency cosmonauts Aleksandr Samokutyayev, Andrei Borisenko, and Sergey Volkov. 2011. Credit: NASA*

This mindset severely limits the pieces of the puzzle that we allow onto our playing board and the possible solutions to shared problems. It can lead to hatred, racism, discrimination, violence, and war. It can lead us to ignore anything of merit on the other side or even to attempt to discredit that merit.

I ponder the fact that many of us blindly put our trust in some theory, organization, or pundit and follow wherever they lead. But this only replaces individual ignorance with biased group-think, which solves nothing. The longer I am in space, the more I am convinced that we'll only solve the big problems facing us when we become members of a community that is committed to finding real, long-term solutions in the context of our entire planetary body—a planetary community not unlike our floating little group of six.

Taking in the beautiful moment I am experiencing now with my crewmates, I am filled with optimism for what our species can achieve when we come together and celebrate our shared humanity.

✦

On the next to last day in August, I'm in my crew quarters on my laptop reviewing still photographs from a night time-lapse sequence I shot earlier in the cupola. With Peter Gabriel's "In Your Eyes" singing out from my laptop speakers, one of the photos stops me. In it, a long, illuminated line snakes for hundreds of miles across a large landmass. *This must be the reflection of moonlight on a river.* Out of curiosity, I try to find out what river it is. But when I pull up a program that shows our path over the ground at the time the photo was taken, I realize that the twisting and turning line is actually the illuminated human-made border between India and Pakistan.

I'd always heard that you couldn't see any borders from space, but apparently you can. On a deeper level, I realize that what the photo really depicts is a scar on the otherwise beautiful landscape, a human-made barrier to collaboration. That line, clearly visible from space, is keeping creative, problem-solving minds on either side of it from working together on their shared challenges, despite the fact that they live in the same location.

The motivation for drawing that line on a map was primarily fear. Fear divides us, and anything that divides us makes us weaker, less secure, and less productive. But I believe that love is what we're born with and fear is what we learn. If we can learn to fear, we can learn to overcome fear.

I realize that the line I see in the photo is exactly the same as the line on the map of the world that hangs in classrooms across Earth. I'm struck by the fact that at the moment, our entire civilization is based on that map, a two-dimensional landscape of

*The Illuminated human-made border between India and Pakistan. This scar on the otherwise beautiful landscape served as a compelling call to focus on the need for international collaboration to overcome the world's problems.* Credit: NASA/Garan

nation-states fighting and competing over resources and ideologies—a landscape where not only nations compete but also corporations, nongovernmental organizations, special interest groups, and political parties.

What's clear from my view in space is that when we use a two-dimensional landscape as the guidepost for our actions, we wind up with a two-dimensional mindset. This leads to a narrow, flat perspective of the world that encourages an us-versus-them mentality, which is prevalent in many political, business, and interpersonal situations. This mindset attempts to undermine emerging cooperative agreements by ignoring or discrediting any merit in the position of the other side. It says, "If we acknowledge merit, they will gain and therefore we lose."

Our prevalent two-dimensional mindset considers common ground as leverage to force the things in contention upon the other party. This mindset is counterproductive and leads to stagnation and a defense of the status quo at all costs. Our successful international cooperation in space exploration has taught us that a proven path to a more peaceful and productive world is to seek the things we agree on and use that common ground, however small it may be, as a launchpad to propel us toward unified action. In the ISS program, once we began to work on things that we agreed on, personal relationships were built, trust developed, and this platform can now potentially be used to address the things that we don't agree on. This is a model for success that the world can and should follow.

What's obvious up here is that the *real world* is not reflected in the two-dimensional map. It is reflected in the *Earthrise* image taken by the *Apollo 8* astronauts.

On some level back in 1968, we realized the territory had changed. What should have been apparent was the necessity to have a new map to navigate the reality of the territory. Once again, I reflect on the fact that the image of *Earthrise* proclaims that we are one people traveling together on one planet toward one shared future. From that perspective, you can't see nation-states. All you see is the fragile oasis of our home planet, Earth.

Some visionary people didn't need to go to space to realize that. On December 24, 1967, Dr. Martin Luther King Jr. gave a prophetic sermon at Ebenezer Baptist Church in Atlanta, Georgia. Dr. King put words to the truth of *Earthrise* even though the sermon was given exactly one year *before* the *Apollo 8* astronauts experienced Earth rising from behind the lunar horizon.

In his sermon, Dr. King started off by illustrating the obsolescence of war. He said, "Wisdom born of experience should tell us that war is obsolete. There may have been a time when war served as a negative good by preventing the spread and growth of an evil force, but the very destructive power of modern weapons of warfare eliminates even the possibility that war may any longer serve as a negative good." Later in the sermon, he proclaimed what was necessary to have true peace when he said, "It really boils down to this: that all life is interrelated. We are all caught in an inescapable network of mutuality, tied into a single garment of destiny. Whatever affects one directly, affects all indirectly."

Dr. King then summed up perfectly the truth that is derived from the image of *Earthrise*: "We aren't going to have peace on earth until we recognize this basic fact of the interrelated structure of all reality." *The basic fact of the interrelated structure of all reality* is not a philosophy or a cliché. It is the reality of the world that we live in. It is a fact. But the world at that time was not ready to recognize this. We were too tied up, and identified too much, with the two-dimensional map.

We cannot continue as a species with this map as our model.

Just like it's done every day for the last four months, the beeping alarm of my Omega Speedmaster watch wakes me from sleep. The first thing I do is open my laptop computer and check the schedule. Today, I see a vertical red line that marches from left to right, passing over all my daily tasks. As I finish tasks, I will mark them "completed" on this program, and the ground will be able to keep up with my progress. My job today, as it is every day, is to keep up with the red line.

My first task is to reconfigure a toolbox that arrived a couple of weeks ago on an unmanned cargo spacecraft. Basically, I need to consolidate two toolboxes into one. That may sound simple, but in zero-g, with tools floating all over the place, it can be a nightmare. I scan through the procedure and note that it is long, complex, and highly choreographed.

This procedure, like all procedures on the ISS, assumes a certain starting condition. Starting conditions assume that the equipment I'm to work on are in a certain configuration—that switches are set a certain way, cables were routed a certain way, etc. Many times, these conditions do not accurately reflect the actual situation and configuration on board the ISS. Today is no exception. The problem is that few of the tools are in the starting place assumed by the procedure writers. It doesn't take me long to realize that the highly detailed procedures cannot be executed as written because they assume the wrong starting conditions. To accomplish the task, I will have to request a change in the procedure.

I will have to be particularly diplomatic when I bring up this observation. In the past, when I pointed out discrepancies and offered an alternative approach to ensure I could achieve desired objectives, I, at times, met stiff resistance. So, after I dress, brush my teeth, and get a bite to eat, I call the on-duty capcom on our onboard phone so that we can talk privately.

On the call, I notice that the capcom is getting irritated. I ask him why.

"Someone worked a long time to come up with these detailed procedures, and now you're throwing them out the window," he says.

In the calmest and most diplomatic way I can muster, I try to explain that although a great deal of work went into the procedures, that doesn't change the fact that because they assume an incorrect starting condition they cannot possibly be used to accomplish the task. I offer an alternative approach. He tells me they will consider my request.

About an hour later, I receive word over the main ISS radio frequency. In a stern and somewhat disgusted tone, the capcom transmits, "We discussed your toolbox issue, and we are going to allow you to do it *your* way."

The response confuses me. The hostility is obvious, and I try to figure out where it's coming from. To me, it indicates that despite my best efforts, I didn't effectively communicate the reality of the situation.

The ground controllers and the capcom thought that one reality existed, but I knew that what I could see with my own eyes differed greatly from the ground's perceived reality. I couldn't understand why they refused to change their perspective in light of the new facts I presented. I remember a quote from Archbishop Desmond Tutu: "We cannot succeed by denying what exists. The acceptance of reality is the only place from which change can begin."

In this toolbox situation, I believe the capcom became combative because, for whatever reason, he couldn't bring himself to believe that the reality spelled out in the procedure was inaccurate. The fact that someone worked hard to produce the procedure clouded his judgment and created a bias in his perception of reality.

There are countless examples of this happening in everyday life. Every day, people have heated, emotional arguments simply because each has a different perspective. It has become so severe that when facts don't agree with our perceived reality, we change the facts rather than change our opinion. "Alternative facts" are simply tools used to keep an inaccurate perceived reality intact.

As I finish reconfiguring and consolidating the toolboxes, I realize that sometimes the common ground that is missing is a common starting condition. When we dolly zoom to the starting condition that the orbital perspective provides, people naturally are drawn together into a more aligned vantage point. In other words, if we zoom out to the point where we consider the implications of our decisions and opinions over the widest feasible geographic area and over the longest feasible time frame, things become clearer and we can make better decisions.

That thought reminds me of the first movie in the *Matrix* trilogy. In one scene, Morpheus says to Neo, "The Matrix is a system, Neo. That system is *hampering our progress.* But when you are inside and you look around, what do you see—businessmen, teachers, lawyers, carpenters, the very minds of the people we are trying to save. But until we do, these people are still a part of that system and are still *hampering our progress*. You have to understand that most of these people are not ready to be unplugged and many of them are so inured, so hopelessly dependent on the system that they will fight to protect it. Were you listening to me, Neo, or were you looking at the woman in the red dress?"

In actuality, Morpheus didn't really use the words *hampering our progress*, he said *our enemy*, which, to me, is the same thing. In the toolbox situation, the capcom couldn't understand the problem because he was part of the problem. He was part of the false reality, and he couldn't rise above it.

In a sense, in 1961 and then again, more profoundly in 1968, humanity had out-of-body experiences that enabled us to rise above our problems. As representatives of humanity, Yuri Gagarin, and then the crew of *Apollo 8*, left the physical aggregate body of Earth and looked back upon ourselves. They were unplugged from the Matrix, or unchained from the cave, which enabled them to dolly zoom to see what we have always been: one single human family with a common origin traveling together toward a shared future—for better or for worse. But the mere fact that those experiences were made possible by the ingenuity and cooperative nature of humanity should give us hope that we can build a shared future that we would all want to be a part of—a future where all people can live in harmony with one another and with the planet, where all people can live in peace and dignity, and where the needs of all will be met.

As I seek refuge in my favorite thinking spot on the ISS, the cupola, the path to this visionary and restorative future becomes clear to me: Humanity must metaphorically launch itself into orbit. To do this, we must capitalize on the opportunity that the evolutionary phase shift sparked by the *Apollo 8* inflection point gave us. We, as a planetary society, have been given the

*Ron Garan takes in the orbital perspective during the*
*Expedition-27/28 mission, 2011.* Credit: NASA/Fossum

opportunity to ascend to incomprehensible heights, literally and figuratively.

Floating effortlessly in the cupola gazing at the snowcapped majestic mountains of the Himalayan Plateau drifting slowly and silently below me, I imagine a rocket. On top of it sits an unconscious superorganism representing all of humanity and every living thing that inhabits Earth. This precious cargo represents not only everything that presently lives but everything that will ever live.

As the rocket's first stage fires, tremendous brute force lifts it from the launchpad and starts the acceleration upward. Eons of competition and conquest push it farther. Dynasties and dictatorships align and organize human effort on a massive scale. In response, tremendous suffering is expelled from the rocket's exhaust nozzle. Greed and conflict serve as catalysts, sparking tremendous technological acceleration. The collective insanity of the First World War produces radios and airplanes. The Second

World War produces nuclear power. The Space Race and Cold War produce satellite communication, personal computers, and solar power.

Blind independence and unconstrained growth consume enormous amounts of natural fuel as the rocket approaches staging. The noise is deafening. The vibration is violent and unpredictable. As it continues to climb, the rocket approaches the inflection point between the first and second stages. As the first stage of the rocket burns out, the lone passenger, the superorganism representing all living things, awakens and is faced with a choice: Jettison the weight of the first stage and fire the second stage engine, or hold on to the first stage and fall back to Earth in a fiery crash.

The superorganism, having just awakened, is confused. It knows that the first stage brought it to this point and is reluctant to jettison it. It does not yet realize that it can't make it to orbit carrying the extra weight of the first stage. But even now, a spark of awareness rises within it.

Just as the rocket is about to start tumbling back toward Earth, the superorganism realizes the futility of hanging on to the first stage and finally lets go. Instantly, the second stage engine fires and the rocket is exponentially thrusted upward and onward, leaving the noise and vibration behind.

But the awakening superorganism realizes that no one is steering the ship. Quickly, it establishes the processes to steer the rocket on its ascent. The superorganism bases its decisions on the most accurate data possible, enabling the most accurate predictions of its effect on the trajectory of the rocket. The decisions it makes are in the context of the entire superbody considering the big-picture implications, not just in reaction to its loudest parts. The superorganism determines the impact of a decision beyond the immediate area of concern and determines if harm would be caused elsewhere.

Decisions cease to be driven solely by party lines or other parochial or tribal factors. The greater good becomes the driving force of a decision, not party or national loyalty. Those motivations were jettisoned with the first stage after they were recognized by the superorganism as fundamentally misguided and destructive in the long run. All actions taken consider the long-term multigenerational effects on all.

When considering a course of action, the resultant trajectory is projected out to the decision maker's great-grandchildren. Only those actions leading to a positive and restorative world for our great-grandchildren are taken. No longer do we sacrifice our progeny for our own present short-term benefit. During this second stage acceleration, course corrections are made with open and transparent inputs and courses of action. All proposed solutions permit everyone to see "how the sausage is being made" and can survive having a spotlight put on them. No longer do decisions require secrecy to be successful.

As the rocket continues its acceleration to orbit, a planetary consciousness arises within the superorganism. This consciousness can be thought of as an embedded system. At the core is social consciousness, where we truly understand the meaning of one human family, where the false notion of separation is finally overturned and we embrace the "basic fact of the interrelated structure of all reality." Encompassing this social consciousness, like the rocket fairing cocooning our spacecraft, is the awareness of our interdependent place within Earth's biosphere. Together, these two nested systems are the emerging planetary consciousness.

With all of this in place, the superorganism can now steer the rocket to orbit. What is orbit? It is where we no longer need our engines. It is where we have accelerated to the speed where, with no additional effort, we can remain at our present altitude. Or, if we so choose, we can continue our ascension farther out into the universe.

Orbit is where we enter into abundance. It is the long-awaited post-scarcity existence where goods can be produced in great abundance with minimal-to-no human labor required. Our metaphorical orbit is a place where everyone has what they need, and it is where everyone can choose for themselves how they will contribute to society. Imagine what the world could look like in the next fifty years if the superorganism that represents all life on Earth, which has as its brain the embedded superorganism known as humanity, were awakened and jettisoned all those things that are no longer needed. What would happen if our true starting condition were realized and we were able to make a course correction to steer our trajectory toward an unlimited future?

*Andrei Borisenko (left), Ron Garan (center), and Aleksandr Samokutyayev (right) climb into their Soyuz spacecraft to start the journey "home," 2011.* Credit: NASA

# CHAPTER 13

# Rock, Flower, and Blade of Grass

✦ Sasha, Andrei, and I float through the hatch between the ISS and the habitation module of our Soyuz—our ride home. It's September 16, 2011, and we've come to the end of our mission. Sergey, Mike, and Satoshi remain on the other side of the hatch. I fight the urge to give these guys one last hug, one last handshake, remembering the Russian superstition that it's bad luck to embrace or shake hands through a doorway.

Sergey starts to close the station's hatch as Sasha unlatches the hatch to the Soyuz. *"Paka! Da stretcha,"* shouts Sasha through the partially closed passageway to the station—"Bye! See you soon." *"Da stretcha, ooh dache vam rebrata!"* replies Sergey—"See you soon. Good luck, guys!"

As the hatches fully close, our crew is cut in half—two separate crews dissected into two separate missions. Our mission now becomes returning from whence we came. While Sasha finishes securing the hatch, I think back to my time sitting nuclear alert in West Germany. *Did Sasha, a fighter pilot earlier in his career, also sit nuclear alert? Did he think it was his duty to serve his country in that way? Did he ever worry about getting shot by his own security guard?*

After we all struggle into our space suits, we each take turns floating down into the descent module and into our respective seats. I go first and wiggle into the right seat, then Andrei into the left, and Sasha into the center, closing the hatch between the habitation module and the descent module on his way.

Months before launch, I traveled to a dilapidated factory building in Moscow to be fitted for my seat liner. Wearing only long underwear and my communications cap, a cloth head covering containing small speakers and a microphone, technicians lowered me into a bathtub-looking container where I assumed the fetal position on my back. Then a technician meticulously poured a white gooey substance around me and into the tub, filling it until the liquid covered all but the forward half of my body. After lounging in the milk bath for what seemed like hours, the goo was hard enough for me to be extracted from the tub, leaving a perfect imprint of my "backside." That molded goo now serves as my perfectly contoured cocoon for my journey back to Earth.

Now, all three of us, with our knees in our chests, lying in the fetal position, each in our own specially designed cocoon, are about to enter into a new existence. We are leaving our weightless home in the heavens to return to a home anchored to Earth by gravity. I am being drawn back to Earth while part of me is clinging to stay here in this marvelous perspective-shifting outpost.

At the predetermined moment, our Soyuz with a painting of Yuri Gagarin just outside our window undocks from the ISS with a gentle push of some springs in the docking mechanism. The last time Gagarin flew, I was in a different cocoon—the cocoon of my mother's womb. I strain as hard as I can to keep the magnificent International Space Station in view through my window. I want to savor the last moments with our *home in the heavens*. Slowly, as *Gagarin* backs away, I lose more and more of my view of the station. All I can see now is the outboard edge of golden solar arrays. It's almost as if I can feel the heat of reflected sunlight from those massive energy converters.

*Will I ever see our home in the heavens again?* I miss it already. Life can be both harder and easier up here. It's the easier parts I'll miss most, although I will miss it all. While I was never really alone in space, a strong desire to be with others is coming alive within me, particularly those I love.

Before we head home in earnest, we will need to make a couple of orbits around our planet to line things up. We've flown around Earth one and a half times since we've undocked from the ISS, and we are presently on the dark side of the orbit. Right now, there's not much for me to do but stare out into the darkness just beyond my window. I marvel at how little separates us from the rest of the universe—just a few millimeters of aluminum between us and the vacuum of space, between us and a realm of vast boundaryless nothingness. The boundaryless world, just outside the window, provides a signpost to the reality that everything is intimately tied together and dependent on each other while not losing the realization of the distinct existence of each individual being.

We've now completed a couple of orbits around our planet and have everything lined up to begin our deorbit. We pass the southern tip of South America, and Sasha maneuvers the spacecraft to point our engines forward into the direction of our travel. As our craft yaws toward the proper orientation, a beautiful crescent moon drifts into view, hanging in space close to Earth's horizon. *What a beautiful sight!*

All three of us dive into our checklists. We have a really important event coming up that has to go right, or we won't be making it back to the planet. At the predetermined time, our main engine fires. Since Sasha pointed the engine in the direction we are traveling, this means that the engine is slowing us down just enough to enter the upper atmosphere. The deceleration gently pushes us down into our seats. I lift my arm and can sense its almost undetectable weight. Each of us is laser-focused on the constantly changing velocity reading on our displays. After about four and a half minutes, the engine abruptly shuts down. From here, the molecules of air in our upper atmosphere will do the rest of the deceleration for us. Dust and small debris that were gathered together in an area behind our seats by the invisible hand of deceleration floats back into the weightless realm.

Right on cue, with the force of a sledgehammer smashing directly behind our heads, explosive bolts fire, separating our spacecraft into three deorbiting projectiles: the habitation module, the instrumentation and service module containing our main engine, and the descent module containing our three fragile and flammable bodies. There's no turning back now. No matter what, I now know that at least the molecules of my body will return to Earth. There's no longer any chance of being trapped in space. If all goes as planned, our descent module will be the only one of the three pieces to survive as it's the only one with a heat shield. Through my window, I see all kinds of debris tumbling out into space in all directions. I hope we don't need any of that stuff.

The moon, Earth, and tumbling space debris are now nowhere to be seen. All I can see is the blackness of nothing-ness. But as I stare off into that darkness, I notice a faint red glow developing in slow waves. The view outside of the window alternates between pitch-blackness and a dim red light. The frequency between darkness and red light accelerates as the red light gets brighter. It must be getting really hot out there as we descend farther into the blanket of air covering our planet.

Then I see a spark shoot past my window, then another, and another, until just outside my window, a fountain of sparks develops. This reminds me of the fireworks my father would light for us on the Fourth of July that shot a fountain of sparks toward the sky. Then the sparks burst into flames as I sense a faint vibration developing. I am gently squeezed down farther into my molded seat as the first bit of gravity hints at what's to come. The vibration builds in intensity, and I am squeezed down into my cocoon even more. I tighten my harnesses. I know that there's going to be a crash at the end of this ride.

*From the orbital perspective this is how Andrei Borisenko, Ron Garan,
and Aleksandr Samokutyayev would have looked as they reentered
Earth's atmosphere in their Soyuz spacecraft. But this photo is actually
a photo of a meteor during the Perseid meteor shower that was taken
by Ron Garan. At the time the photo was taken, the ISS was above the
China–Mongolia border, August 12, 2011.* Credit: NASA/Garan

The vibration has increased so much that I wonder if the
spacecraft will hold together. The flames outside of my window
have also grown in intensity, but I can still see through them.
I see the West Coast of Africa whiz by in a blur. It appears as
though we are coming in very steep. After what seems like less
than a minute, the East Coast of Africa shoots by. Then in a flash,
the entire window turns pitch-black with soot, ending my view
of the world outside for the time being. Seconds later, a call from
mission control in Moscow is cut off midsentence, replaced with
nothing but static. The furnace just outside our spacecraft has
cut off our communications.

The g-force has grown significantly. I feel like my insides are
pulling in from my core. A great pressure is building up outside
of me, and I have to fight to breathe, taking short, quick gasps
like a fish out of water. I look over at Sasha and Andrei, and they
seem to be doing as well as can be expected under the circumstances. As I bring my focus back toward the instrument panel,
which is vibrating too violently for me to read, I feel another
bang, this one from behind the panel. *Must be the drogue chute.
Hang on!*

As the drogue chute—a parachute designed to slow the spacecraft down—deploys to its full length, the capsule is yanked violently. It spins, twists, and pulls in every direction. *You have got to be shitting me,* I think as my body rapidly cycles between being yanked out of my seat against my straps and slammed back down into the seat while my head bounces around like a helmeted watermelon rolling down a hill. I try to look over at my crewmates, but everything is a complete blur.

Just as I start to think that if this violent motion continues much longer, we won't survive, things start to settle down. Our capsule stabilizes under the chute, and the random, violent, chaotic motion is replaced with gentle circular rocking. All of us start laughing. We're laughing because we can't believe we're still alive after that—at least that's why I'm laughing. Andrei yells out in Russian, "That was just like an American amusement park ride!" *That was worse than any ride I've ever been on,* I think. But our respite is short-lived as the main chute—a larger parachute that takes over for the smaller drogue chute—deploys and the violent gyrations start all over again.

Shortly after our second "E" ticket ride on Space Mountain comes to an end and we stabilize in descent under the main parachute, the heat shield is jettisoned, taking with it a layer of protective covering on our windows. Bright white light streams in through my window like a spotlight searching across the instrument panel for a target. The light is noticeably different from the red glow of the superheated plasma that only minutes ago was flowing past.

A radio call from Moscow crackles through our headsets as communication is restored. I can't make out exactly what they are saying, but apparently our communications outage was significantly longer than expected and everyone was quite concerned about us. Rescue forces aboard Russian helicopters join our radio discussion. We're getting close. I raise my gloved hand up toward the window. My arm feels incredibly heavy. Using the mirror

*After a fiery and violent ride through the atmosphere, Ron Garan and*
*his Russian crewmates descend toward "home" (Kazakhstan) under*
*a parachute in what's left of their Soyuz spacecraft.* Credit: NASA

strapped to my wrist, I can see the ground rising up to meet us. I bring my arm back down and prepare for impact.

All three of our seats are simultaneously thrust forward until our faces are inches from the instrument panel, giving our underseat shock absorbers some stroke to absorb the impact. Seconds before we're about to land, I'm conscious of my tongue. I make sure to grit my teeth with my tongue inside. I wouldn't want to bite the thing clean off when we hit. I feel the "soft landing" jets fire behind us with a hiss a split second before we impact the ground. The ground smashes into our backs with the force of a Mack Truck running a red light. I can't believe how hard we hit. I bet the shock waves from our impact were picked up by the Seismological Institute in Sweden! At least it's over. Then I realize that it's not over. We didn't land. We bounced, and we have a few more "landings" to go.

I remember folks telling me that since I've been in space so long, when we land, my sensory system will be all screwed up and it will feel like I'm tumbling. Sure enough, I definitely feel like we're tumbling. Then I see the metal periscope cover shoot past my head as other debris flies around the spacecraft in various directions. I feel like we're tumbling because we *are* tumbling!

After our crash-test dummy duties come to an end and the capsule comes to rest, I look around to survey the damage. Everything seems more or less in one piece. I'm being pushed down into the right side of my seat. *We must have landed on our side*, I think. Looking at Sasha above me—*above me* defined as away from the gravity vector—and Andrei above him confirms my orientation estimate. I am being squeezed between Sasha's weight pushing down into my left shoulder and the resultant force pushing up into my right shoulder by my molded seat liner. It's not unbearable, but I hope we don't have to stay like this too long.

I feel so heavy. It's as if every part of me is immersed in a very sticky glue. If I try to raise my arm, I have to fight against this glue that is pulling my arm toward Earth. Although I know I'll again get used to living within its gravitational pull, it disheartens me that this is probably my lot for the rest of my life. I will probably be tethered to the planet for the rest of my days. I've only been back on Earth a few minutes and I already miss the weightless freedom of life in space.

With my face pinned against our spacecraft's starboard window, which is now pointing at the ground, I see what appears to be a beautiful painting visible within its metal frame. The background of the painting is formed by alternating waves of tan and brown soil illuminated by reflected sunlight seeping in from under the hull of our toppled craft. Three distinct objects that appear to be arranged in a purposeful formation make up the rest of this masterpiece—*a rock, a flower, and a blade of grass.*

Six months ago, I would have described the rock as dull, just your average rock. But now it proclaims a uniqueness and time-worn majesty. It appears stable, solid, and firm. It seems fundamental and strong.

Six months ago, I'm sure I would not even have taken the time to describe the blade of grass. It would have been just another one of the countless miracles that I would have taken for granted. Looking at it now, I see life. I see evidence of an ancient contract, a transfer of energy from our star to this precious living creature, to us.

The focal point of the painting though is a white and yellow flower. Somehow, this delicate creature survived the assault of our landing jets and toppling spacecraft to welcome us. The six white petals of the flower are all reaching up toward us like fingers of a small hand. Its palm is holding the bright yellow center part of the flower. For a brief period back in eighth-grade biology class, I probably knew what the center part of a flower was called, but at the moment, the name is beyond my reach. Whatever it's called, it looks like a jewel. It looks like the flower is reaching up to present us its priceless welcome-home present.

I just hang here for a while, taking in this simple, beautiful scene. As I do, the same emotional thought washes over me again and again: *I'm home.* Not long afterward, the significance of that thought dawns on me. *I'm home, but I'm in Kazakhstan!* In this moment, my home isn't just Houston, where my family is waiting for me to return—my home is Earth.

As I lie here against the starboard side of our spacecraft, I let that thought sink in. *Home—what does that word really mean?*

Has my definition of *home* changed into something new, or has it retained the meaning it had before I launched and has simply broadened? All the former manifestations of the word "home" flash through my mind in rapid succession—family, Yonkers, Roosevelt High School, US Air Force, New York, church, America. I think of all the squadrons I belonged to and all the houses I've lived in. These are places and things that I identified with home, places and things to defend and protect. If I now define home as Earth, do I have to abandon all those places and things that I once thought of as home? The answer comes immediately and forcefully, "Of course not!"

Broadening my definition of "home" does not come with a requirement to abandon where I came from or my national, religious, or cultural affiliations. It simply means seeing those things in the context of the bigger picture. In my first few minutes back on Earth, I realize that they are two sides of our dolly zoomed coin. The definition of home has profound implications for how we problem-solve, treat our planet, and treat each other. If we could find a way to see the things that we've identified with, in the context of the bigger picture— that is, in the context of our planetary community—this would provide a true foundation to solve the world's problems and challenges.

I snap out of my reflection as I hear the muffled voices of the rescue crew just outside the capsule. This fills me with excitement and a longing to trade our artificial world for the world of my birth. Before long, the rescue crew opens the hatch. Bright sunlight streams in accompanied by a wave of cool, fresh air. I disconnect my space suit umbilical, severing my connection with our spacecraft air supply. I inhale deeply, which reconnects me to Earth's life-support system. I am once again sharing in the exquisite and ancient blanket of air covering our planet. *How have I never noticed how wonderful it feels to take in a big breath of fresh air?*

After some words of welcome from the rescue crew, I look back over at the beautiful painting visible just outside the metal frame of our Soyuz spacecraft's starboard window. As I do this, the rock, flower, and blade of grass retreat away from me. The rescue crew decided to roll the capsule clockwise to aid the extraction of the three crash-test dummies. I feel lightheaded as they roll us into the heads-up position. Sasha is pulled first through the hatch and out into the sunshine by a burly Russian with white gloves. This leaves just Andrei and me.

I look over at Sasha's empty seat as I ride on a wave of gratitude. Our Soyuz dubbed *Gagarin* has served us well. Apparently, I'm next, as another member of the rescue crew pokes his head through the hatch and says, "Ron *gatoff?*"—"Are you ready, Ron?" *"Da ya gatoff,"* I respond as he reaches toward me, unbuckles my harness, and grabs my space suit by the shoulders and pulls. He drags me out of the fetal position headfirst toward the hatch. I have to wiggle left and right to avoid hitting various parts of our spacecraft that are blocking my exit. As I approach the hatch, more hands reach in and grab me and pull me out into the bright sunshine.

As my upper body emerges from the capsule, the rescue crew rotates me counterclockwise. I am now facing the sky with everything from the waist down still inside the capsule. I have to close my eyes for a couple of seconds. I wasn't expecting such a bright sun. Upon opening my eyes, I see that one of the rescue guys placed a photograph of a smiling Yuri Gagarin and Sergei Korolev on top of our capsule. As the rescue crew extracts more of my body, more hands reach underneath me to carry me away from the capsule. I'm surrounded by many people wearing the different uniforms of the rescue crew, some with baseball hats adorned with elaborate "scrambled egg" embroidery, others in white medical coats. Video cameras are pointing at me from all directions.

Once I'm completely out of the capsule, four of the rescue personnel carry me through a field of knee-high amber grass

*The Expedition-28 crew Andrei Borisenko (left), Aleksandr Samokutyayev (center), and Ron Garan (right) moments after the rescue crew extracted them from their toppled Soyuz spacecraft. Ron is seen talking on a satellite phone to his wife, Carmel. 2011* Credit: NASA/Ingalls

to a roped-off area adorned with various flags and sporadic boom microphones rising up above a crowd of people. They gently place me in a reclined seat next to Sasha. Immediately, medical personnel, including a NASA flight surgeon, swarm around me. A Russian nurse gently wipes sweat from my brow as another takes my pulse while a Russian doctor affixes a blood oxygen dosimeter to my finger. A blur of activity surrounds me, including Russian MI-8 helicopters taking off and landing. I'm content to just sit here and enjoy the sunshine and fresh air. I'm also enjoying being surrounded by people who are concerned about our well-being and seem genuinely happy to welcome us back to Earth. I look forward to sharing our stories with them from this amazing adventure.

After a brief period, the three of us are moved to a temporary medical tent that a support crew rapidly erected. NASA medical personnel help me out of my space suit and into a more comfortable flight suit. After Sasha, Andrei, and I complete our medical exams, we board three separate MI-8 helicopters for a ninety-minute ride to the Karaganda airport in northeastern

Kazakhstan. I climb into a bench seat on the starboard side of the helicopter and lie down.

I awaken as the helicopter lands at the airport. I must have slept the entire way. I don't even remember the chopper taking off. I'm led by medical personnel into the international departure terminal, where I reunite with Andrei and Sasha as traditional Kazakh music plays over loudspeakers.

Each of us is then seated in an ornate chair behind a shiny hardwood desk set up with microphones and Russian and American flags. My attention focuses on the background music as Carlos Santana's "Europa," one of my favorite songs, starts playing. After local officials welcome us to the airport, three beautiful young Kazakh women—dressed in traditional blue Kazakh dresses and pointy white hats with a fuzzy cloudlike ornament at the top—present each of us with flower bouquets and small ornate trophies. Then the women bring us Kazakh robes and hats. The folks around us wrap the robes around our shoulders and place the hats on our heads. The hats remind me of the captain's hat on the box of Cap'n Crunch cereal I ate as a kid.

Russian space program officials provide some opening words of welcome, and we are each presented with chocolates with our crew photo on the box and matryoshka dolls, which have a hand-painted likeness of each of us. With that, the Russian press conference begins.

The press, seated across from us in the departure terminal benches, asks each of us a question. When my turn comes, I'm asked, "How did you feel in microgravity conditions, and how do you feel right now back on Earth? Maybe you feel like a baby who was just born when you came back on Earth?" I reply by listing some of the things I will miss most about space, like the freedom of the weightless environment. I also share how wonderful it feels to be back here.

Then, when the press conference concludes, after nearly three years of training together and sharing a mission during this milestone fiftieth year of human spaceflight, Sasha, Andrei, and I say farewell. I'm led to a NASA jet, and Andrei and Sasha are led to a Russian Space Agency jet to continue our respective journeys home. And, just like that, our mission ends.

I climb aboard the NASA Gulfstream III aircraft and find my seat, which is actually more like a bed. There waiting for me is a can of cold German Bitburger beer with "Ron" written on it, which makes me laugh. Joining me for the journey to Houston are a couple of NASA managers and medical personnel. I settle into my seat, and shortly after takeoff, I take my first sip of beer in six months. Delicious! I feel home pulling me westward.

After a long but unquantifiable length of time—because I've slept most of the way—we start our final approach to our first refueling stop, Prestwick, Scotland. Lush green countryside passes below us. We are low enough that I can make out individual trees in a sea of green, something that I haven't been able to do for the last six months. Each of those beautiful trees serves as an integral part of the life-support system of Spaceship Earth.

But now I realize the significance that Spaceship Earth does not have a closed life-support system. We are presently using up resources faster than we replenish them. Now, in a very real way, I understand that this means if we continue on our present trajectory, we will reach a point where the life-support systems and resources of our planet will be insufficient to sustain life. After I ponder this on a brief stop where I was able to get out of the aircraft and spend some time in the fresh Scottish air, we're off again.

As we approach our second and last refueling stop, Bangor International Airport in Maine, we are treated to a stunning sunset. I stare out from the windows of the G-III at its beauty, contemplating the difference between this sunset and the countless orbital sunsets I watched during my stay on the ISS. Besides the realization that I will see only one sunset each day, instead of sixteen, I really notice the differences in the vibrance and the thickness in this sunset's band of colors. Although still breath-takingly beautiful, it seems less vibrant and less luminescent than the orbital sunsets I've gotten used to.

Now, the last bit of sun dips below a relatively flat horizon, and I think about the future. I think about a world in a target year 2068. We will arrive at our target after we have completed a hundred-year journey through space—a journey that began at the first earthrise. As I look at the setting sun, I'm hit once again with the thought that it is within our power to create a world-wide movement inspiring a positive vision of the future where our planet is a bold and thriving home for all. We have the ability to come together and design and build a future based on the true interdependence made clear in the *Earthrise* image.

Once we have taken the preliminary steps of determining our state vector and target, we can apply the corrective inputs of a course correction to propel our society on a trajectory to arrive at our desired target. We can then start to build a new civilization. It will be the unity we experienced in space taken to its logical conclusion.

The vision will communicate that Earth isn't flat. We don't live in the two-dimensional world depicted on maps. We live in a beautiful, iridescent, interconnected, and interdependent biosphere teeming with life. The vision will make it clear that we are stronger together and can accomplish the most when we rally behind a common cause. Through the vision, we will come to know that empathy, understanding, reason, and truth are keys to real progress.

As the landing gear is lowered on our final approach into Bangor, I think back to my time in Desert Storm. In 1991, I was asked to fight a war for my country and the world. Although I believed and still believe that war is humanity's biggest failure, I had no moral reservations about going into combat at that time. I was willing to give my life, if need be, to a cause that I believed was just. I truly believed that overturning the aggression and atrocities that Iraq was perpetrating against its neighbor Kuwait was key to creating a safer and more peaceful world. When I returned home to the US after Desert Storm, I was disillusioned with the status quo I encountered. As I've now been returned to Earth, I am again returning to an undesirable status quo, one that I refuse to accept.

I once again feel a calling to devote my life to a cause. I once again feel a calling to fight a just war, but this is not a conventional war. This is not a war of aggression, not a two-dimensional fight between us and them. For the first time in my life, I am filled with deep concern for our future. A critical mass of people around the world has descended into an exceedingly narrow and dangerous worldview. This, coupled with decades of pilotless drift toward environmental and social cliffs, has led to a perilous trajectory. I believe that mindsets, actions, and policies that are being "sold" as beneficial to us are actually leading us to the brink of destruction. These are mindsets that overly focus on the short term and put the complete focus on competition, conquest, growth, and profit maximization at all costs. I truly believe that what we do in the next few years will determine whether humanity evolves and thrives or destroys itself.

The war I feel called to fight will not employ guns and bombs but an arsenal of compassion, empathy, understanding, patience, love, awe, and wonder. Unlike Desert Storm, this war will not end in weeks. Victory cannot be won without decades of battle. But unless we act now and begin our march toward adopting an orbital perspective, the war will be lost before the battle really begins.

As our aircraft takes off again after our brief stop to refuel, I realize that to come out on the other side of the divisive turmoil that is all around us, we must completely flip our perspective. We need to understand that the stakes have never been higher, and it's not embellishment to say that the fate of humanity hangs in the balance. We need to end the cancerous selfishness

*Moments after touching down at Ellington Field in Houston, Ron is joined on board a NASA G-III. Ron is finally "home." Carmel is seen with Ron above. Bottom image (left to right) are: Joseph Garan, Ron Garan, Ronnie Garan, Jake Garan.* Credit: NASA

of parochialism, tribalism, nationalism, racism, sexism, and limited short-term thinking. We need to all become the immune cells of an immune response that is shifting people's perspective to the bigger and more accurate picture. With thoughts of a visionary future in 2068 rattling around my mind, I drift back off to sleep on this, our last leg of the journey.

After sleeping for practically the entire flight from Bangor, I'm awakened by the sound of the flaps being lowered in preparation for landing at Ellington Field in Houston. We have a smooth nighttime landing, then we taxi up and park next to rows of NASA T-38 jets, where I see a small gathering of people waiting for us. After the aircraft engines shut down and everyone leaves the aircraft for the tarmac, I am allowed to remain on board to greet Carmel in private. Minutes pass before my angel walks through the door. Just like when we met a couple of decades ago in the Hahn Air Base officers' club, her smile knocks the wind out of me. I have missed her so much. We embrace. It feels so good to be back in her arms. After a few more minutes, Ronnie, Joseph, and Jake board the plane. Our family is reunited. I am truly home.

# Return to Earth

## STARTING CONDITIONS

✦ In the introduction to this story, I shared with you that humanity and all life on Earth face a crisis that threatens the survival of life on the planet, a crisis that humans are being challenged to overcome. A crisis that requires a giant leap in humanity's evolutionary process. A life-or-death crisis that we won't solve until humanity transcends individual and collective ego and embraces the true nature of its interdependence with every living thing on the planet and the planet itself.

Humanity faces a choice: evolve or perish.

Indeed, we are heading down a dark road. I phrased the first sentence of the first chapter of this book, "My Casio G-Force digital watch silently rolls to thirteen hundred as I drive northeast on Taxiway Alpha under a dreary grey sky" as an homage to the first sentence of the first chapter of George Orwell's *1984*: "It was a bright cold day in April, and the clocks were striking thirteen." I started this book with an allusion to Orwell's prophetic masterpiece because I believe the only thing he might have gotten wrong in it was the date. On the dark road we're heading down, truth no longer matters. It's a road where, in the words of Orwell, "Who controls the past controls the future. Who controls the present controls the past." But we should take courage in the musical promise made by Led Zeppelin's Robert Plant: that there is still enough time to change the road we're on.

Fundamental systemic injustices in our society—racism, sexism, entrenched corrupt concentration of wealth and political power, the inequities of the global economy, and many more blights—have put us on this road. These injustices are holding us back, keeping narrow, self-centered interests in power, keeping the impoverished in poverty, and leading the biosphere toward collapse. The social status quo is not working, at least not for everyone.

Many brilliant, talented people are working on specific prescriptions to counter these systemic issues, aiming them at fundamentally reinventing the structure of our society. I did not write this book to dive into the details of these prescriptions, however, but to illustrate that embracing our implicit wholeness, the idea that we are *one*, is the only true foundation from which our problem-solving process can start. Any impulses we have toward dignity, solidarity, or protecting the planet arise from our identification with our underlying basic oneness.

We are in a time of intense worldwide political upheaval, a time of great transition that could lead to a new human epoch. Though our current trajectory is leading us toward disaster, by connecting to our implicit wholeness we will have the power to take another path, one that will lead to a positive and restorative future.

I see a future where individuals, organizations, and nations set aside differences and work together for the benefit of all of humanity. A future where all people have the tools to understand the long-term economic and environmental effects of their actions on our world and the overall planetary ecosystem. A future where leaders and decision makers across all disciplines use the best data available to ensure that the long-term impacts of their decisions keep us on a positive trajectory. A future where businesses serve the needs of civilization first and foremost and do not operate in a wholly self-serving vacuum but as interdependent nodes in a fabric of prosperity where everyone can live a good life in harmony with our planet's biosphere and one another.

I see a future where openness and transparency fuel tremendous restorative economic growth and enable profound collaboration between scientists, politicians, and nations. A future where education instills in every student the awe and wonder of our beautiful world and where every student is afforded the opportunity to engage with this wonder in a way that contributes to the well-being of our world.

Awe and wonder can dismantle fear and clear a path toward reunification of ourselves, our species, and our planet. Awe and wonder can reconnect us with the underlying intelligence that permeates and maintains the universe. I'm speaking of awe and wonder that we find not only in the physical beauty of our world but awe and wonder that we find everywhere. We find it in falling in love, facing death and surviving, experiencing and embracing diverse cultures, and seeking and finding answers to the important questions. We find awe and wonder in self-sacrifice and selfless acts. In the quest to overcome obstacles and achieve our dreams, the generosity of the human spirit, a baby's coo, and a child's innocent smile. In shared humanity and discovering humanity's place and role in the universe.

## DETERMINING OUR CURRENT STATE VECTOR

To arrive at the potential future I just described, how do we make a course correction to get there? To know our current state vector, we must know our starting condition. To do that, we must engage in large-scale profound collaboration to understand the millions of intersecting interdependent variables of a planetary community containing billions of people. Problems have become significantly more complex since the days when we were foraging in groups of twenty or thirty. Our civilization has evolved to consist of an incredibly interdependent series of related processes, systems, and living creatures.

Our current technology, which makes it easier to distribute knowledge, will allow us to work together on a massive scale to determine the true state of our societal affairs. We can progress and succeed only by incorporating the most accurate data possible from *all* available sources no matter how inconvenient the truth. This will provide us our true state vector.

To accomplish a course correction, we also need to know our target—where we want to be and when we want to be there. Focusing on a destination where all of humanity and the entire living ecosystem can thrive will lead folks to think collaboratively and interdependently for the long term. This will allow all of us to serve the greater cause. We can all play our distinct notes in the cosmic symphony while not losing our individuality.

## THE BEAUTY OF HAVING AN ORBITAL PERSPECTIVE

Imagine that you are on the International Space Station looking through the windowed cupola at our beautiful planet turning slowly below. From space, I believe that you would be struck by the sobering contradiction between the beauty of our planet and the unfortunate realities of life for a significant number of its inhabitants.

But I also believe that seeing the planet from space would fill you with hope. Seeing the unlimited potential of what we could accomplish when we work together, as demonstrated by the International Space Station itself, would extend your optimism. Your definition of "home" would rapidly expand to encompass Earth in its entirety, and for the first time, you might fully understand what it means to be part of one human family.

What does that really mean? In the most superficial terms, it means if we go back far enough, each and every person can be traced back to the same mother and father. It literally means that we are all related. It also means much more.

We are interconnected and interdependent on a dimension beyond the physicality of DNA. We are tied together in ways that are not normally evident. At some point in the evolution of our species, we developed individual egos that can only survive in us by masking our true unity. Our egos deceive us into believing that you and I are separate and distinct and nothing more. Yes, an aspect of each of us is separate and unique, but a higher, more real, and more important aspect exists where you and I are not separate. Our egos mask the fact that each of us is more than a single life. We are life itself.

I believe that if you traveled to space you would realize this, but I don't know this for a fact. The only thing I can say for certain is that traveling to space started me on a journey toward this understanding. Separation from the natural world enabled me to become a detached witness to its splendor and unity.

## WE CREATED IT, WE CAN CHANGE IT

We created the two-dimensional map that hangs in classrooms around the world, but we did not create it based on the reality of our world. That map is the guidepost of the old human epoch—the epoch before *Earthrise*. That map might have served us in the past. It might have been appropriate before we realized that humans could destroy the very life-support systems of our planet. It might have been appropriate when nation-states could operate in relative isolation. It might have been appropriate when it was not apparent how interdependent we all are. It might have been appropriate before we recognized the *"basic fact of the interrelated structure of all reality."* But it is no longer appropriate. Humanity needs a guidepost for our actions that will lead to greater unity.

To achieve this unity, we must broaden our tribe. When we were children, our social circle, our tribe, consisted of our family, normally those with whom we shared a home. Society too tends to define the members of our tribe as those with whom we share our home. In this broader context, that can refer to our national, cultural, ethnic, or religious identity. But as children mature, their social circle and tribe expand rapidly beyond their mom, dad, brothers, and sisters.

It is long past time that we as a species start to cross the bridge into adulthood and to see that our tribe extends beyond those in our immediate family. And just like entering adulthood and realigning our social circles doesn't mean that we have to lessen our relationship or identification with our immediate family, taking a planetary view will not make us any less American, or Russian, or German, or Rwandan, or Chinese. In fact, seeing how our national identity fits into the larger planetary community should only strengthen all of our communities through diversity of approach to problem-solving. It should enrich all national cultural heritages too.

Humanity can initiate a course correction by dolly zooming to the point where we all realize that we are, in fact, one collective superorganism. In doing so, we must zoom out to the orbital perspective without losing the details of the individual communities that make up our planet. We must zoom out from the individual to the collective without causing the individual to be reduced to a statistic or a cog in the wheel of Orwell's *1984* world.

To execute our required course correction, the human superorganism must awaken and act collectively for the betterment of the entire social body. Antibodies must be deployed to fight off our cancerous self-centered, two-dimensional, winner-take-all mindset. We need to understand that each and every one of us is a unique and beautiful cell in the larger living body called humanity. The home of this body is Earth. We will find meaning in life by being an immune cell, not a cancer cell. We will find purpose by propelling humanity forward on the path of evolution toward a more peaceful and harmonious future and by keeping our home in order.

The illusion that we are all separate has led to a great deal of the turmoil you read about in this story. The first chapter illustrated how this illusion pushed humanity to the brink of utter self-annihilation. Throughout the story, you saw how the shadow illusion of separation has led humanity time and time again to exile members of the human family, to consider them less than human and as deserving of our ridicule and violence. But throughout the story, you also saw how an awakening awareness of the awe and wonder that surrounds us constantly is the foundation to overcome millennia of humanity's misguided pursuits.

Once we shine a light on the shadow illusion of our separation, we will finally understand that we must cooperate on a planetary scale. Many species work together on a massive scale—ants, bees, schools of fish—but all species limit their sphere of cooperation to their community, however that is defined, such as the ant colony, the beehive, the political party, the nation. For life to survive on this planet, one specific species, *Homo sapiens*, must figure out how to be the first species in the history of life on Earth to cooperate on a planetary scale. We must figure out how to define our radius of cooperation and broaden our community to encompass the entire Earth, leaving no area uninvolved. Although recent technological developments are accelerating civilization's ability to cooperate, large-scale cooperation is written into our DNA. Evolutionary processes that put a high value on flexible large-scale cooperation transformed us from a weak, insignificant species to the most powerful force on the planet.

As we identify with larger groups and eventually take on a planetary identity, we will have come full circle. We will realize that perceived separation is nothing but a mental construct. We are simply life expressing itself as discrete, interdependent nodes called "persons." Love, in part, is the realization of this truth. It is the recognition of your sharing in the totality of life with another person. It is a recognition of the interdependent nature of all life and all matter. Whether it is the love of a parent, child, spouse, friend, or squadron mate, love is the connective tissue of life. Our egos keep these truths from us.

At some level, we all realize this, but realizing it and living it are different things. Living this truth, however, unlocks the chains that have kept us in the cave. It expands our awareness of the true reality, helping us understand that a larger, more accurate reality exists just beyond our perception.

## MY JOURNEY AND WHAT IT MEANS

Becoming an astronaut and flying in space was not the be-all and end-all. It was a catalyst for a much deeper and important journey to discover the transformative and unifying power of awe and wonder, that we are all responsible for our own awe, wonder, and adventure. Now, I try to live in a constant dolly zoomed state. Every morning I wake up in my bed, but I also wake up on a planet. I deal with all the aspects of "real life"— commutes, bills, and deadlines—but I try to notice the awe and wonder that surrounds me constantly too—the miracle of life, the path to love.

Ironically, it took the crucible of combat to make me realize and internalize the unifying power of love. I now understand that combat was a pivotal moment where pursuing the unity of a continuously expanding tribe became the guiding force in my life. This was my true—but at the time, unrecognized—calling. This moment compelled me to search for something missing in my life that I couldn't quite put my finger on. It made me realize that our real enemies are internal. Collectively, we need to channel our martial instincts inward. We need to transmute all those things holding us back into the fuel to move us forward. Unlike the unrealized quest of alchemists to turn lead into gold, we can actually transmute our negative inclinations into positive ones.

As I write this, I am well into my fifty-eighth year on this planet, minus a brief stint in low earth orbit. When I think back over my life's journey, I feel like I've lived most of it as a prisoner chained to Plato's Cave. All I've really seen are the shadows cast on the cave wall. I have been somewhat blind to a higher truth, to an expanded reality, immersed in a world of darkness, fragmentation, division, selfishness, and narrow-mindedness.

As I hung there chained to the cave ceiling, I was floating in darkness. Most growth occurs in darkness. Our bodies and minds are rejuvenated during the darkness of sleep. A seed grows in the darkness of the earth to become a bountiful fruit-bearing tree. A fetus grows in the darkness of the womb to become a beautiful sentient creature capable of pondering infinity and the meaning of life. So too the dark times of our lives have a sacred purpose—to bring us closer to the truth, closer to freedom, closer to true potential.

Another way to put this is that growth can come from discomfort and suffering, which can be transmuted into wisdom and awareness that replaces the darkness and illuminates the real world. We tend to get comfortable in our understanding of our world and our universe. We've worked hard to identify and classify the shadows on the cave wall, and anything that upsets that comfortable balance can be seen as a threat. We have become entrenched in our perceived starting conditions. But all growth comes with some discomfort, from a willingness to step outside of our comfort zones and open ourselves up for what comes next. It comes from a willingness to step outside of the self-induced darkness of our own ignorance.

While in my darkness, I have glimpsed something more. Each time I got a taste of the sublime, it increased my desire to experience more. At this point in the journey, I feel like I've been unchained from the cave. I'm still in it, but I've turned around and can see an exit. Light is streaming in from a world beyond. It's the light of compassion and human solidarity that illuminates our implicit wholeness. This journey has led me to understand that the basic structure of our society pulls us away from the wholeness that is our true calling as a species. It sets up walls that prevent us from fully realizing our wholeness and fracture us along artificial lines.

I want to devote the rest of my life to exploring what's beyond those walls. I want to be content on my death bed, in the certainty that I made the most of my allotted time here, that I did everything I could to leave this place a little better than I found it. I want to be content that I am prepared for what comes next.

When I die, my tombstone will display the number "1961," representing the year of my birth. To the right of that, another number will denote the year of my death. A dash will fall between the two numbers. That dash will represent my entire life, the entire timeline of my successes and failures, gains and losses, heartache, pain, joy, love, and beauty. The life of everyone who has ever lived or will ever live can be represented by that same small dash—every king, warrior, poet, artist, and great statesman. Every accomplishment great and small and the entirety of human history is contained within that small dash.

That horizontal line represents an infinitesimal span of time in the context of the age of the universe. But there's more to that dash than a short horizontal line. When we dolly zoom out from it, we see that it has depth and height. There's another dimension where time has no power, an existence beyond transience, beyond rust and decay. The dash is a horizontal signpost pointing to our allotted span of time to walk on Earth. But it also has an infinite vertical dimension that serves as our common bond. Dolly zooming out to that vertical dimension merges those billions of dashes into light, unity, and love. We are so much more than that dash. We are simultaneously a discrete individual and an infinitely larger part of a much bigger picture.

The vertical dimension of our collective dashes, of our lives, is weightless unity. In a graveyard, individual tombstones give the illusion of separate lives once lived. But in reality, all life is connected.

Like you, my dash is still being drawn. It may continue for a few more decades or a few more minutes. Regardless, what's important is now, this apparent moment in time. The *now* is all that is real and our entry point to life. On the surface, my dash appears to represent a continuous succession of individual *nows*. In each of these *nows*, I have consciously or unconsciously chosen to participate in the blossoming of life or to obstruct it—a choice to nudge the trajectory of the world toward renewal or toward destruction, toward light or toward darkness. But I don't control the *nows* that have been or the *nows* to come. All I can control is this now, the now that exists between an inhale and exhale in our world inside the cave—the now when I am writing these words to you.

## THE BREATH OF EVOLUTION

In the dream I had on the ISS, I described arriving back at the point where the unimaginably large meets the unimaginably small and the unimaginably fast merges with the unimaginably slow. This occurred as I arrived at the *continuity* where an inhale becomes an exhale. I believe we exist to continue down the path of evolution. The first giant leap of evolution was the development of our ability to self-reflect. This was evolution completing its first inhale. When we inhale, we expand outward, we become, we take in. When our consciousness expanded to the point where we could self-reflect, we became human. But we can only take in so much before we need to exhale.

It's time to exhale.

Exhaling allows us to let go, to give of ourselves. Presently, we are beginning our first exhale as a species, the next giant leap of human evolution—that is, to realize that the self that you are self-reflecting on is not just an individual being but a part of a larger cosmic journey. To realize this, we must have the courage to let go of part of what we believe to be ourselves, to be willing to leave the comfortable and familiar behind and step into the dark forest without a clear path. We must bring into our everyday awareness the primordial fact that the molecules of our bodies were forged in stars. We are the universe becoming conscious of itself.

The evolutionary process will bring us to the point where we all realize that we are not just alive, we are life itself. This awareness will lead us to incorporate the basic truth that we are all interrelated—every thought, word, and action. We will be allowing God—or if you prefer, "the universe"—to work through us. In doing so, we will fully tap into the awesome creative power of the universe and therefore fulfill our potential and purpose. Each of us will play our unique musical note. We will align ourselves with the collective life that inhabits this planet.

## OUR PURPOSE

The purpose of life is to seek, in every moment, the connective tissue of all of creation. To seek it in your neighbors and your "enemies." To seek it in those you meet and the countless other members of the human family you will never meet. To seek it in all who currently walk on Earth, in those that came before, and in those yet to come.

The purpose of life is to seek out what's important, and that is to be a functioning and contributing cell in the societal body, the overarching human superorganism, to avoid becoming a cancer cell, pathogen, or toxin.

The purpose of life is to realize that you are vastly more than what you perceive as yourself, that we truly are all in this together, and that together, we are far more powerful than we realize.

The purpose of life is to live.

## HOW TO UNLOCK OUR PURPOSE

To unlock our purpose, we must overcome our egos and false identities. We must discover that underneath our ego-created insecurities—fear, greed, and selfishness—unfathomable strength and power exist.

Ego enables us to function in the material world. We use it to identify what we perceive as ourselves. It is who we think we are. It is our appearance, stature, nationality, profession, and ethnicity. It is our talents, possessions, personality, and above all else, our thoughts. But the ego falsely associates all those things as our true identity.

The one key thing that we must have before we can begin our societal course correction is easy to state but difficult to accomplish: We must transcend the false idea that we are nothing but our individual egos. Before we can steer toward our desired future, a critical number of humans must do this. Every single person counts. When we reach that critical number, our species will have a fighting chance at transcending its collective ego. Until then, we will not do much more than slap temporary Band-Aids on our problems.

> As we reach critical mass, a primordial certainty will echo throughout creation in a loud, simultaneous proclamation: *We are one!*

## IT'S TIME TO DISCOVER WHO WE TRULY ARE

If you peel back layer upon layer of personal ego, eventually you will get to the core of a person. Once free of the delusion of ego, even if just for a moment, we will realize that each and every one of us is a precious drop in the infinite ocean of universal consciousness—the mind of God. I did not realize this while in space. Only after years of processing my sublime orbital experience did this fundamental truth about our nature reveal itself to me. I now understand that this realization is the fulfillment of the "great commandment"—the great commandment of the particular spiritual path I have chosen to follow, though I recognize and respect the fact that more than one spiritual road exists.

In the Gospel of Matthew, Jesus was asked, "Master, which is the great commandment in the law?" Jesus replied, "Thou shalt love the Lord thy God with all thy heart, and with all thy soul, and with all thy mind. This is the first and great commandment. And the second is like unto it, Thou shalt love thy neighbor as thyself. On these two commandments hang all the law and the prophets."

This is the prescription for banishing ego, for acting from the foundational unity of who we truly are.

What we perceive as differences among people and other living things is the extent to which we realize our true nature. Every problem, challenge, and all suffering on the planet can be found in the gap between the truth of who we are and who we think we are. Every atom and subatomic particle, every solar system and galaxy are the material manifestations of universal consciousness, an infinite intelligence that imbues every part of the material universe. The process of evolution is the awakening of the material universe to this reality. It is our awakening to this truth.

How can we overcome our egos? We can do so by observing the ego when it injects itself into our daily lives. The false identities of the ego cannot survive the light of our conscious observation. They only survive when the ego deceives us into believing that we are our egos—that we are our thoughts. We will overcome our egos when we realize that an awareness beyond thought exists. It is you who realizes that you're having a thought. You are not the thought itself, and you are not your perceptions, sensations, or feelings. You are that which is aware of those things. That simple realization starts a chain reaction that neutralizes the destructive force of our egos. It equips us with the tools to transcend them and see past them, to know for the first time who we really are. The awareness that we are aware is the bridge that will lead us back *home*.

Being in space can be a humbling and ego-dissolving experience. Back in 1969, *Apollo 9* astronaut Rusty Schweickart, in describing his time there, said that he felt as though he was "a sensing element for man." He felt as if he was literally experiencing our planet from space on behalf of all humanity. I too experienced that connection in space. In broader terms, I realized that all of us, regardless if our feet are floating in space or planted firmly on the ground, are the sensing units of the universe. Through us, the universe will come to know itself. Through us, we will come to know ourselves.

There is but one universe, and we are it.

# The Quiet Revolution—A Call to Action

✦ I wrote this book as an autobiographical narrative to serve as an allegory for the evolution of society—not only where we've been, but where we need to go. I purposely refrained from being overly prescriptive. As I mentioned in the Epilogue, countless talented people around the world are working on specific solutions to our shared problems. In this book, I wanted to avoid offering solutions that may change with time. Instead, I set out to present timeless basic principles that any solution should be built upon in order to be effective.

Remaking the world for the better won't come from prescriptive policy or legislation alone, and it won't be found in the latest exponential technology designed to bend our planet's biosphere to our will. It won't come through a blinding upheaval or violent revolution.

In the planetary community of the new human epoch, the dismantling of the old stacked playing field and the remaking of our world will usher in as a quiet whisper.

Although in the end, massive systemic change is required, no real systemic change will occur until a critical number of people identify and challenge their own starting conditions. Once again, I stress that this will require people transcending their individual egos and realizing our underlying unity. But you can't do any of that if you don't know where your next meal is coming from. This is the reality of life for a very large portion of our fellow humans on this planet.

We must dismantle the *global* systems that are keeping the status quo of destitute poverty in place and create systems that allow people to rise above a sole focus on surviving. We must do this not only for the benefit of those who are living in poverty but also for the benefit of us all. Only when we finally embrace the truth that there is no *them*, there is only *us*, will real change be possible.

We can achieve this with the *nudge* of a billion feathers. We must first realize that beyond the surface layer of imperfections, you and every person you meet is a perfect miracle. As a perfect miracle, each person—regardless of their profession, political identity, or any other perceived difference—deserves our respect, compassion, attention, and concern—even if those things are not reciprocated. Using the ISS program as an example, we need to look for the common ground—the things we agree upon—and use it as the jumping-off point to address our differences of opinion. In any proposed solution or systemic restructuring, we need to ensure that those prescriptions cause no harm anywhere within the biosphere of Earth or to future generations. We also need to ensure that those prescriptive measures work on a local scale and a planetary scale. We need to hold policymakers accountable for adhering to these principles.

Here is my challenge to you: In your every thought, word, and action, strive to be a positive part of our required course correction. Every day, provide countless small, positive, unifying nudges to the trajectory of our society. You are more powerful than you can imagine, and together, we are unstoppable.

In loving gratitude to you,
*Ron*

# Endnotes

✦ I derived this story from my memory, a journal I kept during my quest to become an astronaut, letters to Carmel during Operation Desert Shield/Storm, and interviews I conducted with those involved in the story.

After completing the manuscript, I was exposed to several spiritual teachers who, through their teaching, confirmed insights that I shared throughout this book. Two of those teachers are Eckhart Tolle and Rupert Spira. In deference to them, I went back into the manuscript and changed some of the story's lexicon to align with common language used to describe the concepts I was sharing.

In the Prologue, the periodic insertions of historical events were derived from published sources. I variously paraphrased and used exact quotations from those sources to fit into the style and voice of the story. Other historical quoted material is part of popular American culture and is found in duplicate form in numerous sources, variously broadcast, print, and online.

The Prologue insertions originate from the following:

1.  Elizabeth Hanes, "9 Tales of Broken Arrows: Thermonuclear Near Misses Throughout History," updated August 22, 2018, History.com, https://www.history.com/news/9-tales-of-broken-arrows-thermonuclear-near-misses-throughout-history.
2.  Lillian Levy, "Russian First Man in Space," *Science News Letter*, April 22, 1961, https://twitter.com/sciencenews/status/852161929162498048.

3. "First U.S. Spaceman Rockets 302 Miles on 5100 M.P.H. Journey in 15-Minute Flight," *Fitchburg Sentinel*, May 5, 1961, http://www.rarenewspapers.com/view/561048?imagelist=1.

4. History.com Editors, "Freedom Riders Face Bloodshed in Alabama," History.com, http://www.history.com/topics/black-history/freedom-rides.

5. "East German Troops Seal Border with West Berlin to Block Refugee Escape," *The New York Times*, August 13, 1961, https://archive.nytimes.com/www.nytimes.com/learning/general/onthisday/9908130nthisday_big.html.

6. "1961: World Condemns Russia's Nuclear Test," *On this Day, 30 October*, BBC News, http://news.bbc.co.uk/onthisday/hi/dates/stories/october/30/newsid_3666000/3666785.stm.

# Acknowledgments

✦ Many people are part of this story who I want to thank and acknowledge, some who were mentioned and some whose names wound up on the cutting room floor. First and foremost, I thank Carmel and our three sons, Ronnie, Joseph, and Jake. Without their love and support, this story would not have been possible. They were with me on every part of the journey, and I am eternally grateful to them. I also thank my mom, Linda Relis-Lichtblau; father, Ronald J. Garan Sr.; stepfather, Peter Lichtblau; and all of my friends and family members who encouraged me not to give up on my seemingly impossible dream to become an astronaut. Additionally, I thank my mom for sharing her motherly wisdom with me and for stressing the importance of setting out on a sincere search for truth.

In this book, I tried my best to capture the heroism of the men and women whom I had the honor to serve with in the Air Force. On that account, I fell short. I would need many volumes of this story to come close to recognizing them properly. But I do want to single out some folks whose names did not make it into the final version of the book—all of whom served with honor. I thank Tom "Wheels" Wheeler, Bryan "Stew" Turner, Dave "Fingers" Goldfein (who would later command the Air Force as the twenty-first United States Air Force Chief of Staff), Eric "Neck" Dodson, John "Buck" Burgess, Chris "Tuna" Peloza, Gary "Flash" Conlon, Bill "Westy" Westberry, Jeff "JC" Connors, Steve "Cobber" Caine, and Al "Big Al" Shawcross.

I thank Cheryl Ross for her tireless hours editing the manuscript. Thank you for being tough with me even when

I whined and complained that specific stories and passages were being cut. The overall story benefited greatly from your literary guidance. I want also to acknowledge the contribution of Jonas Salk and Jonathan Salk for the concepts of Epoch A and Epoch B.

I also thank the following people who reviewed the manuscript and helped me focus my message: Guy Reid, Wendy Neal, Evan Thomas, PhD, Arta Dobroshi, Andrew Antonio, Jan "Tav" Tavrytzky, Rob Van Sice, Rhonda Cornum, Ed Van Cise, Todd Manza, Paolo Nespoli, Pete "Abner" MacCaffrey, John "JP" Reilly, Bill "Kanga" Rew, Nina Burleigh, James Talacek, Otto Rutten, Jim Buckley, and Carmel Garan.

I also want to thank Milton Menezes and Lightfarm Studios for the use of their compelling image *The Verge* on the cover of the book and to Dragan Bilic, and Tarver Lowe for incorporating the image into the cover design. For me, the image perfectly captures the literal and metaphorical messages contained in *Floating in Darkness*. Thank you for sharing your creativity and vision.

I thank the many people who preordered this book and helped get it published. I want to specifically thank Anousheh Ansari and the XPRIZE Foundation, Hans Reitz and the Grameen Creative Lab, Jim Van Eerden and the 5th Element Group, John Garan and Doctor Auto, LLC, Dr. Evan Thomas and the Mortenson Center in Global Engineering at the University of Colorado Boulder, Amit Aharoni and Mélanie Pereira from Talent.io, and Wendy Neal and Neal Law, PLLC.

Before this book was published, I put a call out for folks to answer three questions about our future. I want to thank the following people who responded to the call and whose answers I compiled below: Eico Neumann, Al Seay, Quan King, Keith Cowing, Beshoy Onsi, Maia Buljeta, Loucaros (Luke) Eleftheriou,

Susan Oh, Deston Tanner, Ann-Marie Bybel, Timothy Gagnon, and Emilie Sydney-Smith.

**Question 1: *What do you want the world to look like in fifty years?***
A world where:

- The well-being of society and individual well-being are better balanced.
- People from all nations can live in harmony and work together for the common good, and there is no war, hunger, or poverty.
- There is a system for greater equality. Where the playing field is leveled and everyone is afforded an opportunity to achieve their dreams and make their unique contribution to society.
- Environmental/ecological sustainability is restored, and technology is used to reverse the damage we've created, leading to clear skies, clean water, and verdant lands, with people living peacefully on Earth and above the sky.
- Facts are respected and when presented with new data, we alter our views and the resulting actions accordingly, without denouncing each other.
- There is no racism.
- We understand that a good idea can come from anywhere.
- Renewable and sustainable approaches are implemented across all aspects of human life on Earth: energy, food production, waste management, protection of our oceans, land, and atmosphere.
- Human consciousness evolves, enabling us to look beyond our dangerously myopic selfishness and make proactive decisions based on long-term cause and consequence.

**Question 2: *What is currently preventing us from steering toward that desired future?***

- Ego.
- Reduced attention spans; the twenty-four-hour news cycle and social media push people toward extreme views and facile insights instead of deep critical and nuanced thinking. Partisan journalism and targeted content reinforces those entrenched positions.

- Fear, which leads to greed, hatred, tribalism, intolerance, selfishness, lack of imagination, and a blind pursuit of power.
- Reluctance to really listen to one another with respect and empathy.
- Gross centralized, opaque, hierarchical global systemic injustices and inequalities.
- Not embracing the reality that our entire planet is a single biosphere.
- A political system that is disproportionately skewed to advance the desires of those with the money to purchase political favor.

**Question 3:** *What do you pledge to do to help nudge our trajectory in the direction of that desired future?*
- Help companies and governments establish Massive Transformative Purposes in order to improve the lives of millions or billions of people (which is predicated on environmental health).
- Provide equal opportunities for all that are qualified, regardless of gender, age, ethnicity, or sexual orientation.
- Speak truth to power.
- Awaken to and implement a greater awareness of the cause and effect implications of our decisions and actions.
- Implement hope through action.
- Help build a circular economy and business models leading to a financially inclusive global economy.
- Vote for candidates who will promote the common good.

In closing, I thank you, the reader, for hanging with me during this journey. I thank you for all that you have done and all that you will do to help make life on our planet as beautiful as our Earth looks from space.

# Index